Special Edition

The

PSYCHOLOGY

PEDAGOGY

of Reading

EDMUND BURKE HUEY

With a new introduction by Michael L. Kamil and Elizabeth B. Bernhardt

INTERNATIONAL
Reading Association
800 BARKSDALE ROAD, PO BOX 8139
NEWARK, DE 19714-8139, USA
www.reading.org

The International Reading Association attempts, through its publications, to provide
a forum for a wide spectrum of opinions on reading. This policy permits divergent
viewpoints without implying the endorsement of the Association.

Executive Editor, Books Corinne M. Mooney
Developmental Editor Charlene M. Nichols
Developmental Editor Tori Mello Bachman
Developmental Editor Stacey L. Reid
Editorial Production Manager Shannon T. Fortner
Design and Composition Manager Anette Schuetz

Project Editors Wesley Ford

Cover Design Snyder Creative

The publisher would appreciate notification where errors occur so that they may be
corrected in subsequent printings and/or editions.

Library of Congress Cataloging-in-Publication Data
Huey, Edmund Burke, 1870–1913.
    The psychology and pedagogy of reading / Edmund Burke Huey.
        p. cm.
    Originally published: Cambridge [Mass]. : M.I.T. Press, [1968].
    Includes bibliographical refernces and index.
    ISBN 978-0-87207-696-9
  1. Reading, Psychology of.   I. Title.
    LB1573.H88 2009
    418'.4019--dc22

                                                                    2009004591

CONTENTS

INTRODUCTORY

PART I
THE PSYCHOLOGY OF READING

PART II
THE HISTORY OF READING AND OF READING METHODS

PART III
THE PEDAGOGY OF READING

PART IV
THE HYGIENE OF READING

CONCLUSION
READING AND THE PRINTING OF THE FUTURE

INTRODUCTION

Michael L. Kamil and Elizabeth B. Bernhardt
Stanford University

WE can only describe the honor we have in writing an introduction to Edmund Burke Huey's 1908 *The Psychology and Pedagogy of Reading* as a lesson in humility. In writing such an introduction, we follow in the footsteps of John B. Carroll and Paul A. Kolers who set about a similar task in 1968 when they wrote the Foreword and Introduction to the MIT Press reprint of this very work. In his introduction, Carroll provided a history of the career of Huey. A more complete history was provided by Reed and Meyer (2007).

Edmund Burke Huey was born in 1870 (according to Carroll) or 1871 (as reported by Reed and Meyer). He pursued doctoral work in psychology at Clark University where his doctoral advisor was E. C. Sanford. In 1899, he was awarded a PhD and published his dissertation (*On the Psychology and Physiology of Reading*) in 1900 and 1901 in *The American Journal of Psychology*. He published *The Psychology and Pedagogy of Reading* in 1908. A second book, *Backward and Feeble-Minded Children: Clinical Studies in the Psychology of Defectives, With a Syllabus for the Clinical Examination and Testing of Children*, was published in 1912. Notes for a third book on clinical psychology were lost in a fire and never published. Huey died at a young age when he succumbed to Tuberculosis on December 30, 1913.

Our careers have spanned the time since the last reprint of Huey's work in 1968 and we both have clear recollections of reading and re-reading the work as part of graduate study and research in reading. Re-reading this classic work once more has evoked astonishment, wonder, laughter, awe, sadness, joy, and as we noted above, most pointedly, humility. It sparked extensive conversation about what Huey did and didn't mean in particular passages, what were the most important issues Huey addressed, and what we could say about the state of reading research today. After re-reading Huey, we repeatedly asked "How did he get it so right, so often?" coupled with, "He was so smart and so right. How did he miss this?"

In addition to these questions, we have asked ourselves what Huey would be impressed by in the modern era of reading research. Have we answered any of the challenges that he put forth? Have we failed in ways that he had already warned us of? We have also asked ourselves which direction of reading research Huey would be pursuing now, were he alive. Given his deep concern for classroom instruction, would he continue with programmatic work on comprehension; work in teacher education; or would he be conducting policy analysis, reinforcing his conviction that "we are all working toward daylight in the matter, and many of the discrepancies of facts and theories are more apparent than real"? We organized this introduction around these questions.

An overwhelmingly striking theme in *The Psychology and Pedagogy of Reading* is Huey's caution against reading as a "fetich." Among the 13 times that he uses the word, Huey admonishes us to avoid "the insidious thought of reading as a formal end in itself." He worries that an overemphasis on technique—which he refers to as "debris"—and an overemphasis on detail and hyperanalysis in instruction do not lead to effective reading but only to more fetichness. In spite of the admonition, he cheers us with his assurance that "the slightest improvement...means the rendering of a great service to the human race."

We can only speculate that Huey would have despaired at the "reading wars" of the past decades as examples of 'fetich'. Those internecine disputes over methods and perspectives would truly have qualified as Huey's debris. And we can only suspect that he would have viewed those activities as distractions from "rendering the great service to the human race." We firmly believe that we have made substantial progress in both the psychology and pedagogy of reading, and we turn to a few of the things that we believe that Huey would admire in contemporary reading research and practice.

What Would Huey Have Cheered Us on About?

Huey stated his explicit intentions of collating all the knowledge about reading "for the guidance of present and future practice in reading and learning to read." Huey even reflected our current concern for methodology that is apparent in recent research, practice, and policy when he wrote "we need to pass in review all the methods that have been tried…take a profound survey." And as many academics do, Huey underscored the need for more research.

> There yet remain to be written many most interesting chapters on the psycho-physiological phases of reading, which will be made possible as investigation proceeds further. The work that has already been done by many hands and in many lands illustrates well how the federated science of the world is making solid progress with specific problems, and bears promise of a day when education shall rest on foundations better grounded than were the individual unverified opinions about "Reading," for instance, even twenty-five years ago.

In anticipation of future research, Huey also calls for "organized research" and "committees of competent specialists." In particular, these last sentiments presage the emphasis on efforts to synthesize research that the field has seen in the past two decades. The 1968 reprint of this work had little to add in the way of large syntheses of extant research. The situation is vastly different with the current edition.

Among the recent efforts at synthesizing reading research are the *Handbook of Reading Research* (Pearson, Barr, Kamil, & Mosenthal, 1984); *Handbook of Reading Research, Vol. 2* (Barr, Kamil, Mosenthal, & Pearson, 1991); *Handbook of Reading Research, Vol. 3* (Kamil, Mosenthal, Pearson, & Barr, 2000); *the Report of the National Reading Panel* (National Institute of Child Health and Human Development, 2000); *Reading for Understanding* (RAND Reading Study Group, 2002); *The National Literacy Panel for Language Children and Youth* (August & Shanahan, 2006), and *Preventing Reading Difficulties* (Snow, Burns, & Griffin, 1998). All of these are in their own way direct outgrowths of Huey's early attempt to synthesize the research on reading and teaching reading a century ago. The trend appears to be accelerating as these syntheses (as well as many others in progress) form the basis for research funding, policy, materials development, and practice.

However, Huey clearly realized the enormity of the task of synthesizing, even in 1908:

Of course no two authors would select the same material for such a work upon reading. I have endeavored to present the most meaningful facts, and those researches in which more or less definite results have been reached. Completeness of treatment and of reference is out of the question in a subject having such various and intricate ramifications.

It is difficult to know what Huey would have made of developments like the What Works Clearinghouse (http://ies.ed.gov/ncee/wwc/) or the Campbell Collaboration (www.campbellcollaboration.org/) in which serious attempts are made to set forth criteria for accepting research. Given the enormity of the reading research literature, compared with its size in 1908, Huey would probably have appreciated the ability to be more selective and, perhaps, objective by establishing criteria for quality of research. Given his penchant for rigorous research, he might well have appreciated the ability to be able to have objective criteria to evaluate the research literature.

A common thread among all of the contemporary reports on reading research and one of the clear areas of instruction in which current practice is the same as it was in Huey's time is the emphasis on oral language: "the child comes to his first readers with his habits of spoken language fairly well formed, and these habits grow more deeply set with every year. His meanings inhere in his spoken language and belong but secondarily to the printed symbols." He notes this clearly as he writes that "printed characters are rendered into living speech in reading." We believe he would have been in full agreement with current thoughts on the importance of fluency for progress in reading comprehension.

However, Huey did acknowledge that the ultimate goal of learning to read was to learn to read silently. In that vein, he plainly thought that phonics was not the way to conduct reading instruction—"too often the line between phonics and reading is not drawn"—and that it took away from the emphasis on reading for meaning. The belief that oral reading was not the most efficient way to teach reading persisted and reached its zenith with the non-oral method adopted in Chicago in the 1930s. A description of this program can be found in McDade (1950). The program persisted for some time, but was eventually abandoned in the 1940s. We have nothing like this method in the pantheon of instructional methods in classrooms today.

Another common thread across the century between Huey and contemporary syntheses is the awareness of the impact of prior knowledge, "the reader's familiarity with what is read" in the comprehension process. Huey's work foreshadows the importance of "previous context mak[ing] the line easier to read" and that "in reading the deficient picture is filled in." The current emphasis on the centrality of meaning making at the core of comprehension is also emphasized when he writes about the reading process beginning with meaning, with the proposition. He also notes, "But meaning *leads*, and the idea of the whole dominates the parts, composed of a protoplasm of total meanings."

While understanding the facilitative nature of prior knowledge and context, Huey also wrote that it limits the trend of association at the start: "The limitation extends farther when the reader has caught the general topic discussed." Perhaps the most modern of all of Huey's descriptions of reading is his notion of "reading as thought-getting" and his recognition that it is important to read actively and constructively. He worried about the "inanity and disjointed nature of reading content"; about the role of information text; and about an overemphasis on literature—all of which are topics that appear in contemporary syntheses about research and instruction and about linking literacy to the lives of all children.

Huey also foreshadowed the contemporary research and instructional focus on adolescent literacy and modern-day efforts at high school reform. He wrote, "It is high time that high schools should live for their own pupils and come out of the shadow cast backwards upon all pupils by college entrance requirements and examinations that will be taken by comparatively few."

While Huey might have despaired that we have not made more progress in teaching all students to read, he would have welcomed the relatively recent emphasis on adolescent literacy. He believed that at high school instruction should be committed to the efficacy of individual school subjects in a way that suggests current emphasis on content reading in high school and beyond.

Yet another intriguing insight of Huey is akin to our modern notion of metacognition. He writes,

> So much for the part played by imagery in reading, a part that is far larger in the reading of young children than in that of adults and that is far larger in some than in others, but a part that is always secondary or auxiliary to the suggestion and control of meanings themselves. The *consciousness of meaning* [emphasis added] itself belongs in the main to that group of mental states, the feelings, which I regard with Wundt as unanalyzables, or at least as having a large unanalyzable core or body. Each meaning-feeling is very much itself and unlike every other.

A final arena in which Huey was involved and would have cheered recent research and instructional directions is the area of second-language reading. We were struck in re-reading Huey by his repeated references to languages other than English. He was obviously well-traveled and, consequently, respectful of the languages spoken by his fellow scientists. In fact, he reminds his readers that "the acme of scholarship, until quite recently at least, has been stated in such terms as 'Why, he reads seven languages'." He returns repeatedly throughout the book to the experiments conducted by German scientists and English-speaking visiting researchers who would examine each other's reading behaviors in their dominant and non-dominant languages—usually restricted to relations between German to English or English to German—noting how these cross-linguistic experiments helped to bring light to the process of reading. He references eye movement and reading rate in particular. Rather than relegating languages other than English to the sidelines, which modern reading research has done over and over again, Huey actually highlighted them. He refers also rather matter-of-factly to children's learning to read other languages and that students should recognize the "power of reading the difficult languages and the remote literatures."

By and large, Huey is on target regarding the process of learning to read in languages other than the mother tongue. Throughout many of his commentaries, he is careful to interpret research data as being generated "in English," acknowledging that languages other than English may not subscribe to the same processing strategies.

He notes that foreign language reading is more labored using the evidence of pauses per line and reports on the

> comparative ease with which a reader may paraphrase the thought of what he reads. This is especially noticeable in the case of a person reading in a foreign language which he does not pronounce easily but which he comprehends rather rapidly.

We have come to believe that Huey would look on the field of reading research and instruction with great pride and, although we of course can only speculate on this, with some degree of smugness. The field has come to hold dear many of the thoughts that he articulated without an elaborate research budget, graduate student assistants, conference presentations, international organizations, refereed journals, and Federal policymakers. He was Professor Huey, carefully observing the readers around him and listening to and interacting respectfully with his colleagues.

What Did Huey Miss?

Arguing that Huey missed very little that we consider important today is not to say that he did not leave some gaps to fill—gaps in theory, in instruction, and in the nature of language itself.

Paul Kolers made note in the Introduction of the 1968 reprint of the rudimentary and incomplete theory of meaning under which Huey operated. We have little to add to this, other than that the fields of discourse analysis and pragmatics have had a substantial effect on contemporary theory and practice in reading. Huey, despite all of his emphasis on prior knowledge and context, did not account for the effects of higher level language processes in reading. Without a well-developed theory of meaning, Huey could not focus on comprehension and comprehension research as reading researchers have in the past several decades. Huey did understand the importance of meaning and its centrality in reading. He also understood the idea of what we now call metacognition. What is missing, for example, is the notion of strategies for comprehension. In contemporary research on comprehension, strategies are a focal point.

One of the stark contrasts in Huey's synthesis is that he relies heavily on empirical research data when he discusses basic processes but feels at ease in recommending or praising instructional materials without the same sort of data. While Huey would have applauded the current emphasis on instructional research, very little of his discussion of instructional materials does more than describe. This is not surprising, given the dearth of such research in 1908. What is surprising is that there is at least an implicit approval of methods related to those of John Dewey insofar as instruction is concerned without evidence akin to that on basic processes. While there is unmistakable emphasis on doing basic research with the aim of informing instruction, Huey does not call for programmatic research into the efficacy of instructional materials or methods. This is a true contrast with the current emphasis on scientifically based reading research.

Huey surveyed a great array of instructional materials. The history is interesting, but more complete versions of this history are available to us today. Mathews (1966) provided an engaging, updated history, but perhaps the most extensive examinations of instructional materials from this era can be found in the work of Venezky (1984, 1986a, 1986b, 1987, 1990a, 1990b, 1991, 1994).

Huey's attention to and mention of languages other than English also leads us to a two-dimensional blind spot. First, he was so focused on the visual mechanics of reading that he never gets as far as understanding the role that grammatical or constituent structures or word valence play in eye movement control during the reading of second languages. An example is his analysis of eye movement protocols in which he repeatedly references the drift of eye fixations to the right. His interpretation remains fundamentally at the physiological level although he mentions "close grammatical connection." Huey never explores the thought that perhaps it is the nature of English (as a right-branching language) that stimulates the drift, a feature of understanding, not of physiology, even though he admits that "our words are thoroughly organized according to these general associative habits of language."

Second, Huey fell into the same trap that educators for the past century have fallen prey to—the belief that "there is no other age when a child may, with so great economy of effort, gain a lasting knowledge of a foreign language as when he is from seven to eleven years old." He seemed to be blinded by the surface manifestations of oral language in young children, namely the pronunciation of a foreign language. Research has indicated that accurate pronunciation is the only area in which children actually outperform adults in the learning of foreign languages (Herschensohn, 2007). The arena of second languages is a key example in which Huey got much right, but also fell short of the target in the long run.

In summary, Huey did miss some important issues, mostly through no fault of his own. What he did miss does not detract from all that he got right.

What Would Huey be Doing as a Researcher?

Huey spent many, many pages in the early section of *The Psychology and Pedagogy of Reading* discussing eye movements in reading. In fact, he embarks upon his lifetime investigation of reading with eye movement. There is no question that his understanding of that particular technology for providing insight into the reading process was profound. He was fully aware that he did not have the apparatus to measure fixation duration, for example, but appropriately mentions everything that ultimately should and could be measured. He wrote that, in 1897–1898, the thought of such measurement accuracy was "impossible." Again, we can only surmise the quantity and quality of research that Huey could have continued, had he had modern instrumentation.

He clearly remained engaged by this level of research. Carroll, in the 1968 Foreword, reports that after publishing *The Psychology and Pedagogy of Reading*, Huey turned to doing neurological research. We can only conjecture that Huey would have been thoroughly taken by the available technologies that allow for neuroimaging of brain functions with MRI or fMRI techniques. The kinds of work summarized by Shaywitz, et al. (Shaywitz, et al., 2000) provide for very different ways of measuring cognitive functioning. While the inferences are clearly at a similar level to those for eye movements, the new technology gives researchers another converging measurement to work with.

At the same time, there is renewed interest in using more sophisticated methods of eye movement technologies. (Updates and examples of current research on eye movements can be found in Beymer & Russell, 2005; Beymer, Russell, & Orton, 2008; Rayner, 1998) The improved technology to measure many more physiological functions concomitant to eye movements allows for more sophisticated inferences about cognitive processes. Many of these efforts have been used to analyze reading in detail with regard to the length of lines on a page, the types of fonts, and the presence or absence or relevance of graphics on a page. We speculate that Huey might have enthusiastically taken up these new technologies in pursuit of examining reading more precisely than he was able to in 1908.

And, of course, we believe that Huey would also have been involved in the research synthesis efforts that are so much a part of contemporary efforts to understand reading. His mantra would have been Where is the evidence for that conclusion?

What Would Huey Have Been Surprised by?

While Huey writes about the possibility of "gramophone" technology to allow students to listen to text, he made no comments about the use of incorporating moving pictures or what we today call multimedia elements with conventional text. Would he have been surprised at iPods or webcasts, or would he have simply assumed that these technologies were a natural outgrowth of progress? We speculate that the internet would have intrigued Huey for its myriad possibilities for providing more natural experiences of meaning.

Computers would have also been an astounding development. The malleability of text provided by computers, Kindles, and other devices for presenting electronic text would certainly have changed his thinking about the production and use of materials for reading. The careful specification of different font sizes and line lengths that Huey describes in Chapter XXI can now be easily provided for any electronic text. We have to believe that Huey would have been engaged in employing new technologies to study reading of electronic and multimedia texts with all of the new technologies that he had not had access to in his brief career.

Nor could Huey have conceived of the vast amount of information available on the World Wide Web, although he certainly would have been appalled at the enormous amount of irrelevant material that accompanies it. The ease with which information and research can be shared would probably have amazed him and yet presented him with yet another tool that would have made his task of synthesizing the research literature far easier than it was.

Summary

The longevity of Huey's work is impressive. It is as relevant today as it was in 1908 or 1968. Much of what he wrote could be found in many contemporary works on reading as well as in the reading research literature. In rereading Huey, we can truly see how far we have come in answering the questions surrounding how we read and learn to read. It is clear that in 1908 the conduct of instructional research in reading was of interest to a great number of psychologists. With a far smaller body of instructional research to draw upon, Huey is less concerned with data when he analyzes instruction than he is when he reports on empirical research into basic reading processes. In this he reflects the psychological assumption that understanding the processes will dictate the pedagogy. Despite this, Huey was quite prescient in his enumerating the concerns of modern scholars and practitioners in reading research and instruction.

We trust that another generation of scholars will be inspired and encouraged by Huey's work in reporting the *Psychology and Pedagogy of Reading* from a century ago. Certainly, Huey does leave us a number of questions that still require research. We believe that he will serve as the same stimulus to future research as he has served in the past. As we humbly complete this introduction, we urge readers to recognize the wisdom and erudition contained in Huey's legacy, to contemplate reading research in the years ahead, and to imagine what we will know about reading by the publication of the next milestone anniversary of *The Psychology and Pedagogy of Reading.*

References

Barr, R., Kamil, M.L., Mosenthal, P.B., & Pearson, P.D. (Eds.). (1991). *Handbook of reading research* (Vol. 2). New York: Longman.

Beymer, D., & Russell, D.M. (2005, April). *WebGazeAnalyzer: A system for capturing and analyzing web reading behavior using eye gaze.* Paper presented at the CHI '05 Conference on Human Factors in Computing Systems, Portland, OR.

Beymer, D., Russell, D.M., & Orton, P.Z. (2008, September). *An eye tracking study of how font size and type influence online reading.* Paper presented at the HCI 2008 Conference, Liverpool, UK.

August, D., & Shanahan, L. (2006). *Developing literacy in second-language learners: Report of the National Literacy Panel on Language Minority Children and Youth.* Mahwah, NJ: Erlbaum.

Herschensohn, J.R. (2007). *Language development and age.* New York: Cambridge University Press.

Kamil, M.L., Mosenthal, P.B., Pearson, P.D., & Barr, R. (Eds.). (2000). *Handbook of reading research* (Vol. 3). Mahwah, NJ: Erlbaum.

Mathews, M.M. (1966). *Teaching to read, historically considered.* Chicago: University of Chicago Press.

McDade, J.E. (1950). Method in non-oral beginning reading. *The Elementary School Journal, 50*(9), 497–501. doi:10.1086/459183

Pearson, P.D., Barr, R., Kamil, M.L., & Mosenthal, P.B. (1984). *Handbook of reading research.* New York: Longman.

RAND Reading Study Group. (2002). *Reading for understanding: Toward an R&D program in reading comprehension.* Santa Monica, CA: RAND.

Rayner, K. (1998). Eye movements in reading and information processing: 20 years of research. *Psychological Bulletin, 124*(3), 372–422. doi:10.1037/0033-2909.124.3.372

Reed, J.B., & Meyer, R.J. (2007). Edmund Burke Huey (1870–1913): A brief life with an enduring legacy. In S.E. Israel & E.J. Monaghan (Eds.), *Shaping the reading field: The impact of early reading pioneers, scientific research, and progressive ideas* (pp. 159–175). Newark, DE: International Reading Association.

National Institute of Child Health and Human Development. (2000). *Report of the National Reading Panel: Teaching children to read: An evidence-based assessment of the scientific research literature on reading and its implications for reading instruction: Reports of the subgroups* (NIH Publication No. 00-4754). Washington, D.C.: U.S. Government Printing Office.

Shaywitz, B.A., Pugh, K.R., Jenner, A.R., Fulbright, R.K., Fletcher, J.M., Gore, J.C., et al. (2000). The neurobiology of reading and reading disability (dyslexia). In M.L. Kamil, P.B. Mosenthal, P.D. Pearson, & R. Barr (Eds.), *Handbook of reading research* (Vol. 3, pp. 229–249). Mahwah, NJ: Erlbaum.

Snow, C.E., Burns, M.S., & Griffin, P. (1998). *Preventing reading difficulties in young children.* Washington, DC: National Academy Press.

Venezky, R.L. (1984). The history of reading research. In P.D. Pearson, R. Barr, M.L. Kamil, & P.B. Mosenthal (Eds.), *Handbook of reading research* (Vol. 1, pp. 3–38). New York: Longman.

Venezky, R.L. (1986a). Literacy, literacy instruction, and the history of the book. *The Book*, no. 10 (November), 5–6.

Venezky, R.L. (1986b). Steps toward a modern history of American reading instruction. *Review of Research in Education, 13*(1), 129–167.

Venezky, R.L. (1987). A history of the American reading textbook. *The Elementary School Journal, 87*(3), 246–265. doi:10.1086/461493

Venezky, R.L. (1990a). *American primers: Guide to the microfiche collection..* Frederick, MD: University Publications of America.

Venezky, R.L. (1990b). The American reading script and its nineteenth-century origins. *Publishing Research Quarterly, 6*(2), 16–28. doi:10.1007/BF02683808

Venezky, R.L. (1991). The development of literacy in the industrialized nations of the West. In R. Barr, M.L. Kamil, P.B. Mosenthal, & P.D. Pearson (Eds.), *Handbook of reading research* (Vol. 2, pp. 46–67). New York: Longman.

Venezky, R.L. (1994). History of reading instruction. In A.C. Purves (Ed.), *Encyclopedia of English studies and language arts: A project of the National Council of Teachers of English* (pp. 583–587). New York: Scholastic.

TO

MY FELLOWS IN RESEARCH

WHOSE INVESTIGATIONS OF READING AND LANGUAGE

ARE HERE JOINED WITH MY OWN

THIS VOLUME

IS PRESENTED BY THE AUTHOR IN THE HOPE THAT

IT MAY RENDER SERVICE, AND WITH

RESPECTFUL APPRECIATION OF

THEIR PART IN ITS

PRODUCTION

PREFACE TO ORIGINAL EDITION

THE writer's studies upon reading began nearly ten years ago, being first suggested by a question concerning the possibility of reading without inner pronunciation, raised by my friend and fellow-worker in the laboratory, now Professor G. M. Whipple of the University of Missouri. The reading process had long seemed to me to mirror the processes of thinking, and thus came to seem an appropriate subject for psychological analysis. Besides, the peculiar fatigue occasioned by reading caused a curiosity to know its sources, and the great variations and limitations in speed of reading suggested possibilities of improvement here.

Such considerations gave birth to my experimental research. The field seemed clear. Diligent search in the literature showed only the preliminary experiments of Javal and his pupils, and those by Romanes and by Quantz, upon reading properly so called. Erdmann and Dodge were then completing their research, but I did not hear of their work until a year later. Reading thus offered to the experimentalist a practically unoccupied field.

Ten years has given a development here of which experimental psychology may be proud. Dodge, Zeitler, Messmer, Dearborn, and others have thoroughly investigated important phases of reading, and the collected studies now present a very tolerable account of the main processes involved. It has therefore seemed to me that a conspectus should be made of this work, not to close the story but to furnish a new point of departure for further study, and to give perspective for new researches.

Then it is due to education that from time to time the psychological investigations that have pedagogical bearings be edited, for such applications as education can helpfully make of them. And while engaged in this latter task, for reading, and falling in with much of the pedagogical literature of the subject, it became ever more evident that there was great need of bringing together the data not merely from the psychology of reading, but from the history of reading and of reading methods, from the current practice and points of view in the subject, and from the side of hygiene, drawing finally such conclusions as these collected data might warrant for the guidance of present and future practice in reading and learning to read.

So the present volume has taken form, typical of books which, it seems to me, should be written for each of the more important school subjects, however poorly this volume may exemplify the type. Consider the need of this in the various subjects. Not to mention writing, a branch in which there is perhaps the most of needless confusion and in which perhaps the greatest benefit would be derived from such a concentration of data, and number, in which certain phases have already been well presented, consider, for example, the value of such a treatment of geography. The psychological section would be mainly an outline of researches to be, but it would be of the greatest value to have these suggested, with our graduate departments full of men looking for problems. The school subjects, ordinarily, involve some characteristic modes of mental and physiological functioning which furnish to psychology problems fruitful for psychology's own purposes. But pedagogically, what sort of symbols, for instance, are most effective instruments for thinking the earth, its divisions and dependencies? Are actual experiences, the very appearances of mountains and cities seen in reality or constructed in miniature, the best geographical furniture for life's uses? Or do symbols utterly unlike the realities, marks and colors upon maps and charts and globes, give us the most compact and convenient scheme for mind's dealing with the earth's forms? Or are words, though totally unlike their objects, the best manipulators of meanings here, as they certainly are in some divisions of thinking? And what is the order in the development of capacity and interest, in the child and the race, for the various modes of symbolic presentation here, and for the various phases of geographical knowledge?

Such problems, but the first of a host that will suggest themselves to any competent investigator, are capable of at least partial solution from the data even now accessible, if these be gathered from the various sources. And then, as every one knows, the history of geography and of geography teaching is full of valuable suggestion; and when presented with a review of present-day theory and practice and with the psychological data upon the subject, the whole cannot fail to give us a far better orientation and the possibility of distinct advance in this much-abused branch of study. It is to be hoped that the various departments of educational psychology, now becoming popular in our universities, will recognize the great service which they can render, both to psychology and education, by such organization and concentration of data concerning the various school subjects.

Of course no two authors would select the same material for such a work upon reading. I have endeavored to present the most meaningful facts, and those researches in which more or less definite results have been reached. Completeness of treatment and of reference is out of the question in a subject having such various and intricate ramifications.

Some of the pedagogical principles suggested by the psychological work are still in the "recept" stage. In working over the material one comes to feel their truth and their applicability, but to attempt their logical statement or derivation would in many cases be premature and would tend to arouse useless polemics. Teachers will usually be better satisfied to find them well founded empirically, and psychological values have guided me, at least implicitly, in their selection and use.

In the work of collating and editing the data presented in the present volume, I have been greatly aided by the large number of writers and publishers who have courteously permitted me to publish so many extracts and illustrations from their works. To them is justly due a considerable share of the credit for whatever success the book may have. Professor Reeder deserves the main credit for gathering material and suggesting sources for my section on the history of reading methods and texts. The excellent volumes by Isaac Taylor, Hoffman, and Clodd were indispensable in preparing my sketch of the history of reading and writing. My thanks are especially due to Messrs. D. Appleton and Co., and to Kegan Paul, Trench, Trübner, and Co., for permission to use so many of their valuable illustrations. The American Book Co., the Funk and Wagnalls Co., and the Macmillan Co. have also been especially indulgent. It will be noted that one of the chapters on the Hygiene of Reading has already appeared in the *Popular Science Monthly*.

I wish to thank Professors E. C. Sanford, W. H. Burnham, W. F. Dearborn, and Henry D. Sheldon for suggestions from the reading of parts of the Ms., and Mr. Louis N. Wilson for efficient and kindly assistance in the library and otherwise. I am also indebted to the genius of President Hall for much more than text or bibliography can well indicate.

Professor and Mrs. Will Grant Chambers have given valuable criticisms and suggestions from a reading of the proofs, and the book owes much to their unfailing encouragement and assistance. Mr. E. H. McClelland and Mrs. H. H. Fisher have kindly assisted with the revision of the proofs, and Miss Grace Kerr deserves special mention for patient care in typewriting most of the illegible Ms. To these and the other friends who have lightened the labor of the book's production, I express my grateful appreciation. In conclusion, it is a pleasure to acknowledge the intelligence and cheerful courtesy of the Macmillan Co. and of the J. S. Cushing Co. in carrying out the plans of the author.

E. B. H.

PITTSBURG, PA.,
Christmas, 1907.

INTRODUCTION

CHAPTER I

THE MYSTERIES AND PROBLEMS
OF READING

READING, for our Anglo-Saxon forefathers, meant counseling or advising oneself or others (A.-S. *rædan*, to advise). To read was to get or to give counsel from a book, originally from a piece of bark on which characters were inscribed, at least if the reputed connection of *book* and *beech* can be sustained. The accessory notion of talking aloud seems to have been implied in the word, as it was also in the Roman word for reading. To the Roman, on the other hand, reading meant gathering or choosing (*lectio*, reading, from *lego*, to gather) from what was written, suggesting that constant feeling of values which goes on in all effective reading.

But reading had a meaning and was a common practice long before the times of Anglo-Saxon or Roman. Men read in North Babylonia as long before Abraham's time as the latter precedes our own. In that land reading and writing had passed the pictograph stage eight thousand years ago. In Egypt, alphabet signs were used at least seven thousand years ago, and we know that with races the attainment of an alphabet is just the opposite of the A B C stage of reading and writing. Indeed it is certain that even in that early period, in Egypt, Babylonia, and Crete, reading and writing were already of hoary antiquity, and had for these peoples already lost their beginnings in the mist and myth of a still more distant past.

To the early peoples, reading was one of the most mysterious of the arts, both in its performance and in its origin. We recall how, even in modern times, Livingstone excited the wonder and awe of an African tribe as he daily perused a book that had survived the vicissitudes of travel. So incomprehensible, to these savages, was his performance with the book, that they finally stole it and *ate* it, as the best way they knew of "reading" it, of getting the white man's

1

satisfaction from it. Among early peoples the mystery of reading naturally led to reverence for the printed word and book and for reading and the reader. Reading became a holy office, performed by individuals who possessed divine powers, and the book became a fetich. The written word was always of mysterious significance with the savage. It carried meanings through distances in space and time in such an utterly incomprehensible and apparently lawless fashion that he could not but fear and venerate it. A man might even be destroyed by doing certain prescribed things to his written name. The "winged words" of spoken language traversed the air unseen and were indeed objects of mystery, but they needed their written symbols, more tangible and thus better fetiches, to become the objects of primitive worship.

And the man who could deal in these symbols and use them for his purposes, he was next to the gods and might rule in their stead. And so reading was long mainly in the hands of the priesthood, and written language, bearing the records of civilization and becoming the tangible subject-matter of learning, ministered to forms of worship and remained in the hands of the Church. Written language became the currency of civilization, and so of learning and education. It was thought of as value in itself, and most commonly the Church "kept the bag." And so through this mystery of the printed word and this reverence for reading and for the book it came about that learning and education have ever been more or less holy things, and that the core of education, the reverenced part of it, has not been the arts, nor even the sciences as first-hand studies of reality, but language and books. People's reverence for reading and writing helped to bring this about at first, and the clergy, always conservative, preserved this ideal in the face of a "better reason," even until now.

How dominant and ingrained is this ideal of education is evident in our names for, and common expressions concerning, learning. The learned man is a "man of letters," while the ignoramus is "unlettered." To say that one "cannot read and write" is to outlaw him in the commonwealth of learning, while the acme of scholarship, until quite recently at least, has been stated in such terms as "Why, he reads seven languages," "He reads Greek at sight," "He is well read," etc. "Learning" is still largely the ability to read and the reputation of having read, and reading keeps the momentum of the ages in which it was identical with learning.

The modern dominance of this ideal is not merely because reading, especially reading of the classics, was for centuries the only road to culture if not to station. But to this day reading carries with it the faint but instinct-starting aroma of its old religious significance. Book is still Bible, perhaps as much as Bible is Book, to the average reader. All of us believe a little more readily if it can be said of the doctrine, "It is written." Students still worship the "power" of reading the difficult languages and the remote literatures, and theological education, true to its history, still clings to reading and language as its main food. Little wonder, then, that Professor Dewey calls reading the Fetich of the Primary Grades. It is a mystery and a fetich with us all, and has not only blinded us to comparative values in the primary school course, but as subtly warps the judgment in a dozen other important directions. The written or printed "word," and especially, as of old, if it be written in *strange characters*, still awes us and controls us by its appeal to the old folk-soul, which is the deepest soul in us all.

Perhaps there is nothing that has been greatly venerated for long periods that is not really very wonderful, if one considers the essence of what is wondered at. And after all it does not seem so absurd that reading and the book should have been the worshipful wonder of the ages, and that they should still be reverenced. Real reading is still the noblest of the arts, the medium by which there still come to us the loftiest inspirations, the highest ideals, the purest feelings that have been allowed mankind, — a God-gift indeed, this written word and the power to interpret it.

And reading itself, as a psycho-physiological process, is almost as good as a miracle. To the average reader the process by which he gets his pages read is not understood very much better than was the performance of Livingstone by the savage. Indeed, until twenty-five years ago, science could not give a very much better specific account. The psychological part of the present study has grown mainly out of my own simple wonder at the process of reading, and out of my curiosity to know its mechanism; and this wonder has simply expressed itself in a different procedure than that of the African, has used the better tools of science and of scientific coöperation with other wonderers, in the endeavor to solve this mystery of the ages. Problem enough, this, for a life's work, to learn how we read! A wonderful process, by which our thoughts and thought-wanderings to the finest shades of detail, the play of our inmost feelings and desires and will, the subtle image of the very innermost that we are, are reflected from us to another soul who reads us through our book. And a wonderful, awe-inspiring instrument, this book, that keeps this subtle likeness of its author, unfolding it part by part, changing it in phase at every page or sentence, yet all faithful to the original impress. Not in a day, not in ten thousand years even, as we shall find, has man been able to contrive the making of such a book or the manner of reading its pages.

And so to completely analyze what we do when we read would almost be the acme of a psychologist's achievements, for it would be to describe very many of the most intricate workings of the human mind, as well as to unravel the tangled story of the most remarkable specific performance that civilization has learned in all its history. The beginnings of such an analysis and description are attempted, with the help of many co-workers, in the psychological chapters which follow. The strange and fascinating story of how the book and page have grown to be is sketched in the chapters on the history of reading, using the records of many patient scholars.

So much for the appeal which reading makes to our psychological and historical interests, to our naïve curiosity and the concern which we have for the penetration of mysteries. Perhaps most of my psychological and historical chapters owe their origin to this motive, the basis of much of our science for science' sake. But reading and books are of even greater concern to us for the reader's sake. What a habit, this, that has fastened itself upon us in modern times! While the art of reading is indeed so very old, and while the practice was even so prevalent among certain ancient peoples that learning to read is recorded to have been compulsory at one time upon all free Chaldeans, yet the absence of printed matter, in all early times, made it impossible that reading should be anything like the habitual practice of the present, except among very limited numbers and special classes of individuals. But since the invention of printing, the reading habit has steadily grown upon the whole civilized world; and, furthered by modern laws for compulsory education, this habit has become the most striking and important artificial activity to which the human race has ever been moulded. Printed matter has been so diffused, and all that we do is so concerned with it, that a very considerable proportion of most people's waking time is taken up with the contemplation of reading symbols. This applies, of course, not merely to the reading of books and papers; but in the car or on the driveway, in the street or at the railway station, advertisements, signs, notices, — what-not of printed matter, — keep one reading. At the opera or concert there is the libretto or program, and when interest palls, these are read and reread, even to the last silly advertisement. One is seldom out of sight of some sort of matter to be read, and having formed the reading habit it has become second nature to read all that appears. Printed matter has become a stimulus which sets off, reflexly, a sensori-motor activity which goes off on sight anywhere, and which continues until there is no more to be read or until one is checked by disgust or by a counter-interest.

And yet this habit to which we subject ourselves and our children for so considerable a part of the time is an unnatural one, intensely artificial in many respects. The human eye and the human mind, the most delicate products of evolution, were evolved in adaptation to conditions quite other than those of reading. Such functionings as reading requires not having been foreseen in the construction of these organs, we need not be surprised that our continued and careless exercise of these unusual functions causes fatigue and, in very many cases, certain dangerous forms of degeneration. The very evident inheritance of some of the more disastrous effects, such as myopia and nerve exhaustion, warns us of the danger of race degeneration from this source.

For the sake of millions of tired readers, then, it may well be asked, and until recently the question has scarcely been raised, What are the unusual conditions and functionings that are enforced upon the organism in reading? Just what, indeed, do we do, with eye and mind and brain and nerves, when we read? And what may be done to avoid or minimize the dangers that come with this most universal and most artificial of habits? The answer can only be given by an analysis of the process of reading and an examination of the essential nature and history of the page and book.

And then, as a school subject, reading is an old curiosity shop of absurd practices. Until as late as thirty-five years ago, in America, the blind devotion to the unreasoned and unreasonable A B C method of learning to read was as universal and as fetichistic as the worship of reading itself had been. Within this thirty-five years the A B C fetich has been put away in most quarters, and the results of trial and error with new devices have given us somewhat better methods, and best of all have put us in an inquiring and more humble frame of mind. But after all we have thus far been content with trial and error, too often allowing the publishers to be our jury, and a real rationalization of the process of inducting the child into the practice of reading has not been made. We have surely come to the place where we need to know just what the child normally does when he reads, in order to plan a natural and economical method of learning to read. We have come to the place where we need to pass in review all the methods that have been tried in all the centuries of reading, and to learn any little that we can from each. We need, too, to take a more profound survey, and to learn from the tortuous yet ever progressive path which the race has followed, in the hundreds of centuries in which it has been developing reading and writing, the significant suggestions which this ethnic experience may have for our own further development of methods in reading and writing and printing.

Whatever side of reading we consider we are challenged to investigate. For instance, we have long known that some readers read four times as fast as others of equal intelligence, and yet obtain better results. Yet we have remained content to completely ignore the question of rate, in teaching to read; the only times it is mentioned, usually, being when the pupil is cautioned "not to read too fast." We know that the reading of life is almost exclusively silent reading. Yet in preparing for life we are instructed almost exclusively in reading aloud, and have not troubled ourselves to ask whether habits learned in reading aloud may not be hurtful in reading silently. We have learned comparatively recently that nearly if not quite all readers say over again within themselves all that they read. Yet no one has thought to determine whether purely visual reading, omitting this complex functioning of speech, may not be learned and be most economical of time and energy. We have made a fetich of our doctrine of formal discipline, and formal reading has kept its artificial place in our curriculum supported in part by this now fast-decaying prop. But when have competent persons taken the trouble to really analyze what in mind is exercised or disciplined when we read or when we learn to read? And above all, how we have most wastefully failed to use the real opportunities that reading offers for discipline, the opportunities for training pupils to effective use of books and library, to selective reading, and to the prompt feeling for and use of values in what is read!

Indeed, when we ask seriously why we do, as we do, almost anything that we commonly do in reading or in learning to read, the answer is that so it has always been done. Why, indeed, should we read from side to side along a narrow line, as the printers have found it convenient to print, and not down or up like the Chinese and old Egyptians? Why have we not turned inventive genius to the entirely possible task of making a page that can be read with one-fourth of the eye-work required by the page of the present? So slowly does thought find its way to the rationalization of the common things that we do in life. So rich are the possibilities for research in many lines. So vital to economy in education and in life is the particular group of preliminary researches on reading, the results of which we attempt to bring together in this volume. Though but the beginnings of what is to be done, and but faintly suggesting, if at all, the answers to many of the questions raised, we shall at least break ground for the more complete work that is to follow. And first we shall attempt an analysis and description of the reading process itself.

PART I

THE PSYCHOLOGY
OF READING

CHAPTER II

THE WORK OF THE EYE IN READING

IF we sit directly before one who is reading and watch his eyes closely; or, more conveniently, perhaps, if we have him hold a hand mirror flat on the adjoining page as he reads, while we look over his shoulder, we will notice that his eyes move pretty regularly from side to side along the printed lines. We may count these sweeps from left to right, as a page is read, and at the end will find that they correspond to the number of lines on the page. The reader may insist that he reads several lines or even a paragraph with one sweep of the eye. He has perhaps grasped the thought of the lines or paragraph in one unitary act; and being quite unconscious of the movements of his eyes, he may very naturally suppose that he has taken but one "look" at the lines. However, I have been able without fail to count the lines of the page from the movements of the reader's eyes, whenever the whole page was actually read, not skimmed; and in using apparatus which recorded every movement, the eyes have been found in every case to move from side to side, line by line, without missing any line.

As you watch the reading, you notice, too, that the eyes do not move continuously from left to right along the line, is but proceed by a succession of quick, short movements to the end, then return in one quick, usually unbroken movement to the left. You find all this very evident. And yet most of those who have studied the eye have curiously failed to note that the movement was discontinuous; and up to about 1879, when Professor Javal called attention to it, I find no mention of the fact in the literature. Indeed, I have not myself seen mention of these reading movements until 1898, except in the writings of Professor Javal and some other French authors who took up his discovery, and in a paper published in 1895 by Professor Alexander Brown, of Edinburgh. It is a curious instance of the failure of scientists to make first-hand observations except along certain lines that have become habitual.

You will find that there are at least two pauses for every line, and almost always more than that for lines of this length, — from three to five pauses, usually, and even more when the reading proceeds very slowly. The movements are so very quick that you may wonder as you try to follow them whether the reader has time to see anything during the movement, and you may forecast, as Professor Javal did, what later experiments have seemed to prove, that there is practically no reading, or rather no direct seeing of the words and letters, except during the pauses.

You will find it impossible to determine just what word is being looked at, or fixated, as we say, at any moment; and the reader himself cannot give a much more accurate account of this than can the onlooker, although he often supposes that he can.

An attempt to count the pauses for each line will give rise to some curious difficulties, in case you "lay it on your conscience" to get the number right. If the movements occurred at regular time intervals, so many per second, you might get on very well with them; but it has been found that they vary greatly in extent, and that some of the pauses are very much longer than others. This irregularity prevents the rhythmic grouping which helps so much in counting, and forces one to make a particular counting reaction, say to tap with a pencil or to inwardly say "one, two," etc., for each movement. One may do this for a reader who is not very speedy, but I doubt if it is possible, even with special training, to make accurate counts, by this method, of the movements of the eyes of persons who read rather fast. Besides the difficulty of the counting itself, there is always the possibility of losing movements that occur while your own eye is in motion, as you are practically blind to what occurs while you are changing your own fixation; just as in boxing, one may be startled by a blow that started while his eye was moving, attracted by a feint. And we know the rule, as Professor Dodge observes, that the fencer should look his opponent *in the eye*, trusting to indirect vision for information about his movements.

Professor Javal, of the University of Paris, seems, as has been said, to have been the first to note the actual character of the eye's movements in reading. He concluded that there was a pause about every ten letters, and thought that this was about the amount that could be seen clearly at one fixation. He found that after reading he had after-images of straight gray lines corresponding to the parallel lines of print, and concluded that the eye's fixation point did not leave the line as it moved forward in reading. Finding that the upper half of the line was most important for reading, as can be seen at once by dividing a line in halves horizontally and comparing the legibility of the upper and lower halves, he concluded, from this and other observations, that the fixation point moves along between the middle and top of the small letters. He also stated that the movement was such as to prevent the seeing of what was read except during the reading pauses.

While not all of Professor Javal's observations are conclusive, he deserves more than does any one else the credit for making the initial discoveries in this field, and for initiating a considerable number of later studies. His own further work was prevented by his losing his sight, although, upon calling to see him a few years ago, I found him busily engaged in experimenting upon the reading of the blind.

M. Lamare, working with Professor Javal, found it simpler to count a series of sounds produced, in a microphone, by the eye-movements. The eyelid is displaced a little at each movement of the eye, and this gave the necessary stimulus in an electric circuit. Some information about the movements was thus obtained, although the author is careful to acknowledge the inadequacy of even this method of counting, and guards himself against making more than general conclusions. M. Landolt, continuing the study at the University of Paris, and observing the movements directly, concluded that on an average 1.55 words were read per reading pause, at the ordinary reading distance. Reading of a foreign language required more pauses, as did also the reading of detached words, numbers, and lists of proper names. He found that the small movements were very fatiguing, and that, since the angular excursion increases as the reading matter is brought nearer to the eye, this may account for the tendency of children to bring their books too near the eye. Relief is thus obtained from the fatigue incident to small-angled movements, but the work of the muscles of accommodation and convergence is correspondingly increased, with the resulting tendency to myopia. Doubling the distance of the page from the eye increased the number of movements in the ratio of nine to seven, the number of eye-movements seeming to depend upon the 1 number of words per line rather than upon the visual angle subtended. Landolt's method obliged him, as he states, to have his readers read slowly, and more movements are made by the slow readers.

Dr. Ahrens, at the University of Rostock, Germany, attached a light ivory cup to the cornea of a reader's eye; and fastening a bristle pointer to the cup, he attempted to get from this a tracing of the eye's movements written on a smoked surface. He was unsuccessful, but he had given a valuable suggestion.

Dr. Lough, at Harvard University, and Professor Delabarre, at Brown University, at a considerably later time, attached a plaster of Paris cup to the cornea and obtained some records of the movements of the eye, but apparently obtained no record of the movements in reading.

Erdmann and Dodge, in an extended investigation of reading made at the University of Halle, Germany, and published in 1898, studied the movements of the eye in reading, using the mirror method of direct observation referred to on a previous page. They found that the number of pauses did not vary greatly from line to line, for the same reader and with easy familiar reading matter. There were fewer pauses with familiar matter. In reading lines from a familiar philosophical treatise, printed in English, with lines 83 millimeters in length, Dodge, an American, averaged from three to five pauses per line, according to the familiarity of the passages read. Erdmann, a German, averaged from five to seven pauses per line, under the same conditions, in reading a familiar German scientific work, with lines 122 millimeters in length. In the initial readings, Dodge averaged five pauses per line and Erdmann seven. The variations above and below these latter averages were small and infrequent. More pauses were made in reading a foreign language. Proof-reading required about three times as many pauses as regular reading, in the case of Erdmann. In writing there seemed to be a pause for about every two letters, but they could not be sure that they noted all of the movements here.

By watching a reader's eye through a telescope arranged to permit measurement of horizontal distances observed, they found that the first pause was almost always within the line, and that the last was still farther from the end of the line. The more familiar a text, the greater was the indentation at the left, and more especially still at the right. They consider that the greater indentation at the right is because the previous context makes it easier to fill out the end of the line apperceptively, and also because the last section of the line is seen longer in indirect vision than is the first section, the reader getting no data from the beginning of the line until he arrives at it.

These authors made some observations which seemed to indicate that the fixations of the eye in reading were almost exclusively upon words, upon the middle of the word usually. However, the experiments were not conclusive, and did not permit of the marking of the actual places fixated.

Erdmann and Dodge did not measure the speed of the eye's movements in reading. Lamansky had measured the speed of the eye's movements in general, by counting the number of after-images produced during a given movement of a pencil of light flashed into the eye at regular intervals through the perforations in a rotating disk. Dodge repeated these experiments, and then carried over the results obtained for the speed of eye-movements as they occur in moving voluntarily from one fixation point to another, to the movements that occur in reading. The results, as published in 1898, did not agree with those of Lamansky, and indicated that the time required for an eye-movement in reading was about .015 second. These experimenters had no means of measuring the duration of the reading pauses, but seem to have supposed them to be of tolerably uniform length for a given reading. The pauses have later, however, been shown to vary greatly in length.

Professor Dodge has later succeeded in photographing upon a moving plate a beam of light reflected from the eye at different angles during its movement from one fixation point to another, thus permitting a computation of the rate of movement. The tests that he made of the movement in reading showed that the forward movements varied from two to seven degrees, and that the time occupied by these was, on an average for three readers, nearly .023 second. The return movement through twelve to fourteen degrees required a little less than .041 second. As the lines subtended an angle of sixteen degrees, the eye evidently passed over but three-fourths to seven-eighths of each line.

In experimenting upon the psychology of reading, in 1897-1898, it seemed to me impossible, from my own observations and from those of all earlier experimenters who had tried direct observations of the reader's eye, to get trustworthy account, by direct observation, of the speed, nature, and even number of the eye's movements in reading, of the length and variation of the reading pauses, etc. Nor could the reader himself give even so good an account. For him the succession of movements and pauses is practically non-existent, except when the eyes are very tired or in some way abnormal. In certain cases of abnormal vision, it is true, some valuable observations may be made by the reader. For example, a patient who had no use of the left halves of his retinæ and thus could not see any letters that lay to the right of the point fixated, was quite conscious of the jerky forward movement of his eyes as section after section of new matter came into view. Again, some readers become quite conscious of the presence of the muscæ volitantes, or flitting spots that appear more or less in the vision of most people; and these give some notion of the jerky character of the movements.

Most of us, however, find ourselves getting over the page rather smoothly and continuously, apparently seeing distinctly a considerable portion of it at once, and without interruptions of any kind. Words, letters, and letter-groups flash into greater distinctness from moment to moment, and there is some thought of a mental traversing of the lines. If we watch closely, we are apt to find some sort of inner utterance of what is being read, and we have a notion of the meaning of it all, although we cannot very well describe this consciousness of meaning. Thus reading appears to the casual introspection of the reader. We find, however, that underneath this apparent simplicity, there is an astounding complexity of processes. These have been built up slowly, and by an immense amount of practice, until they have organized and settled into the smoothly running machinery of our present-day reading. The psychologist's analysis discloses a condition which impresses one, to use Francis Galton's figure, as "when the basement of our house happens to be under thorough sanitary repairs, and we realize for the first time the complex system of drains and gas and water pipes, flues, bell-wires, and so forth, upon which our comfort depends, but which are usually hidden out of sight, and with whose existence, so long as they acted well, we had never troubled ourselves."[1]

As a beginning of such analysis of reading, it seemed important to obtain a definite description of the work of the eye. For this purpose I arranged apparatus as follows: A little plaster of Paris cup was moulded to fit the cornea accurately and smoothly, sand-papered until it was very light and thin, and placed upon the front surface of the eye, the cup adhering tightly to the moist cornea. No inconvenience was felt, as the corneal surface was made insensitive by the use of a little holocain, or sometimes cocaine. A round hole in the cup permitted the observer to read with this eye, and the other eye was left free. A light tubular lever of celloidin and glass connected the cup to an aluminum pointer, flat and thin, which responded instantly to the slightest movement of the eye; and, suspended over the smoked-paper surface of a moving drum-cylinder, the aluminum point traced a record of the eye's movement as the observer read. The drawing (Fig. 1) shows the arrangement in the earlier and simpler form. The observer's head rested in a frame which was arranged to prevent movements that would interfere with the record, and which held an attachment to prevent the eyelids from interfering with the cup. The weight and friction of the recording apparatus was reduced to a minimum, the weight of all the parts moved by the eye being but a little more than half a gram, while the weight resting directly upon the eye was less than one-seventh of a gram. During the reading, the reader was usually quite unconscious of there being an attachment to his eye, and the reading proceeded as glibly and easily as could be desired.

Records were made from a large number of readings, with various lengths of line, sizes of type, distances of reading matter, etc. Sometimes the reading was at normal speed, sometimes as fast as the reader could possibly read. The apparatus seemed to work equally well under all the various conditions, even when the speed reached an average of twelve words per second. In order to measure the speed an electric current from an induction coil was passed through the pointer to the drum. This current was interrupted at

---

[1] "Inquiry into the Human Faculty," p. 186.

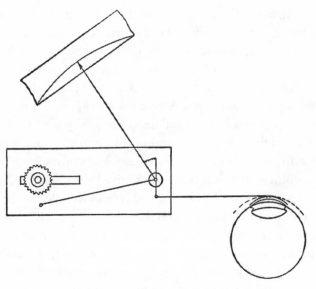

Fig. 1

very regular short intervals by the vibrations of an electrically driv-
en tuning-fork, the snap of the spark from the pointer's tip thus
displacing a dot of soot on the paper record at each interruption. As
the pointer flitted over the drum during the reading, a tracing was
thus produced like that shown in Figure 2. The tracing as taken of
course magnified the actual movement several times.

The tracings showed that the eye always traversed the page line
by line, and always in a succession of quick movements and pauses
when moving from left to right. Movements in retracal occurred
but seldom, averaging about once in seven lines. Apparently the eye
did not wander far above and below the line that was being read,
although the arrangement of the apparatus could not show this
certainly. As we have seen, Professor Javal thought that the eye's
fixation point moved along the line between the middle and top of
the small letters, but I do not think that his experiment with after-
images establishes this. It seems to me probable that the fixation
point varies more widely than this, but there is nothing to indicate that it wanders perceptibly above or below the line. The return
sweep when a line was finished was usually without interruption, although about once in six lines a halt would be made near the end

of the movement, apparently for the eye to get its bearings in the new line. These halts in the return movement are more numerous in reading long lines. The eye is apparently guided in making the

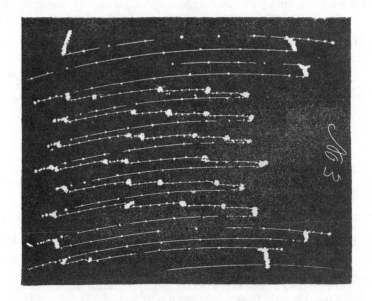

Specimen Curve of 'Spark' Record.

This reproduction, cut by a careful engraver upon a block on which the original tracing had been photographed, shows with great accuracy the sort of record from which the times of the eye movements have been determined. The chief difference between the original and the reproduction is in the breadth of the horizontal lines which are finer in the original.

The curve shows the movements of the eye in reading six lines, preceded and followed by two free movements of the eye each way, in which it was swept from one end of the line to the other, the beginning and end alone being fixated. The broad vertical lines and the round blurs in the reading indicate pauses in the eye's movements, the successive sparks knocking the soot away from a considerable space. The small dots standing alone or like beads upon the horizontal lines, show the passage of single sparks, separated from each other by 0.0068 sec. The breaks in the horizontal lines indicate that the writing point was not at all times in contact with the surface of the paper though near enough for the spark to leap across, as shown by the solitary dots;

The tracing shows clearly the fixation pauses in the course of the line, the general tendency to make the "indentation" greater at the right than at the left, and the unbroken sweep of the return from right to left.

NOTE. The cut and description are reproduced from the *American Journal of Psychology*, Vol. XI.

FIG. 2

return by the consciousness of the next line's beginning, seen dimly at the left as it starts. Such guidance would of course be less accurate as the line is longer, and this may necessitate both the haltings and the distraction that we notice introspectively when we lose the line.

In reading lines of the length shown in Figure 3, the subject-matter being of only ordinary difficulty, the smallest number of

Each page thus honey-combed, was fastened closely upon a white paper background. The page was then marked off into four divisions. Two readings were taken, separated by sev-

Fig. 3

movements for any line was two, the largest seven. Usually there were from four to six. One reader averaged four and a half pauses per line for fifty-one lines. Another averaged a very little more. These readings were at the ordinary reading distance. Doubling the distance did not appreciably lessen the number of pauses per line.

ney very seldom paid any attention to it. If they wanted to do cer-ain things, they would do it whether the constitution allowed them o or not. The only reason they had a constitution was because they

Fig. 4

Of course this means that the angle of each eye-movement grows smaller as the book recedes, possibly with the increased tendency to fatigue that comes with small eye-movements, as experienced when you look along the pickets of a fence or the letters of a line, although in these latter cases the conditions are somewhat different.

Using the smaller type shown in Figure 4 slightly increased the number of pauses and movements. Using shorter lines of course reduced the number. A magazine article, with lines of the length and type shown in Fig. 5, gave an average of 3.6 pauses per line, there

give the murderer the benefit of a doubt, he felt as a man that the doubt could not really exist, and that Tebaldo had in-tentionally put him under the seal of con-

Fig. 5

being always either three or four pauses for a line. A newspaper article, of lines and type as in Fig. 6, gave 3.8 pauses per line for one reader and 3.4 for another.

The records for lines of all lengths show that the eye seldom moves along the whole extent of the line, but makes the first pause somewhat within the line and the last still farther within. From 78 per cent to 82 per cent of the line, on an average, was actually traversed by the eye, in reading such lines as are shown in Figures 3 and 4. The indentation was usually in the vicinity of

> American citizens could not have a
> part. But I am satisfied that it is all
> right. Every one of tne great races
> that are blended in our national life has
> its own glorious traditions which it

Fig. 6

18 per cent of the total line length, varying considerably from line to line, and being usually considerably greater at the right, although occasionally it was greater at the left. In some readings the first pause must have been in the first half of the first word in most of the lines, while in other passages it must usually have been in the second or even in the third word. For a given passage, the reader seemed to fall into a way of indenting a certain amount at the beginning or end of a line, and kept this tendency through the passage.

The extent of the forward movements in reading varied greatly in all cases, and the conclusion of Javal that the eye moves over the extent of matter that can be read at one pause, about the space of ten letters in his opinion, was shown to be unfounded. The specimen tracing above shows the great difference found in the extent of the movements, and is typical. A slight movement may be followed by one four times as extensive, and the movements are in general very irregular. The movements averaged from three to four degrees of arc in the various readings, with lines of the length shown in Figures 3 and 4. With these lines the return sweep usually traversed twelve to thirteen degrees.

The forward movements of the eye in reading were found to occupy a relatively constant time, somewhat irrespective of their extent. In one reading, the movements of the eye varied in extent as from four to twenty-six, while the times for these movements ranged from four to seven. Excluding three exceptionally short movements, the others in this same reading ranged in extent from seven and a half to twenty-six, while their times ranged only from six to seven.

The spark record indicated that the absolute time required for each movement forward varied usually between .04 second and less than .048 second. The return movements usually required a little longer, usually from .051 to .058 second. Later experiments indicate, as we shall see, that the times are actually considerably shorter than this.

The reading pauses were of very variable duration. In one of the readings the pauses averaged about .19 second, but the average variation was nearly .05 second. Another reading by the same observer showed an average pause of less than .11 second, with one-third less variation. This latter record was taken under circumstances which may have sometimes permitted the current to snap twice at the same spot, and if so, the pauses were really a little longer than as above. The other times given here for the pauses were measured from the displacement of the drum as measured by an electric time-marker connected with the laboratory clock and writing its record beside that of the eye's movement. Two additional readings by different observers gave an average pause of a little more than .18 second for each. The pauses in retracal and at interruptions of the return sweep are usually shorter than the reading pauses proper and are not included in the averages above.

For rather fast readers, then, the pauses seem to average in the vicinity of .185 second; but the variation is so very great that any average is misleading, and the pauses may really be of almost any length. The averages, however, show the interesting fact that the most of the reading time is used in a fixed gaze at the page and but an inconsiderable portion of the time is used in the eye's movements.

In all the experiments whose results are given above, the readers read at their usual rate, silently, and for the thought. In another series of tests they were asked to read as fast as possible. This decreased the number of pauses per line, and also the duration of the pauses. The extent of each eye-movement was correspondingly increased.

The speed of the movements was not increased in the least, and there was nothing in any of the experiments to indicate that the rate of movement is subject to direct voluntary control. Fast readers thus seem to perform less eye-work, their movements are less fatiguing in so far as large-angled movements may be easier than small ones, and they take less time for visual perception of the printed matter.

These results are fairly congruent with those of Erdmann and Dodge as to most points, except as to the rate of movement. Rather fewer pauses per line were found in my experiments than in those of either Erdmann and Dodge or of Javal and Landolt, for the reading of new matter. But the fact that Landolt's readers read slowly would account for the more numerous pauses in his case, and the method of counting may have led to reading that was slower than normal in all these cases. On the other hand, my records were from rather fast readers, and they may have made somewhat fewer pauses than occur in ordinary reading.

As to rate of movement, we have seen that the early measurements by Lamansky gave times that were not in agreement with the later ones by Dodge, using the same method. Dodge's still later photographic measurements show a still slower rate of movement, and with considerable individual differences. His times are still considerably shorter than those found in my own experiments, averaging nearly .023 second for forward movements of from two to seven degrees, and nearly .041 second for return movements of from twelve to fourteen degrees. While a part of this difference may be due to individual variations, the larger part of it is doubtless due to error somewhere. As we shall presently see, the recent measurements by Dr. Dearborn, using the Dodge method of photographic registration, confirm the later results of Dodge as stated above, and I accept these, therefore, as trustworthy conclusions on the rate of movement. I am unable even yet to certainly locate the source or sources of error in my own measurements of rate. All of Professor Dodge's criticisms of my apparatus were in my own mind in its construction; and it seemed to me, as well as to several psychologists and physicists who were experienced in the manipulation of delicate apparatus, that there was little likelihood of any considerable error. Error, however, there evidently has been; and I am at present inclined to think that most of it arose through a slight yielding of the corneal surface under the movement of the recording attachment.

Very accurate determinations of the rate of eye-movement are of considerable importance along several lines of psychological inquiry, which, however, do not concern us here. The essential problem as to the movements in reading is to know whether they are of such a speed as to prevent our perceiving letters or words during the movement. This question is already practically settled, provided we can carry over to reading the general requirements for fusion of visual stimuli. The rate of reading movements is much too fast to permit our getting such data during the movement as can appreciably help us in our reading, granting that the laws of fusion apply. Various experimenters have shown that when retinal stimulations are given in rapid succession, as when a disk of white and black sectors is rotated before the resting eye, the impressions fuse into one continuous impression when a rate of thirty to sixty stimulations per second is reached. But in reading at even a very slow speed, and supposing the rate of the eye-movement to be the slowest found in any of the measurements, the succession of black better-strokes and white interspaces occurs at a rate which is far faster than even sixty per second, and which would inevitably produce nothing but a light-gray blur, if the eye were still and the line shifted horizontally at a corresponding rate. The experiment may be tried by holding a pencil tip near to a sheet of printed matter, as a fixation mark, and giving the paper a fairly rapid movement from side to side. If the movement is in the direction of the lines of print, the latter will appear as homogeneous gray bands, with no letters or words recognizable.

But why do we not see these gray bands as we read? Scarcely a trace of them has been reported by any experimenter, except that Professor Dodge believed that he could detect faint traces. I have found no reader who had any consciousness of them, and have none myself. We seem to see the letters and words as distinctly during the movements as at the pauses, and the visual field is unbroken to consciousness.

Professor Cattell advanced the hypothesis that the visual organs respond to retinal changes more rapidly when the eye moves than when the objects are in motion, and that we really do see objects distinctly during the eye's movement. He believed that when we look from one end to the other of a row of books, for instance, we can note titles, etc., that were outside the range of distinct vision before the movement began. Indeed, in moving the eye over black and white surfaces, it seemed to him that no fusion occurred "even when one thousand stimuli per second fall upon each retinal element."[1] However, careful observation reveals the fact that in looking along a row of books or any other objects which we attempt to perceive, the eye makes a succession of short pauses and quick movements, as in reading, and it is not at all necessary to suppose that there was anything perceived during the movement. Professor Cattell supposed that a very large number of pauses would be necessary to allow of distinct perception, if no data were obtained during the movement; but his estimate of one degree as the limit of the "field of distinct vision" is much too small, as will be seen later, the pauses even in reading occurring only at intervals of from three to four degrees, on an average.

Professor Cattell's hypothesis seemed to be rendered untenable, as he himself frankly acknowledged in a later note in the *Psychological Review*, by some experiments of Professor Dodge upon the possibilities of vision during eye-movement. Professors Erdmann and Dodge had found that when one watches his own eye in a mirror, it is impossible, when the eye moves, to detect any trace of the movement. This furnishes at least a partial demonstration of the apparent fact that we are not usually aware of what goes on in the field of vision while the eye is in motion. It cannot, however, be said to be a final test.

Professor Dodge made some further experiments to determine whether the eye is quite insensitive to impressions received as it moves. At first it appeared to be so. But after preliminary practice, and with more intense illumination, it was shown conclusively that distinctions of light and shade, and indeed of color, can be made in objects that are exposed only during the movement. Furthermore, under the special conditions of the experiment, it was found that lines of print exposed only during the eye's movement "gave a perfect

---

[1] Psychological Review, 1900, p. 325.

though shadowy series of gray bands in a lighter gray background, in which individual letters or words were absolutely irrecognizable."[1]

Professor E. B. Holt, of Harvard, made a series of careful experiments to determine whether "voluntary movements of the eyes condition a momentary, visual, central anæsthesia," and concluded that they did. However, his results, even if finally conclusive on this point, cannot be carried over to the involuntary movements of the eye in reading.[2]

Professor R. S. Woodworth, of Columbia, on the basis of other experiments, maintains that the eye is not anæsthetic during movement. He finds that an image thrown on the retina during the eye's movement is correctly localized in space, that muscæ, etc., are seen during the eye-movements, and cites the fact that an object which moves with the eye, at the eye's rate, is seen clearly during the movement.[3]

Finally, Professor Dodge, in his article in the *Psychological Bulletin* of June 15, 1905, says that he has "yet to meet with any unambiguous evidence of anæsthesia during eye-movement, either central or peripheral," and thinks the lack of clear perception during eye-movements must rest largely if not wholly on other grounds. Among the more important of these latter he mentions the persistence of the positive after-image for some three hundredths of a second, at about full intensity; the inhibition by the following stimulation from the new fixation point, and the fact that the stimulations during movement are not objects of interest and are, therefore, ignored as are the muscæ, the fencing mask, and other such irrelevant stimuli.

Evidently, then, the retina is sensitive to impressions received during the eye's involuntary movements, such as occur in reading, although it is not shown that it is more sensitive then than at other times. Evidently, too, fusion of impressions may occur during the eye's movement as when it is at rest. There remains the question as to why we are so completely unconscious of any fusion of the letters as we read.

---

[1] *Psychological Review*, September, 1900, p. 463.

[2] *Ibid.*, Monograph Supplement, January, 1903.

[3] *Psychological Bulletin*, February 15, 1906, and *Proceedings of American Psychological Association*, 1905-1906.

A conclusive answer cannot be made until there has been further experimentation; and, perhaps, a better understanding of the
conditions under which the consciousness of fusion arises. However,
it should be remembered that the total stimulation given during
the movement is very brief compared with that of the preceding
reading pause, certainly not more than one-fourth as long in most
cases. We know that a strong memory image of the reading stimulus
tends to persist after the pause, as after any stimulus of such duration; and this would tend to persist in consciousness to the exclusion
of the much fainter and briefer stimulations that occur during the
movement. The stimulations occurring during the movement would
have their own effect cut short prematurely by the intense stimulation of the succeeding pause, and would tend to pass unnoticed in
consequence.

Mainly, however, as has long been known, we habitually ignore
stimulations and sensations which have no meaning for us, in favor of
those which carry meaning. Raw sensations are continually ignored
in favor of their meanings, in all the sense spheres; and indeed there
is a tendency of consciousness to remove in the direction of the more
and more remote suggestions from any given stimulus, at least so far as
such removal is helpful in practice. The gray-blur stimulus produced
during the movement carries no meaning of its own, and leads no
whither as a sign of remoter meanings. It is faint, of most transient
existence, and remains beneath the threshold of clear consciousness.
Our ignoring of the movement stimulations is not exceptional in the
psychology of perception. Stimulations constantly occur in various
parts of our bodies, from pressure of our clothing and of the body's
parts, stimulations which are often of considerable intensity, but
which regularly pass unnoticed. The failure of most people to notice
the entoptic phenomena, —the dark spots and strange shapes that
are usually to be found in the field of vision, is, as Professor Dodge
observes, a case of our systematically ignoring stimuli which would
disturb our clear vision if attended to. I am in general quite of his
opinion that the absence of the consciousness of fusion is "centrally
as well as peripherally conditioned."

These are the conclusions which, I think, the facts would
ordinarily be said to warrant. I must confess, however, that I am,

as yet, not entirely satisfied with them. Several minor facts brought out in the various experiments harmonize well with the view that the stimulations occurring during the eye's movement may be effective both upon the reflex mechanism of movement and upon the conscious content, and that they are correctly localized without fusion. Professor Holt's discovery that a stimulus acting upon the retina during eye-movement caused a reaction of the reflex mechanism in the direction of fixating the stimulus; Professor Woodworth's determination that an image thrown upon the retina during the movement is correctly localized in space; these, with minor indications from various sources, are suggestive of the latter view. Indeed, do we have the consciousness of visual fusion in any case where it is possible to apperceive the stimuli as they occur, where our concern is with apperceiving them, and where the conditions are such as to permit our giving them a correct orientation in space? There is little to indicate that a new orientation with reference to the reading stimuli arises *in toto* when the eye makes a new pause in reading. There is much to indicate that the orientation persists from pause to pause, and indeed during temporary closing of the eyes. A compensatory adjustment of the field of vision would seem to be made as the eye moves forward, and it is doubtful if at any instant of the movement the spatial relation of the body and self to the various parts of the visual field is not felt as truly, although fleetingly, as when the eye is at rest. If so, then there is much reason to suppose that the stimulations received from the page as the eye moves are properly placed in order as they come, with no possibility of a blur. It is true that impressions made by each letter or smaller form upon any given retinal area would be very brief and slight; and yet, if the stimulations are sufficient to be felt as a blur, they may well be also sufficient to serve as cues for their proper projection in space, without blur.

So it may be that Professor Cattell was right in his conclusion if not in his method, and that our thought of the printed line gets the benefit of what stimulations occur during eye-movement, and has no tendency to fuse the impressions because these are taken care of in advance. Fusion may occur only when there is inability to "think" the data given, in which case the consciousness arises of the *data themselves*, the black-white of the sensations. The cases in which fusion occurs have always, perhaps, been cases in which conditions were such as to prevent apperception or compensatory adjustment of the field of vision; and indeed the attempt to make such adjustment is seldom made in such cases as produce fusion. These suggestions, however, are offered as but tentative, and of no scientific value except that they show, to my mind, that the absence of fusion during eye-movement presents a problem which is by no means closed at the present stage of experimentation.

Since most of the above account was written, Dr. Dearborn has published the results of a thorough study of the eye's movements and pauses in reading, based upon experiments at Columbia University in which Professor Dodge's method of photographic registration was used. Dr. Dearborn's results agree, in the main, with those of earlier experimenters, but they give additional information that is of much importance. It was found that "the more pauses there are in a line the shorter their lengths, on the average, and, *vice versa*, the fewer the pauses the larger any one pause is apt to be." "Viewed simply from the standpoint of speed of reading, it is in general an advantage to read a given line with the smallest possible number of pauses, because while the elimination of a pause increases somewhat the average duration of the remaining pauses, the total time for the line is decreased, or remains constant." The number of pauses per line varies greatly, but is greater for the slow readers and when reading slowly. The eye readily falls into a brief "motor habit" of making a certain fixed number of pauses per line, for a given passage, independently of the nature of the subject-matter. "The ease of the formation of motor habits seems to be one of the characteristics of rapid readers as contrasted with slower ones." In making the adjustment for the return sweep at the end of the first line, and sometimes at the end of the second, the dependence is "solely on the peripheral local signs. The longer the line, the more inexact these will naturally be." But, if the lines are not too long, "after the first or possibly the second horizontal movement, the resident muscular sensations of angular displacement govern the extent of movement of the succeeding return sweep. This is the basis of the motor habit." It is important, therefore, that the lines be of only moderate length and that this length be approximately uniform, although Dr. Dearborn agrees with Professor Cattell that "a small indentation of a few millimeters, for example, of every other line . . . would help to differentiate the lines, and prevent their confusion." He finds that the modern primers and first readers constantly violate this principle of uniformity, breaking up the line with their illustrations and often making a paragraph, with its unequal lines, for every sentence. Besides, the lines of the beginners' books are usually too long. A more or less uniform motor habit of eye-movement is to be acquired in the beginning, and the shorter lines of uniform length are necessary for this. Lines of varying length "must naturally lead to a more cautious mode of eye-movement, hard to overcome later, and may cause unnecessarily slow readers."

The average duration of the pauses was found to be uniformly less in the shorter lines than in the long ones. The total time per passage is also decreased in moderately short lines of right arrangement. It was discovered that the first pause in each line is distinctly longer than the others, especially in rapid reading and with rapid readers. Toward the end of the line, also, there is apt to be a pause of greater length than the average, although shorter than the first. At the initial long fixation and at the secondary long one the "attention expands," and by the former "a more general perception is secured of the ideas and words that follow in the line. The succeeding fixations serve to amplify and fill out this general perception. Finally, this expanding of the field of attention is made more frequently and with greater ease in the short line."

In general, Dr. Dearborn thinks that differences in the rate of reading in the same individual and between different individuals depend "largely, when other conditions are constant, upon the ease with which a regular, rhythmical movement can be established and sustained." The peculiarities of such a movement are "first, a succession of the same number of pauses per line, and secondly, a certain fairly uniform arrangement in the order of long and short pauses," in which arrangement the first pause should be longest, with a secondary pause of increased length near the end of the line. When "shorter lines" are mentioned as best meeting these requirements, the reference is to lines of a length common in our newspapers, or a little longer. Dr. Dearborn thinks favorably of "a line of seventy-five to eighty-five millimeters or about a third longer than the ordinary newspaper line of the New York dailies," although he recognizes that his data are not sufficient to warrant any conclusion upon this point.

Dr. Dearborn's measurements of the rate of the eye's movement in reading agree substantially, as we have seen, with those of Professor Dodge, and these may be taken as representative for most readers, although the rate was found to vary considerably. Dearborn, therefore, concludes that there is "no distinct visual impression" during the eye's movement in reading. Some readers, however, were found to make a considerable number of slow shifting movements, often ten to twenty times slower than the usual movement. These shifting movements are really to be classed as unsteady fixations, the eye accompanying the movement of attention as the latter shifted, and gathering data for perception as it moved. "The eye tends to follow each shift of the attention in order to bring the object nearer the fovea," and Dearborn believes that "the unsteadiness of fixations is due to the acute unbalance and general alertness of attention to peripheral excitation." "The attention is ahead and pulling the eye along."

It was found that the "exact point that is fixated may be in any part of the words, or in the spacing between them." "It does not fall predominantly in the first part of words, nor does it occur more frequently in the first part of the sentence than in the last, and apparently pays little attention to many of the laws of apperception or the rules of the rhetorician." The exact points of fixation are "significant only as representing the point about which are grouped the 'block' of letters that are simultaneously perceived as one word or phrase complex. It more often falls in the first third than at the centre of a given perception area." "The short connective and non-substantive words, the prepositional phrases and relative clauses, make the greatest demands upon perception, and thus require most fixations." "They necessitate the eye's coming out quite to the edge of the lines." These "transitive" parts of speech are "not associated in one phrase more regularly than in another, they cannot be fused into a larger apperceptive unit, as the syllables into a word form, or 'phrase whole'; but each stands by itself and must be so perceived." "It is not the short words, as such, but the words which cannot be easily grouped with others, which necessitate separate fixation." Prepositions, conjunctions, etc., "occur now with one word and now with another; they cannot without danger of error be fused into larger wholes, and, for that reason, they must, except where the context gives the connection, be separately perceived." The same was found to be true of numerals, lines of nonsense-letters, etc., and the explanation is similar. On the other hand, nouns, adjectives, and verbs, and especially words and phrases which are familiar to the apperception of the reader, or for which he has a particular memory, "allow of an exceptionally large 'jump' between fixation pauses."

Children of from nine to eleven years, the only ages tested, were found to make more frequent pauses than adults, and generally longer pauses, although quite short pauses occur. While there is "some unsteadiness and refixation" their "accuracy of fixation appears as exact as that of adults." "The more purely physiological difficulties have been fairly well mastered. The rate of movement in the return sweeps and in the inter-fixation movements is not different from that of the adult."

In the reading of a single adult who was tested for the effects of fatigue, it was found that after a hard day's work with the eyes the reader made more pauses and longer ones than when the eyes were fresh next morning. Eye-fatigue was thus found to diminish the speed of reading, for this reader. Some further experiments showed that the eye becomes fatigued very quickly in making movements through a large angle, covering say one hundred and fifty millimeters on the page. At least the rate of movement became from one-third to one-fourth slower in the course of seven movements. This indication of fatigue did not appear to any considerable extent in making movements of about half this length, and thus furnishes an additional argument in favor of using lines of moderate length. I cannot agree, however, with Dr. Dearborn in his belief that these results negative the conclusion of Landolt, that small-angled movements are very fatiguing, as Landolt's reference is to the very short excursions such as are made in the smaller inter-fixation movements.[1] Landolt himself instanced the fatigue which comes when we attempt to count the palings on a closely picketed fence. Of course we must always recognize that such fatigue may be of the attention rather than of the eye-muscles.

We may note in conclusion Dr. Dearborn's agreement with the writer in concluding that Javal's theory that the eye moves along between the middle and top of the small letters is "a physical impossibility," although Dearborn's apparatus did not permit, as mine did not, definite measurement of movements in the vertical plane.

Concluding here our survey of the eye's movements and pauses as mechanical processes, we will next consider the psychic processes of perception which occur in dealing with the data obtained during the reading pauses. And first we shall try to determine the amount of printed matter that can be seen clearly at any moment in which the eye is at rest, say during a reading pause.

---

[1] In a recent letter to the writer Dr. Dearborn tells me that his reference to Landolt rested upon a misunderstanding. On the other hand, I agree with him that Landolt's test is not conclusive for the reading movements.

CHAPTER III

THE EXTENT OF READING MATTER PERCEIVED DURING A READING PAUSE

In looking casually over a printed page, one is apt to think that a very considerable portion of it is seen at any moment with distinctness enough for reading. The amount that can be seen thus distinctly is smaller than is generally supposed. The illusion may come partly from the fact that the retina's ability to discriminate brightnesses, or differences in the light and dark of the page, does not decrease from the point of clearest vision outward as far as is reached by both ends of the ordinary line, when one looks at the middle. So most of the page appears as bright in one part as another. Again, since by long experience we know that we can at once see distinctly any part of the field at will, and since we are usually unconscious of the eye-movements which make this possible, we naturally mistake the "reading range" given by several quick eye-movements, for that which is possible for the unmoved eye.

However, if you will look fixedly at a letter in the middle of the page and will attempt to name the letters or words about it, without moving the eye for a single instant, you will discover that the reading range of the unmoved eye is distinctly limited. Erdmann and Dodge, in trying this experiment on a page of German printed in good type, found that neither of them could see letters or words clearly beyond the ends of the lines represented in the diagram below, when fixating a letter at the central dot. Not all of even this amount could be seen clearly.

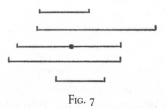

Fig. 7

Some of you will be able to see all the letters distinctly over a little larger area than this; a few will not be able to do so well, for some readers are found to have a curiously limited range of distinct vision. However, if you have tried the experiment, you have doubtless noticed that, beyond the circle within which you recognize clearly most or all of the letters and words, there is also recognized, now dimly, now rather distinctly, an occasional letter of characteristic form, most often a capital, — or even a whole word of striking appearance, and this at a considerable distance from the fixation point. Erdmann and Dodge found this to occur at the distance of nearly or quite an ordinary line-length. Sometimes a word or a letter or group of letters flashes up momentarily from the obscurity of indirect vision. Helmholtz found, in lighting a page for an instant by the electric spark, that particular groups of letters would appear here and there in somewhat the same fashion.

Some of you will see distinctly much farther than I have suggested as possible, because, as you interest yourselves in this or that part of the visual field, unconsciously your eyes move a little in that direction. This not only brings new matter within range, but freshens the retina as well, by changing the position of all its letter-images. It is difficult for an unpracticed observer to prevent such wandering of the eye; and even the most thoroughly trained observer cannot prevent a slight fluctuation of the fixation, which seems to occur almost constantly. We see an accentuation of this normal healthy condition in persons who are troubled with nystagmus, an affection of the eye characterized by a slight but plainly visible and constant change of fixation point, the patient being quite unconscious of the movement and supposing that he keeps his eye steadily fixated as he looks.

The range of clear seeing about the fixation point is really a little greater than as given above. The retina is very quickly fatigued in maintaining a fixed stare for even a moment. The glance of the first instant shows the largest area, the border letters immediately growing indistinct before we have had time to make them out or repeat their names if recognized. In actual reading, as we shall see, the meaning or context fixes them before they fade.

It was found by Cattell, Goldscheider and Müller, Quantz, and various other experimenters, that when printed matter was exposed to the eye for a very short time, about one one-hundredth of a second, more could be read, or the same amount could be read more easily, than when the exposure was longer. Of course in such an exposure the retinal image remains for some time after the exposure ceases, just as you see the incandescent light after you have turned off the current. I proceeded to measure, with as much care as possible, the amount of printed matter that can be read at a single pause of the eye; and in doing so, relying on the experience of the investigators mentioned, I made a clear exposure of the printed lines for the slightly longer period of one sixty-sixth of a second.

In actual reading, we largely disregard the lines above and below the one that is at the moment being read; and as far as the eye is concerned the procedure is a matter of taking a succession of from three to five quick peeps at as many places in the line. How much of the line can be read at a single peep of this kind? I carried through a series of experiments in which just such peeps were given, along lines of printed matter similar to those shown in Figure 3, taken from the *American Journal of Psychology*. The printed lines were pasted on strips of cardboard and were carefully joined from end to end so as to form, on each card, a continuous line of print. The exposures were made with the Cattell Fall apparatus, an instrument in which a thin steel plate containing a rectangular horizontal cleft is arranged to fall close before the printed line, the latter being invisible except while the rectangular opening in the plate permitted a peep at the line in passing. The length of the exposure thus depended upon the height from which the plate had fallen before the cleft reached the printed line, and could be regulated accordingly.

The reader looked at a point close before a marked place in the line, two seconds before the plate fell, and thus had his eye fixed on this known point in the line during the exposure. The lines were seen at the usual reading distance, were well lighted, and the reader sat comfortably in a quiet room of the laboratory.

The first series of peeps was taken at intervals of 1.75 centimeters, eleven and one-half letter spaces, in order as one would read, the reader saying aloud as much as he could see after each exposure. Then the intervals were increased to 2 centimeters, 2.25 centimeters, and so on up to and including intervals of 4 centimeters. The reader always had the benefit of knowing the context up to the section about to be exposed, the preceding sections being read to him if he had not made them out.

It was found that some readers could read continuously for a considerable distance when the peeps were taken at intervals of 2.5 centimeters, sixteen letter spaces, and not repeated. Of four readers tested three were able to do as well as this, except for occasional failure through inattention or the special conditions of the experimenting.

When the peeps were at intervals of 4 centimeters, or separated by twenty-six letter spaces, none of the readers were able to read continuously for any distance, although all but one at one time or another read phrases of greater length than this, and that one read phrases as long as 3.7 centimeters.

When the peeps were taken here and there in new matter without giving the preceding context, it was found, to my surprise, that a little more was read, on an average, than when the context was known. With preceding context known, considerably more was read to the left than to the right of the fixation point, on an average. Without the context a little more was read to the right, although in neither case did this hold for all the readers.

The *average* extent of matter read per exposure was of course much less than the amounts stated above. One reader read an average of ten letter spaces, another fifteen, a third eleven, and a fourth, with a curiously limited range of distinct vision, averaged but five, — the average reading being ten letter spaces for these four readers, from many hundreds of exposures. If we include in our average the cases in which the beginning and the end of a section were correctly read but some intermediate part was lost, the average extent was eleven and one-fourth letter spaces.

Comparing the average amounts thus read in these peeps at the line with the average amounts read at the reading pauses in actual reading, we find that they are nearly the same, two representative readers being found to cover about ten letter spaces per reading pause, on an average, when reading similar lines.

However, a comparison of averages has but a partial value, for the actual amounts read at each peep at the line or in each pause in ordinary reading varies very much from the average. For instance, in actual reading it was found that in rare cases two pauses sufficed for the reading of a whole Journal line (Fig. 3). The exposure experiments cited above show that in similarly rare instances each reader, even the one with the much limited average range, was able to read correctly nearly or quite the half of such a line at a single peep. The readers stated, too, that they actually *saw* the whole extent thus read at one exposure without conscious guessing or estimating. Some of these longest readings are given on page 39.

We may conclude, then, that the reader's eye is usually capable of taking care of as much as nearly half a line of the length and type used in our experiments, provided conditions are favorable. The fact that much less was read at most of the exposures was due to causes some of which can best be stated in our later discussion. It was, of course, inevitable that sometimes the reader's attention would wander at the moment of the exposure, and then little or nothing would be read. Again, parts of the line which were seen clearly for an instant would be forgotten before they could fix themselves in mind sufficiently to be reproduced. Then again, the amount that could be read varied very greatly with the character of the matter exposed. In general, the more the word groups resembled isolated words, as when divided by punctuation marks, the less easily they were read. Prepositional phrases, substantives with a series of modifying adjectives or with a closely linked phrase modifier, and series of any kind which had a rhythmic swing, were preferred. Certain words, usually rather unfamiliar ones, presented peculiar difficulties. It seemed almost impossible to bring about a recognition of them by repeated exposures when the reader failed to recognize them at first. "Titillation" was exposed ten times successively before recognition had proceeded so far as to call it "tililation." All the readers had difficulty with this word. The letters would be clearly seen, but apparently could not be remembered long enough to enable the reader to construct the word. *Raison d'être* caused similar trouble.

It might be supposed that in a momentary peep at a line of print approximately as much would be read on one side of the fixation point as on the other, but this is by no means the case. The averages, it is true, do not show great differences, but it is very different with the results of particular exposures. The following table shows the extent in millimeters read on each side of the fixation point by two readers in consecutive peeps at the line: —

READER A		READER B	
Left	*Right*	*Left*	*Right*
20	25	5	0
7	19	12	6
17	10	13	18
0	0	24	0
9	15	9	15
2	13	14	13
17	4	18	4
10	8	10	8

FIG. 8

Some of the longer readings by various readers in these experiments are given below, with the fixation points marked: —

Condition of consciousness
by a brightly colored
These muscular contraction
Condition of consciousness
So difficult is the
of the relevant ones
the whole body
but also the movements
The whole body converges
by a brightly colored object
typical form, known as
are not of equal value
these muscular contractions

FIG. 9

It is interesting to note that in almost every case in which a large amount is read, far more is read to the right of the fixation point than to the left. We can hardly explain this by attributing it to an involuntary wandering of the eye's fixation toward the right. No tendency to wander to the right rather than to the left has been noted in other experiments, and there is much reason to think that the fixation point did not vary more than a letter space or two at most, except perhaps very rarely. One of the readers who is thoroughly practiced in such matters constantly stated the letter or space which he supposed he had fixated; and in practically all cases his statement was correct. Two of the other readers had had a fair amount of laboratory practice and exercised all possible care in preserving a constant fixation. The fourth, a graduate student in mathematics, was at least as careful as the others.

The conditions, such as close grammatical connection, etc., mentioned earlier as making for larger total readings, tend similarly to give larger readings to one or another side of the fixation point, as they occur there. Then, too, the attention is by no means always directed to the same point as the eye's fixation, and there may then occur a greater readiness for dealing with matter seen at the right or left.

In the case of the larger readings in which so much more is read at the right than at the left, this is probably largely due to the tendency of our words, as of all mental contents, to call up or to facilitate the perception of those associates which have habitually succeeded rather than preceded them. The words far at the right, although dimly seen, are helped into consciousness and preserved in memory by associative links from those that are clearly seen. Then, too, the latter half of a long word seen far at the left is not apt to suggest the first half, and the whole word is lost. The first half of a long word far at the right, on the other hand, is apt to suggest the whole word, both because the flow of association has been in that direction and because the first half of a word is much the more important for the word's recognition, as we shall see later.

The maximum amount which can be read during a reading pause has been measured by various other experimenters, with fairly congruent results. Erdmann and Dodge found that a German reader, in a single exposure lasting one-tenth of a second, read correctly sentences consisting of from four to six words of two to ten letters each, and occasionally recognized a simple word even at the end of a sentence of seven words, containing twenty-six letters. The middle of the sentence was fixated in all cases. The type was larger than that used in the writer's experiments, and the other conditions somewhat different.

Messmer, experimenting at the University of Zurich, found that most of his readers could read nearly as much as this, in certain cases.

But like the writer, he found certain readers with a curiously limited reading range.

Cattell found one reader who could read as much as seven words at a single exposure, when the words composed a sentence and were given in two lines. His other readers, however, were usually limited to four words. Of course all these results show only the maximal amounts which can be perceived at a glance, corresponding roughly to what is read in a reading pause when pauses are least frequent. We have seen that the eye usually makes pauses so frequently as to keep well within this maximum, the average amount covered per reading pause approximating the average amount read in the momentary exposure tests.

My readers will doubtless wonder that so much of sense matter can be read at a single glance or pause, when the particular letters can be made out only, as we have seen, within a limited radius about the fixation point. It is very likely, as I have suggested, that one can really make out letters somewhat farther from the fixation point than the Erdmann and Dodge experiment indicates. But there is no doubt that words of sentences are read at a distance from the fixation point at which letters are no longer recognizable. Similarly, Erdmann and Dodge found that words could be read at a distance from the reader which made the constituent letters unrecognizable when presented singly. Yet in many of these cases the reader states that he sees clearly all letters of the words or sentences read; and in my own experience, as also for Erdmann and Dodge, the letters of words seen far from the fixation point seem about as distinct as the others. Nevertheless it seems certain that in the longer readings the parts most distant from the fixation point are not clearly seen except with the mind's eye; they are filled in mentally by suggestion from what can actually be seen, somewhat as we recognize a friend from a glimpse of his hat and cane or of his bowed form. Not only are words thus recognized when letters can no longer be made out, but Erdmann and Dodge found that even very familiar short sentences were sometimes recognized as wholes under conditions which prevented recognition of their constituent words. Careful distinction will have to be made, therefore, between what is actually "seen" during a reading pause, and what is mentally supplied, and we must review the experiments made to determine the reading range for meaningless letters, words, etc., with the suggestions which these furnish for an explanation of the apperceptive filling in which occurs in reading.

When a series of letters in nonsense arrangement is momentarily exposed to a reader, the exposure suffices, according to Erdmann and Dodge, for the naming of but four or five letters, in the majority of cases, although as many as six or seven letters may, in exceptional instances, be read. Usually, when the series consists of six or seven letters, the first and last letters are clearly perceived, showing that the eye can recognize single letters at least as far into the periphery as this. The intervening letters were possibly recognized, but failed to persist in memory until their names could be stated.

Erdmann and Dodge found that while but four or five nonsense letters could regularly be read at a single exposure, words consisting in the aggregate of four or five times as many letters were read under similar conditions. Their readers recognized, at a glance which lasted but one-tenth of a second, words having as many as twenty-two letters, in one instance, and twenty, nineteen, eighteen, seventeen, etc., letters in other trials by the various readers. They believe, however, that for the words, as for the nonsense letters, only an extent of six to seven letters is clearly perceived, although their readers believed that the letters of the words were seen, as letters, over three times this extent of space. It was found, too, that while nonsense words gave readings that were three or four times as large as readings from nonsense letters, the readings were still uniformly less than when the words were combined to form sentences.

Zeitler, experimenting at the University of Leipsic, found that the most difficult reading was of consonants in nonsense arrangement, such as *v c p f n g l w*. Of these, four to seven were read at an exposure, while with vowels interspersed from five to eight could be read. A series of familiar syllables joined continuously, as *lencurbilber, losverkungwei*, was next easier to read, six to ten letters being read at a glance. Progressively larger readings were obtained from series of unfamiliar words, familiar words, sentences, and familiar expressions or proverbs. Sentences consisting of four or five short words, with a total of twenty to thirty letters, were readily read. Single words having as many as nineteen to twenty-five letters each, as *Bewusstseinszustand* and *Aufmerksamkeitsschwankung,* were read at a first glance of one one-hundredth second.

Evidently, then, the amount that can be read during a reading pause varies greatly with the nature of the reading matter. It may seem strange to some that this should be so, that the amount we see at a glance should depend upon whether the line makes sense, whether it is composed of sentences, nonsense words, nonsense syllables, vowels, consonants, or what not. Let us determine first what the limiting factors may be on the side of eye structure and function, and later examine the psychic factors.

In looking at a line of print, as at any object, an image of the line is formed upon the retina somewhat as is the image which we can see upon the ground glass of our camera when the focusing has been done properly. The image is inverted, of course, in both cases, and the mind at the outset must interpret the picture as representing a printed line that is "right side up" and "right side to." But let us examine further the nature of this inverted picture. We know that the rods and cones, which alone are sensitive to the light impression, are less and less abundant from the central fovea outward toward the periphery of the retina, and that the distinctness of the retinal image falls off rapidly, accordingly, as we go from the center. The visual field corresponds, therefore, as Helmholtz says in his "Physiologische Optik" (p. 87), "to a drawing in which, indeed, the most important part of the whole is carefully executed but the surrounding parts only sketched, and sketched the more roughly the farther they are from the main point."

The little depression in the retina, called the fovea centralis, in which the cones are closely packed together and in which, accordingly, the retinal picture is complete even in its smaller details, is only about one-fifth of a millimeter in diameter. It thus includes not more than perhaps three-fourths of a degree of the retinal image, corresponding of course only to this small extent of arc on the printed line, about three letter spaces at the ordinary reading distance and with this type. The macula lutea, or "yellow spot," in which the fovea lies, is itself not more than about three millimeters in horizontal diameter, including thus about eleven and one-fourth degrees of the retinal image, corresponding to about 6.3 centimeters or a little more than six words on this page, at the ordinary reading distance.

As we leave the fovea there is a marked decrease in the distinctness of the image, a gradual blurring and losing of details, due to the fast-diminishing numbers of sensitive retinal elements. Only the larger and larger figures of the picture appear as we go farther, and finally only the most general outlines of even the forms that are of considerable size are evident in the extreme outer parts. It is somewhat as though our camera plate were comparatively perfect within a very small circle at the center, but were perforated from this outward to form a sensitive netting having larger and larger meshes toward the edges of the plate. A print from such a negative would give some suggestion of the character of the retinal picture, and would be called exceedingly defective as a photograph.

It will be readily understood, then, that, while for a space of six or eight letters the single letters can be made out independently of each other, with perhaps the dots and small marks in most of them, the small marks must inevitably disappear as we go farther from the fixation point; the small letters must gradually disappear except as their presence is suggested by what clews remain in the rough outline; later even the large letters and all but the most general outlines of words must be, in part at least, inferred from such clews of context, etc., as are to be had.

So it is clear that the larger the amount read during a reading pause, the more inevitably must the reading be by suggestion and inference from clews of whatsoever kind, internal or external. In reading, the deficient picture is filled in, retouched, by the mind, and the page is thus made to present the familiar appearance of completeness in its details which we suppose to exist in the actual page. The defective retinal picture, taken in connection with all the other clews available to consciousness at the moment, *means* such a page, and we project this meaning outward, just as we fill in mentally the gap in the visual field left by the blind spot.

Two facts that especially concern us are very evident from what has been said: First, reading may and must go on by other means than the recognition of letters; second, the amount that can be read at a reading pause, and consequently the number of necessary pauses and movements per line and page, will vary with the nature of the matter read, with the associative connections existing between the letters, words, etc., and with the reader's familiarity with what is read, the latter enabling any part that may be clear to help into consciousness other parts that are indistinct.

Turning now to the psychic side, we find certain further limitations upon the amount that can be read during a reading pause. And first, the recognition of any particular object as such necessitates a unitary focusing of consciousness, practically an act of the attention. But it is a well-known fact that but very few acts of the attention can take place simultaneously or within the narrow limits of a reading pause. Let my readers try taking a momentary glance at a number of distinct objects, all of which are in plain view at once, as at a group of pictures, the faces in a passing car, or the jumble of things in a work-basket. You will realize after a few trials that the number of separate recognition acts per moment has rather narrow limits, and is not merely a matter of how many objects can be imaged simultaneously on the retina.

The extent of this span or range of the attention or apperception has been variously stated by those who have attempted to measure it, but is usually found to include not more than four or five unrelated impressions. To attempt to distribute the attention over more than about this number is only successful when we can in some way unitize them, when we can somehow relate them in our thought so that we are conscious of them in groups or as a whole having a unitary meaning. However, when groups of objects, no matter how complex in their details, have these details firmly organized into a unitary whole and are thought of as wholes, then about as many of these wholes can be attended to simultaneously as if they were simple objects. Accordingly we find that readers recognize, apparently in one pulse of attention, four or five unrelated marks of different shapes, four or five letters in which such marks are unitarily combined, or four or five unrelated words which are still higher unitary complexes of these letters. Even two or three short sentences which had come to be thought as units might possibly be recognized in one pulse of attention. Of course it may be said, and it is doubtless in some measure true, that a wandering of the attention may occur during a reading pause, that the recognitions that occur are not all simultaneous but are in some measure successive. This will be considered presently. But all admit that not more than a very few acts of recognition can occur, whether simultaneously or successively, within the limits of a reading pause, and this is our main concern here.

Again, when we consider that the attention must concern itself partly with the meaning, with the images, feelings, and conscious states generally which are aroused by the reading symbols, and in many cases with the articulation of words, we begin to wonder that the mind can deal with so much data, rather than with so little, in any given moment of our reading.

To summarize then, we are limited, in the amount that can be read during a reading pause, by the inadequacy of the retinal structure, by our inability to attend to more than a few parts of the total picture presented, and by the necessity of our attention's concerning itself with interpretations.

CHAPTER IV

THE EXPERIMENTAL STUDIES UPON VISUAL PERCEPTION IN READING

We must next consider the mental processes concerned in perceiving what is before us on the page, and the means by which the mind takes note of what is there at such a very rapid rate. This raises, of course, the time-honored question of whether we read by letters or by words; but we shall find that much more is involved than the settlement of this somewhat scholastic query.

The fact that during a reading pause one may read as much as even twenty to thirty letters when combined in sense matter, and that one averages usually as much as ten letters, suggests, as I have indicated, that the reading must go on by some other means than the recognition of letter after letter as was once supposed. This old and deeply rooted assumption was founded partly on the general belief that the eye passed from letter to letter along the line, the recognitions following the fixation point successively. The letter-recognition theory was strengthened, too, by certain data furnished by aphasic patients, data which were interpreted by specialists in speech defects into a theory of reading by letters which it is impossible to hold in the face of what we now know about the eye's actual movements in reading. The eye being still while most of the data is received from the page, it is perfectly certain that stimulations from letters in various parts of the section before the reader affect him simultaneously, and that there cannot be separate acts of recognition for each letter.

Professor Cattell early concluded, as a result of his experiments at Leipsic upon the amount which could be read in single short exposures, that we read in word-wholes and even, sometimes, in phrase or sentence wholes, and not by letters. This was evidently before the nature of the eye's movement was known to him, although the discontinuous character of the movement had already been determined by Professor Javal and his pupils. Cattell found that when single words were momentarily exposed, they were recognized as quickly as single letters, and indeed that it took longer to name letters than to name whole words, the exposures being made under conditions in which the times could be accurately measured.

It was found that when sentences or phrases were exposed, they were either grasped as wholes or else scarcely any of the words or letters were read. This observation was strikingly confirmed in the writer's experiments in which sentences were momentarily exposed. Rarely were single letters read, even as forming the beginning or ends of words that were but partially recognized. The readings were of whole words, and almost always of words connected in some sense fashion. The words appear very distinct, even, as Cattell says, "when the observer constructs an imaginary sentence from the traces he has taken up." Professor Cattell also found that the shortest exposure which would permit the recognition of single small letters and capitals sufficed also for the recognition of short words, and that long words needed but one one-thousandth of a second more. The time needed for naming a word was considerably less than for naming a letter, and the time needed simply for recognition without naming was "only slightly longer for a word than for a single letter. We, therefore," he adds, "perceive the word as a whole." Again, he found that when unrelated letters or words were read aloud as fast as possible, the reading was about twice as slow as when the letters or words were combined into words or sentences respectively; this indicating that in the latter cases the reading was in larger wholes than letters.

Erdmann and Dodge argue strongly for the theory of perception in word-wholes, on the basis of numerous and varied experiments. The length of the word and its characteristic general form as a visual whole seem to them to be the main means by which it is recognized by the practiced readers. They base their argument mainly upon the following facts: First, words are recognized when lying too far from the fixation point to permit recognition of their component letters. Second, words are recognized when formed of letters so small that the letters could not be singly identified. Third, in about half the cases tried, words were recognized at distances at which the letters, when exposed singly, could not be recognized. Fourth, in the latter experiment the words were more readily recognized when they were long, or of optically characteristic form. Fifth, when twenty-six selected words were learned thoroughly in a fixed order, as the alphabet is known, and then exposed beyond the distance at which the letters could be recognized, the words could be distinguished and recognized in almost every instance. Sixth, words of four letters are named some- what more quickly than single letters, and words of eight, twelve, and sixteen letters need comparatively little more time, the longest words needing only about one-fifth more time than the shortest.

These authors point out that it is not the constituent parts of any given form that make it recognizable, but it is the familiar total ar- rangement. Thus - ı ɔ is not recognized as **5** nor **‹ l** as **K**, although the constituent parts are presented. The arrangement reading (printed vertically bottom-to-top: g n i d a e r) has all the elements of a familiar word and, indeed, in their usual order. But it is by no means the visual form recognized at once in the word reading. Why should not a familiar word-form be recognized and named on sight just as a house or wall is recognized and named? We do not, in the latter cases, take account of the constituent stories and bricks; nor of all the sticks and limbs and leaves in recognizing a particular thicket or oak tree. The arrangement, the total form, is the main thing, whether in the recognition of letters, numbers, words, or objects of whatsoever sort. One may always analyze the whole into its parts and recognize each part singly, as we have done in the figures above. But we do not do this in actual reading any more than in regarding a landscape.

So the argument runs, and much more might be said for it. We shall next consider another view, advanced by Goldscheider and Müller, on the basis of experiments made at Berlin. These experi- menters, working earlier than Erdmann and Dodge, found first that when a group of simple unrelated strokes in various arrangements, as

NOTE. The cuts and quotations from Goldscheider and Müller are from their article "Zur Phys. und Path, des Lesens," in *Zeitschrift f. Klin. Med.*, Bd. XXIII, p. 131 ff.

was exposed for one one-hundredth of a second, only four or at most five strokes could be recognized or described and reproduced. When simple unrelated strokes were grouped into a regular symmetrical form, as

although the whole had no definite meaning and was totally new, seven strokes could be similarly "recognized" and the arrangement given. When the strokes were combined into squares and a group of the squares was exposed in varied arrangements, as

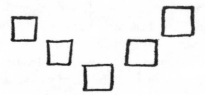

the form, orientation, and relative arrangement of two or three squares could be told at a glance, although this, of course, involved locating and describing eight or twelve strokes. With a symmetrical arrangement and similar orientation of the squares, as

the whole group of five squares could be reproduced at the first glance, although this involved twenty strokes.

Similarly with semicircles, ellipses, etc., the number that could be recognized and correctly reproduced, at a glance, increased regularly with their arrangement into forms that could be grasped unitarily.

An arrangement like

was easily reproduced so far as the general form was concerned, but to state how each particular semicircle faced was very difficult.

From the constant recurrence of various geometrical forms, in the world of things, we come to have a stock of ideas of these forms all ready to use, ready to be touched off by even very slight cues that may appear in any visual complex. This aliveness or acute apperception for total forms makes us negligent of the details that appear. They are too numerous to be attended to, and can come to consciousness with less expenditure of energy as parts or aspects of the total upon which the thought is mainly focused. So recognition by general forms rather than by particular details may be expected and will occur preferably wherever the total arrangement has often recurred, and where attention to certain details is not absolutely necessary for the determination of the recognition. The general form repeats itself oftenest, and so we are most ready for it.[1]

Goldscheider and Müller found that such a group as

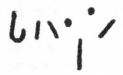

had to be exposed seven times before it could be reproduced, while the same forms arranged into

---

[1] Note. The theoretical view presented in this paragraph is not necessarily that of Goldscheider and Müller.

were reproduced at the first or second glance. So when

was exposed, but four or five characters could be perceived at a glance, but when these same forms appeared as

the whole was recognized at the first or second glance. The habitual association of the parts into a unity, which makes the perception facile and the memory after the exposure easy, and the familiarity of the total form as an unanalyzed whole, work together as factors in these as in all such recognitions.

Goldscheider and Müller went on to expose series of nonsense letters, syllables, words, phrases, etc. They found that "an optical memory image" of a word was readily called forth by an incomplete series of its letters. Certain letters would be disregarded when present in the exposed word, or might be omitted and the recognition would still occur readily. The letters which seemed to be especially used in determining the recognition of any given word were named "determining letters." The others were named "indifferent letters." The places of the absent or disregarded letters would be filled in subjectively when the exposure was made, sometimes filled with the wrong forms even though the right letters were actually there. Whether wrong or right, the letters thus supplied were apt to seem as distinct on the page as did the others, and these authors quote with approval Professor Münsterberg's conclusion[1] that "reproduced sensations under favorable conditions cannot be distinguished from sense impressions." Exposure of C ntr m constantly sufficed for recognition of the German word Centrum, but ent um did not. Klangbild was recognized readily from Kl ngb ld, but not from lan bild. M k do

---

[1] "Beiträge zur Experimentellen Psychologie" H. 4, s. 17 ff.

gave *Mikado*, but *Mik o*, of the same word, gave only *Mikosch*. *Ch té* gave *Charité* at once, and other such familiar words were recognized when a few characteristic letters were given.

To the determining letter class belongs the first letter of a word, almost always. If it is wanting, the recognition is apt to fail, especially if its absence breaks up an initial diphthong. *Autor* was never recognized from *utor*. Here the wrong sound seemed to be suggested for the u, resulting in such completions as *tutor; eweis* did not give *Beweis* as intended, but *edelweiss; weifel* did not give *Zweijel*, but *Weibel; ia n se* was completed to *Wannsee*, and the actual word *Diagnose* could not be made out. If the determining letters are left out of a word, there is left an "indifferent word-form" which sometimes permits a great number of different completions.

Goldscheider and Müller do not find that the consonants are the determining letters as against the vowels as indifferent letters, as some suppose. For instance, *Diagnose* was recognized with greater difficulty when *D gn se* was presented than from *D a nose*. The greater importance of the vowels in such a case may be due to the fact that the vowels give the clew to the number of syllables, and with this they awaken in us the memory of the rhythm and the accent. Or it may happen that the vowel sound is of "determining significance" for the given word. The former would be apt to occur if the reader's inner speech habitually went on in motor terms, the latter if he were of the auditory type. The consonants, however, from their frequently projecting above or below the line, are apt to contribute more than the vowels to the characteristic form of the word.

The kind of words which were usually suggested by the word skeletons presented in these exposures lead Goldscheider and Müller to conclude that the first suggestion from the sight of the determining letters is the sound of these letters, and that these sounds call forth or suggest, immediately, the sound of the whole word. They admit that the visual perception of the determining letters may sometimes be filled out at once with the remaining visual forms, and the word-sound then be aroused from this total visual form. But this, they think, occurs but seldom, and is a roundabout process.

In general, these experimenters conclude that the more unfamiliar a sequence of letters may be, the more the perception of it proceeds by letters. With increase of familiarity, fewer and fewer clews suffice to touch off the recognition of the word or phrase, the tendency being toward reading in word-wholes. So reading is now by letters, now by groups of letters or by syllables, now by word-wholes, all in the same sentence sometimes, or even in the same word, as the reader may most quickly attain his purpose. In the case of reading by word-wholes, they call attention to the fact that the characteristic form of the word is conditioned by certain characteristic letters, namely, the determining letters.

The reading of the blind, in the opinion of these authors, seems to illustrate this combination of methods of perceiving words. A practiced reader of the raised-letter pages goes ahead with the fingers of the right hand to examine the general outline of the word, while a finger of the left hand follows, gliding successively over the letters. Ordinarily, however, only a part of the letters are examined, while the finger passes over the others without touching the points. Intelligent and attentive blind readers state that they thus read but a part of the letters and conjecture the rest.

Zeitler, experimenting at the University of Leipsic, made about six thousand exposures of groups of letters, words, sentences, etc., usually for very brief intervals. By making the exposures very short he thought he could best determine what letters, letter-groups, etc., stand out most prominently and are perceived when others are not. His experiments are therefore important as helping to determine what parts of reading matter are "determining" parts, or "dominating" parts as Zeitler prefers to call them.

Zeitler found that in his brief exposures certain letters or letter-groups of a word, and indeed certain words of exposed sentences, drew the attention to themselves and were apperceived. The apperception of these dominating parts or complexes is, he believes, the basis for the recognition of the word or sentence. These apperceived parts are at once supplemented by, filled out with, an inner mental contribution, associates that belong with the parts apperceived. The result is the blending of the outwardly given apperceptions with the inwardly arising associates into a total "assimilation," which constitutes the recognition of the word or sentence. "The word-form is indeed apparently assimilated as a whole, *secondarily*; but *primarily*, it is apperceived only in its dominating constituent parts." Zeitler admits, however, that ordinarily we cannot distinguish these two processes of apperception and assimilation. His very short exposures, varying to suit the reader, ruled out, as he believed, most of the associative contribution, and caused the reader to strain his attention to the utmost upon the objective factors, the matter actually exposed.

It was found that the letters projecting above and below the line were recognized preferably. The vowels and small consonants were misread most often, the long consonants least often. In general, "the more characteristically" a letter is shaped, the more clearly is it recognized. As in the visual field with objects generally there are dominating points and lines which get the attention, which reflexly attract the eye, and over which the eye preferably moves or rests, just so when we regard words and sentences, the corresponding dominant parts here are these characteristically formed letters, "over whose high relief the eye springs along," although this last is true only figuratively, he says, as the eye does not move during the exposure.

As examples of the dominating letters may be cited the following, found to be the same for all of his (five?) readers: —

Gold	G	ld	
Haut	H	t	
Fliege	F	lg	
Woche	W	ch	(ck)
Streit	St	t	
Minute	M	t	

Cattell had already found that the different letters required different times for their recognition, and that they were of different degrees of legibility. His observations here have a certain significant relation with those of Zeitler. It will be noticed that in the above examples the large letters are the dominating ones throughout, except in the characteristic combination *ch*.

When much is read in the exposure of a sense passage, Zeitler finds that certain dominating "syllable complexes," usually those which contain the sense of the words, are apperceived and the rest is associatively supplied. If quite familiar sentences are exposed, there are dominating words, sometimes, the perception of which suffices for the recognition of the whole sentence. Alterations in the "indifferent" words of the sentences, or even their absence, may go unnoticed. The sentence is "assimilated" just the same.

This experimenter opposes Goldscheider and Müller's conclusion that the perception of the determining or dominating letters arouses first the sound of these letters, the word-sound being filled out associatively from these sounds. Still, some of Zeitler's own experiments show that this occurs sometimes. Regularly, however, he thinks that the dominating complexes, when apperceived, are filled out *directly* into the visual form of the word or sentence. The dominating parts may be silent letters, or letters having a sound that is very different when heard singly than when combined in the given word.

The conclusions of Cattell, Erdmann and Dodge, and others as to perception in word-wholes are also thought to be incorrect. The reading stimulus, when one looks momentarily at the page, is ordinarily not the whole sentence or the whole words printed there, at all. Externally, it is true, they are there and are of such and such total form, word-length, etc. But the real stimulus is the series of dominating letters or complexes. It is these which first affect consciousness and get the attention. It is these that are directly perceived.

In Zeitler's opinion, then, word-length and total form are not very important factors in the recognition. For instance, when the words in the left-hand column below were briefly exposed, the reader was uncertain whether he saw the one or the other of the words on the right, although they are markedly different in length: —

	Phantasie
Phalanstère	or
	Phalanstère
	Skorpion
Skioplikon	or
	Skioptikon
	Pygmae
Pygmalion	or
	Pygmalion

Such readings as

Leoparden for
Lepidodendron,
Retoranda for
Ritardando,
Epimenides for
Epaminondas,
Polarstern for
Phalanstère,
Agraphie for
Agoraphobie

show discrepancies in word-length and, quite often, in total form. The determining letters, however, are retained, only the indifferent letters being changed, omitted, or inserted.

That the total word-form is not very fixed and rigid to the consciousness is indicated by the inversions and permutations of even the letters that are dominant. Thus,

Farbe	was read Fabrik
Meludie (exposed for Melodie)	was read Medulla.
Gefüdl (Gefühl)	was read Gefilde.
Külge (Külpe)	was read Klage.
Fniede (Friede)	was read Feinde.
Analomie (Anatomie)	was read Anomalie.

It would seem to Zeitler that in the first perception of the dominant parts of a word these parts are not seen in any very fixed spatial arrangement, but are later put in place in a total word-form when the full recognition completes itself with the coming of the associative elements. At first "each dominating letter has a certain elbow-room in a space within which it can be changed about with its neighbors." There they hover, oscillating with the play of processes, until they become "anchored" in the places to which they are assigned in the total word-complex when this is once formed. "The letters are throughout not linked so fast to one another as they seem. The sense first welds them together." "The mere optical word-form is continually inclined to fall apart into its elements, is held together only by the framework formed by the dominating letters. In this word-form the small and unimportant letters can be changed about quite irregularly." "The word-form remains uncertain (labile), if it does not immediately receive its signification. First through the sense is the letter-complex established."

Neither does Zeitler find that the perception of what is read during a reading pause occurs simultaneously for the various parts of the section read. The time of such a pause, very considerable as compared with the short times used in his exposure experiments, is quite sufficient to permit a wandering of the attention over what is read, and he finds that such a wandering of the attention actually occurred in the readings of his observers. The attention is upon the dominating letters or complexes, and wanders from one to another until all are apperceived. A dominating complex may consist of two or three neighboring letters, or may even be an entire short word in familiar sentences. In any case it seems to be perceived simultaneously over its various parts. Indeed, Zeitler admits that, when two distinct dominating complexes occur in different parts of a word, the attention may in certain cases divide and be given to both simultaneously. But generally, in reading, "we arrange the dominating complexes successively one after another, similarly as we do the letters in the earliest reading by letters. The progress of the reading is only very fast, but it is none the less successive. With ordinary letter-after-letter reading, however, this has nothing to do; instead, we arrange in a series one after the other the dominating letters and important complexes. This goes on, possibly, in a kind of rhythmic succession, with continued variation in the rhythm."

There is thus, according to Zeitler, a "very quick succession of consciousness processes in reading," which indeed gives one the "illusion" of reading simultaneously what is seen at a glance, or during a reading pause. This illusion comes from long practice and from familiarity with the words. But with less familiar words, even the practiced reader may establish for himself that the "simultaneous reading exists only for the extent of a dominating complex." His reference here is only to visual perception in reading, and he remarks that the inner saying of what is read goes on successively, sound after sound.

The following examples are given by Zeitler to illustrate the wandering of the attention which occurred when these words were exposed for periods of from one tenth to one fifth of a second, approximating the time of a reading pause. The strokes under the words indicate the important parts of the word-form, the bent arrows show the subjectively noticed course of the attention. All his readers seemed to agree that when these longer times were used, the readings were regularly successive and not simultaneous.

That Cattell did not note any wandering of the attention and considered the readings to be simultaneous is due, Zeitler supposes, to the fact that Cattel's exposures lasted but one one-hundredth of a second, making the observation of such a wandering very difficult. Erdmann and Dodge, with their long exposures of one tenth of a second, were misled, he believes, by the illusion of the final simultaneous "assimilation," not distinguishing this from the slightly preceding successive apperceptions.

FIG. 9 ½. Movements of the attention in Zeitler's readings.

They were misled all the more from being mainly concerned with other factors.

Messmer has more recently made a long series of experiments in the psychology of reading, at the University of Zurich. He finds confirmation of Zeitler's conclusions that perception in reading is mediated, for a certain type of readers at least, by "dominating" letters and complexes, and that there is a wandering of the attention over these. He used very short exposures for the most part, as short as two one-thousandths of a second, making the time for each reader such as just sufficed to permit normal recognition. After practice, two one-thousandths of a second sufficed for all his readers.

Messmer finds that the long letters which project above the line are usually the dominating ones. The attention concerns itself most with the upper half of the word, and the letters projecting below are not so important. The latter and the short letters are the ones most often mistaken in the readings from his exposures. Letters projecting below the line would be mistaken for vowels, as *g* for *a*, *p* for *o*, etc. "They possess optically the value of small letters." The dominating parts of words and sentences are most apt to strike the eye and to get the attention. But accidental circumstances may sometimes make other parts more prominent. In the relatively long pauses of actual reading, very many if not all parts of the word can affect consciousness somewhat and thus give clews which help in the recognition, preventing the possibility of errors in filling out from the dominating letters, errors which actually arise, however, in reading from the short exposures. The dominating letters play the main role in recognition, but the others thus play an important part as well.

The experiments indicated that readers may be either of a subjective or objective type. The subjective type is characterized by a wandering attention which travels far from the fixation point, by a large associative contribution in perceiving, and by slight fidelity to the outward object. Readers of this type apperceive words from the total character of the word-form rather than from the dominating parts, these latter not differentiating from the whole. The objective readers, with characteristics which are the opposite of the above, recognize the dominating parts first, and the effect of the total form is minor. They read a smaller amount at a glance than do the subjective readers, but are less liable to error.

It was found that during a reading pause there is first an impression of the whole word, as "lively," "stiff," etc., for example, a feeling reaction to the total word-appearance. This *may* alone suffice to set off the recognition of the word; usually, however, with objective readers at any rate, there follows a successive coming to consciousness of first the high dominant letters, then the low and "indifferent" ones. Small letters adjoining a dominant letter may, by their proximity, help in forming a total configuration and may thus come to consciousness as part of a dominant complex. The effect upon consciousness of the total word-form as such is a simultaneous one, but the dominant parts come to consciousness successively. He agrees with Zeitler that in actual reading these successive acts of recognition follow each other so rapidly that they appear simultaneous. He finds that word-length plays little part in characterizing words for children, and that it is usually less important for children than are the dominant complexes.

Messmer's analysis of the "total character of words" has a considerable value. The three main factors are, first, breadth of the letters horizontally; second, height of the letters vertically; third, geometrical form of the letters. As to breadth, the letters are composed of one, two, or three vertical strokes, as i, h, m, or of forms occupying one or another of these three horizontal spaces. Of one thousand consecutive letters on a German page, seven hundred and thirty are found to be small letters. While these are usually of about the same height, they have a variety of widths, as appears when words are printed in vertical arrangement, as

W
i
m
m   Wimmern.
e
r
n

It might seem, therefore, that letter-width is a very important factor in characterizing the total word-form. However, the differences in letter-width largely disappear in the total impression of word-length given in our horizontal arrangement of the letters. Differentiation in letter-width, therefore, seems to be of comparatively little value. Indeed, Messmer found frequent errors in perception due to combining parts of adjacent letters into a wrongly conjectured letter, or to making still other mistaken groupings of the individual strokes.

The uniform height of the small letters is the measure of the word's height in the main, since these letters are in such a majority. But the long letters relieve the monotony by their projections, and thus characterize the word in the vertical meridian. Viewing the total word-form as to height, these long letters vary it and give a characteristic outline. Considering the total word-length, these letters break it up into sections,—"rhythmize" it, to use Messmer's expression. Note this effect in *Verschiedenheiten*, as compared with *Zusammenreisen*.

The word is characterized, thirdly, by the geometrical form of the particular letters composing it. Disregarding their variations in height and breadth already referred to, the letters may be grouped, first, into those composed essentially of vertical strokes, as i, n, m, t, l, f, h, r, j; second, those composed essentially of curved lines, as o, e, c, s, a, g; third, those composed essentially of both perpendicular strokes and curved lines, as b, d, q, p; fourth, those composed essentially of oblique strokes, as, w, v, y, x, z, k, the last letter having also a perpendicular stroke. The first group includes almost half the letters, 469 per thousand as they occur consecutively on the page. The second group has over one-third, 371 per thousand. Only 61 per thousand belong to the third group, and 46 per thousand to the fourth. The remaining 63 per thousand were capital letters, more frequent, of course, in German than in English.

The predominance of one or another of these classes of letters, in any given word, gives it a characteristic total appearance, as in wimmern and übereinstimmen, for the first group, and ausgeschlossen, psychologisch, for the second. The former words have a unitariness of total character, giving an unbroken total impression. Their total form, however, is too little differentiated, and such words are most often misread and "most uncertainly recognized or falsely interpreted." They are "stiff" as contrasted with the words of the second group, whose letters have more individuality, and whose words are thus better differentiated and recognized with greater certainty. These characteristics of the first two groups are combined in such words as characteristisch, wissenschaftliche, each containing about equal numbers of these two groups of letters. The total impression here is at least agreeable, and Messmer calls it "the most favorable total form," since it gives "the greatest harmony and most agreeable contrast."

Groups two, three, and four include fewer of the alphabet letters than are found in group one. As they also occur less frequently in any given line, they thus have more individuality and differentiate the line better than the letters of group one. This is particularly true of the second group, the others partaking somewhat of the nature of the first group. In words which contain no long letters, as zusammenreisen above, certain letters having the greatest individuality seem to serve as dominating letters, and to some extent break up or "rhythmize" the word. Messmer finds that readers do not get any very distinct notion of the length of the words exposed, very often mistaking a word for some much shorter one, occasionally for a longer one. This was especially the case with his child readers, and he thinks that for them, at least, word-length is but a minor factor in word-perception.

In experiments made some years ago I found that the first half of a word is of considerably greater importance for perception than is the latter half. If the reader will turn to page 66 and will read down the last column of words as fast as possible, endeavoring to avoid lateral movement of the eyes, he will probably find himself fixating the words to the left of the center. If he will then read down the column again, fixating toward the end of the words, say three or four letters from the end, and again fixating near the beginning of the words, he will find the reading much easier in the latter case. Indeed, in ordinary reading, I find myself much more conscious of the beginning of words than of their other parts, although I am not certain that my readers will be able to verify this by their introspection.

It will be recalled that the beginning of a word was regularly found to be a determining or dominating part, in some of the exposure experiments. Indeed, the terminal letters are considerably more legible than the others, perhaps from being partially isolated. Fixate the middle of one of the long words and you will probably find yourself much more conscious of the end letters than of many of the intervening ones. The writer made a quantitative test of the comparative importance of the first and last halves of words by having readers read passages from which the first half of each word was carefully removed in the one case, and the second half in the other. Specimen lines are shown in Figure 10, the unmutilated passage being printed at the end. It was found that more words were made out, and in less time, when the first halves were read than when the latter halves alone

1y	ures f	ch 1	eme?	f	is	es	1t	eal o
1u,	en	ll 1u	dly,	om 1	re	tical		point,
ate	he	1ges	1d	1rms	st	1tly	ded?	1r
pose	so	bine	1se	1ws,		tically	1d	wise,	1d
o	nd 1	1ted	py o	ch		ibutor.
	he 1ms	low	ely	gest	1ing	ics.	ect	1se
1u	re	st	ested n	1d 1d	1y	ers.

a1	feat	o	su	1 sch		I th	do	n1	app	t
y1	th	wi	y1	kiń	fr	1 mo	pract		stand
st1	t1	cha1		a1	ref1		mo	gre1	nee	O1	pur1
	i t	com	t1e	vi1.		statis1		a1	othe1	a1
t	se	1 pri1	co	t	ea	contri·
	T1	ite	bel	mer	sug1	lea1		top	Sel	th1
y1	a1	m1	inter		i	a1	ad	an	oth

H

any features of such a scheme? If this does not appeal 'to you, then will you kindly, from a more practical standpoint, state the changes and reforms most greatly needed? Our purpose is to combine these views, statistically and otherwise, and to send a printed copy to each contributor.

The items below merely suggest leading topics. Select those you are most interested in and add any others.

FIG. 10[1]

remained. The four readers tested averaged .49 words per second when reading from the first halves, as against .33 words per second when reading from the last halves.

Among factors which coöperate to produce this result may be mentioned, first, the tendency of English to place the accent upon the first part of the word, the accented part then tending to represent the word, at least the spoken word; second, the preponderance of the number of suffixes over prefixes, the main root of the word tending to appear in the first part, thus rendering the first part more important. It seems probable also, as a third factor, that the time-order in ordinary inter-association of syllables has much to do with the difference shown. This time-order has almost always

---

[1] Reproduced from *American Journal of Psychology*, July, 1898.

been from the first part toward the latter, and, as has been shown by various experiments, associations do not work nearly so well in reversed time-order.

The upper half of a word or letter is obviously more important for perception than is the lower half. This may be tested by comparing the difficulty of reading the two mutilated passages below, the unmutilated passage being in the same type:—

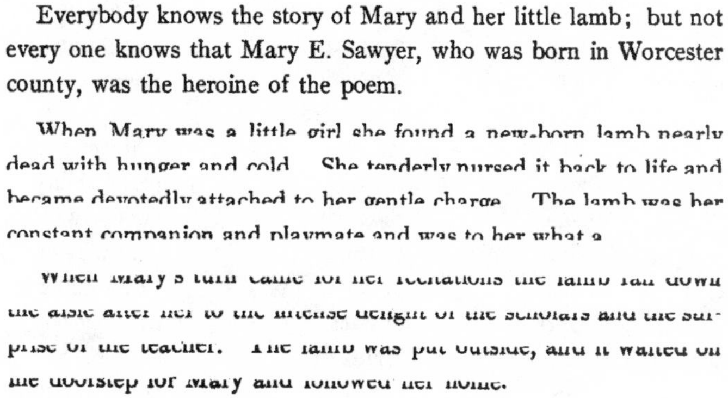

Everybody knows the story of Mary and her little lamb; but not every one knows that Mary E. Sawyer, who was born in Worcester county, was the heroine of the poem.

FIG. 11

Professor Javal, from watching the course of an after-image along the lines as he read, and for other reasons, concluded, as we have seen, that the eye's fixation point moved along between the middle and top of the small letters, thus giving an advantage in perception to the upper half of the line. As already mentioned, I do not consider his experiments final on this point; and it seems to me that the greater importance of the upper part is due rather to the words being better differentiated there than below, as is shown by Messmer's count of two hundred and thirty-eight letters projecting above the line to thirty-two below. Besides, we habitually find most meanings in the upper parts of objects; we ourselves are so placed and so oriented as to bring this about.

In considering whether we read by letters or by word-wholes, my readers may be assisted in their judgment by reading down the column of letters below, as fast as possible, either simply recognizing each or pronouncing it aloud, and then doing the same for the columns

y	pool	analysis	anthropology
w	rugs	habitual	independence
u	mark	occupied	histological
s	send	inherent	astronomical
q	list	probable	tautological
o	more	summoned	paleontology
m	pick	devotion	consummation
k	stab	remarked	concomitance
i	neck	overcome	epistemology
g	your	resolute	irritability
e	dice	elements	somnambulism
c	font	conclude	minimization
a	earl	numbered	malleability
z	whit	struggle	emblematical
x	ants	division	permeability
v	role	research	etymological
t	sink	original	quantitative
r	rust	involved	ascertaining
p	ware	obstacle	definiteness
n	fuss	relative	sociological
l	tick	physical	legitimately
j	rasp	pastness	scientifical
h	mold	lacteals	institutions
f	hive	sameness	governmental
d	four	distract	emphatically

Fig. 12

of words containing four, eight, and twelve letters respectively, comparing the rate and difficulty by the aid of a stop-watch, if one is at hand. It will be evident that the multiplication of letters makes proportionately little difference in the ease or speed of recognition. In my own experiments in which such lists were read aloud as fast as possible, my four readers read the lists in the following times:—

50 letters in an average of 15.7 seconds.

50 four-letter words in an average of 17.3 seconds.

50 eight-letter words in an average of 19.6 seconds.

50 twelve-letter words in an average of 28.5 seconds.

50 sixteen-letter words in an average of 54.1 seconds.

Since part of the slightly lessened speed of reading eight-letter words as compared with those of four letters must probably be due to the utterance of the additional syllable or syllables in the former case, it seems certain that the recognition of familar and comparatively short words is little affected by doubling the number of letters; and this seems confirmatory of the view that such words are recognized in one unitary act, as wholes. The greatly lessened speed of reading the words of sixteen letters as compared with those of twelve is due in part to their being considerably less familiar. It is probably due in much greater part to the need of making lateral movements of the eye, these words occupying a considerable horizontal space when typewritten for use in the experiments.

CHAPTER V

THE NATURE OF THE PERCEPTUAL PROCESS IN READING

It is very difficult to draw final conclusions concerning visual perception in reading, in the present stage of the investigations. I have, therefore, given at some length the views of the various experimenters, and have referred to many of the particular experiments upon which they are based, that my readers may be helped in drawing their own conclusions. I am glad to know that further studies are being undertaken in this field, and by comparing the results of these as they are published with this review of the work thus far, the truth will no doubt gradually appear, as to most of the problems. We are all working toward daylight in the matter, and many of the discrepancies of facts and theories are more apparent than real. A very important section of general psychology must here be worked out, constructed in the new rather than taken and applied. How do we perceive anything? The whole stupendous problem rises at every turn, but is far too large even to be adequately stated here. The following conclusions seem to me to be warranted by the data now at hand.

Goldscheider and Müller were profoundly right when they said that readers perceive in various ways as their purpose can be best attained. We must allow for consider able variety, not merely of individuals but of occasions. The manner of perceiving words must depend, for the child, very largely on how he is *taught* to perceive them in learning to read, and here, as we know, the methods are most diverse. To take a simple example, the writer still finds himself hesitant in naming or recognizing several capital letters of the Greek alphabet, perhaps even incapable of recognizing one or two of them when seen in isolation. Yet Greek was a favorite study with him through years of college and secondary school. The reason for his persistent inattention to the letters is evident enough. He began

Greek with the sentence method, and his attention was seldom called to the particular letters in reading.

The perceptual process in the practiced reader doubtless uses many a short-cut for which there can be no science. Such a reader has grown up with these letter-forms and word-forms as intimate parts of his environment. He has made friends, boon companions, of them, in his own way, and differently with each. Some early absurd way of thinking about A, or about the appearance of the word *cat* or *and*, may have grown to be the invariable feeling reaction which greets this form when it appears, may really be the core of the consciousness in its recognition. Various experiences and associations have been woven in with the appearance of the various word-forms, differing from reader to reader. These determine in part what will stand out most prominently in any given word. They bring out now the general outline of the total word-form, now this or that dominant letter or complex, now the word-length, etc., as one or the other of these may have formed the basis of our individual experiences with the given word.

However, there are general features of the perceptual process which appear as we survey the collected data from all the experiments on reading. In the first place, perceiving is an *act*, a thing that we *do*, always and everywhere, never a mere passive sensing of a group of passing sensations or impressions. It probably always involves actual innervation of muscles, and indeed coördinated and organized, we may say unitized, innervation of muscles. Certainly on the psychic side there is an active and more or less unitized movement of mind, a sense of inner activity.

Perceiving being an act, it is, like all other things that we do, performed more easily with each repetition of the act. To perceive an entirely new word or other combination of strokes requires considerable time, close attention, and is likely to be imperfectly done, just as when we attempt some new combination of movements, some new trick in the gymnasium or new "serve" at tennis. In either case, repetition progressively frees the mind from attention to details, makes facile the total act, shortens the time, and reduces the extent to which consciousness must concern itself with the process. One may say that the "memory image" helps in the later perception of the word; but it may well be that, as Goldscheider and Müller put it, the memory is but an exercise or habit of the apperceptive activity (Uebung der Apperceptionsthätigkeit), — that we perceive better at the later trial just as we shoot better or skate better with practice.

Again, as in the performance of any act, a perception may involve more and more complex constituent acts as these are progressively welded together by practice, and especially as they become synthesized to a total performance which may be set off from a single consciousness cue. It comes about, therefore, that just as the complicated but associatively concatenated and organized movements of hitting a target with a ball may be touched off by the mere sight of the target, in one attention-act, so the various activities involved in apperceiving a phrase or other word-group may become one complex but unitary act, and this act may be set off very simply by this or that cue or set of cues given from the page, and may be done with a minimum of consciousness concerning details.

Again, perception is always a projection or localization outward of a consciousness which is aroused or suggested by the stimulations that have come inward, but which is conditioned strongly, also, from within. We have seen how, when some dominant parts of a word or sentence were exposed without the other parts, the reader would project the absent letters upon the page and would "see" them as distinctly as when they were actually before him. We have seen, too, how in every moment of our reading we project letters and parts of letters to fill up the gaps that are always left in the peripheral parts of our retinal image. We know how we project a consciousness content to serve for what should be imaged on the "blind spot." Such projection is as certain and as common as is any mental phenomenon. The simple fact is that the words and all the other objects that we ever see are thus thrown outward, projected upon a page in the case of reading, somewhat as a lantern might throw them outward upon a screen. In the case of perception it might be said that the mind furnishes the screen as well. It must be remembered that consciousness does not dwell in the retina or in retinal images. Objects may be pictured very well without any retina or optic nerve. For our purposes here consciousness may best be thought of as in the brain, totally in the dark as to physical environment, constructing even its light as well as its forms and meanings according to the excitations that come in to it and their relations with those that have previously come in. I raise here no question of idealism, and there need be no discussion of metaphysics.[1] An outer world may be there and may be quite as I think it, doubtless is a very great deal more than I think it. But it is simply an empirical fact that I do project my thought of it, that there is constructed a consciousness world.

When visual forms, then, affect my retina, there come to the brain certain signs of their presence, position, etc. The character and destination of the incoming excitations from the retinal image are sufficient signs of the presence of the particular form. Its distance, size, and orientation in space are suggested from certain other signs, such as excitations from the muscles of accommodation and convergence, along with others which indicate the bodily position at the moment. The totality of signs, outwardly and inwardly initiated, suggest or awaken a consciousness corresponding to the particular sign-combination, a consciousness which is projected or placed, we say apperceived sometimes, in its proper place and relations, or rather a consciousness which *is* our seen world of the moment, including the page, the letters, etc.

The signs indicative of the presence and nature of an object of perception may be either states of consciousness or merely neural conditions. In the case of a word perceived upon a printed page, it seems likely that the distance and direction of the word from the reader, and the word's arrangement as spread out upon the page, are suggested mainly by states of the eye-muscles and tendencies to innervation peculiar to dealing with such a form in such a place, states and tendencies which are in the main neural only, except under artificial conditions of introspection. On the other hand, certain of the signs suggestive of the perceptual consciousness are themselves consciousness states, having, of course, neural excitations also as correlates if not as causes. Among these consciousness signs are the various intensities of blacks, whites, and grays which

---

[1] Of course the whole matter could be stated equally well in terms of James' radical empiricism, without affecting the argument here. I have come to consider the doctrine of James to be nearer the truth. However, my thought about perception in reading is doubtless more intelligible as stated in terms of my working hypothesis of plain dualism.

occur in the printed form, and the context imagery and feeling from what has just been read and from the general subject of thought and feeling for that moment. Part of these signs are operative precedent to the beginning of adequate stimulation from the particular word perceived. Such are the signs indicative of the word's distance and position, with a certain context consciousness leading the reader to expect a certain kind of word, etc. The word is to this extent preperceived; there is a "set" or "predisposition" in its direction which may need but a few supplemental signs to set off the proper perception.

When we consider that the arrangement on the page, of the words and of their parts, is a construction within from cues which are probably given in non-spatial order, we are prepared for the statement of Zeitler that in the first awareness of the dominating letters of a word they are not seen in any very fixed spatial arrangement, and are only put in place and "anchored" there as the recognition completes itself with the coming of the associative contribution from within. The wonder is that the cues to the arrangement of the letters are not more often fallacious, and that misreadings like Krone for Korne, aneotic for anoetic, Larabee for Labaree, actual cases which I have noticed recently, are so infrequent with most readers. In this view of perception one is inclined to accept what the experiments of Zeitler, Messmer, and others seem to show, that the first factors of perception in reading are not usually the total form, word-length, etc., but certain striking "dominant" parts, the appreciation of total word-form and word-length coming a little later as the recognition is completed at the suggestion of these dominant cues.

However, while the experiments of these investigators indicate the special part which the dominant letters and letter-groups play in setting off the word-recognitions, we need by no means suppose that the former are always or usually apperceived as distinct letters in performing this function of special signs. Through their being the most obvious parts optically, and through habit, they have come to be most quickly operative in unlocking the word-recognitions; but in ordinary reading they would seem to have but a minimum of attention, performing their function automatically and without any apperceptive act that is distinct from that for the larger whole in which their recognition is subsumed. When that total recognition completes itself, however, we are apt to be conscious of these dominant forms as the most prominent parts of the word.

With some readers, however, and perhaps with all of us for many words, the total form, word-length, etc., seem to characterize the word and are apparently the first factors in its recognition. In these cases the stimulations from all the parts and points which signalize this total form are operative simultaneously as cues which set off the projection of this form, and this general out-line rather than a few particular dominant letter-shapes is the aspect of which we are apt to be most conscious in the total recognition. In such cases the recognition could well be set off by a skeleton drawing of the word showing no particular letter forms, and might well occur at distances at which particular letters were no longer recognizable as such. There is no question but that such perception can occur, for certain words and for certain readers, and that it does occur. But Erdmann and Dodge have here apparently mistaken what is possible and many times actual for a usual and almost universal method of recognition. Here the testimony of the majority of careful experimenters is against them.

though

though.

As a matter of fact, the outline form of a word is a rather inconstant quantity. For a considerable part of our reading we concern ourselves with *written* symbols, in which the word's total form is different, often very different, from reading to reading. Not only do the height and slant of the letters vary, but the spacings between them and, of course, the total length. If the reader will place side by side various printed, written, and type-written forms of the same word, the variations in the outline form will be evident, as in the example below. Of course the

though

Though

though

Fig. 13

letter-forms change as well, and it might be difficult to determine whether these or the total form have the greater variation.

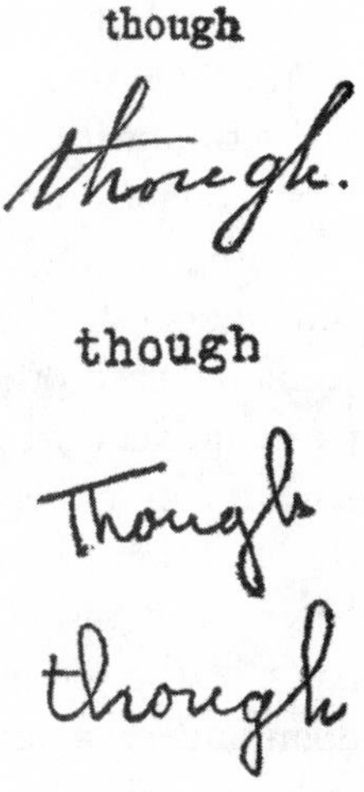

The constant practice of writing words letter after letter, and the use of the letters in abbreviations, etc., tends to increase the consciousness of single letters as they appear in words, and thus to break up the consciousness of total word-form. Of course, too, the school practice in spelling and the synthetic methods of learning to read contribute strongly to the dominance of letter-units in the perception of words. Even in the more pronounced cases of letter consciousness, however, it is perfectly certain that words are not perceived by a successive recognition of letter after letter, or even by any simultaneous recognition of all the letters *as such*. By whatever cues the recognition may be set off, it is certainly a recognition of word-wholes, except when even these recognition units are subsumed under the recognition of a still larger unit. The only question is as to what parts are especially operative as cues in setting off this recognition.

Doubtless, for readers who are familiar with the letters, the recognition of word-wholes and of phrase or sentence wholes involves the inhibition of incipient recognitions which start for the letters or other constituent units. There is a hierarchy of recognition habits, the exercise of the higher drafting away the consciousness that would otherwise serve for completing the recognition of the particular letters. Let us examine the case of perceiving a single letter as such, and then that of perceiving the larger and progressively more complex reading units.

When a single letter is exposed and recognized as a letter, the simultaneously given stimulations from its various parts mutually reënforce each other, having been associatively knitted together in past experience. Doubtless even in the case of the letter certain of its parts are more characteristic than others, and thus, having had the attention oftener, become especially effective in touching off the letter's recognition, and may even do so when the more indifferent parts of the letter are absent or are ignored. Doubtless we have dominant parts of letters as of words. The full recognition of the letter doubtless has in it a slight feeling attitude toward it as a total form, and carries with it some notion of the letter's sound and, more distantly perhaps, the letter's name.

But now consider the recognition of a familiar word in which this letter is contained, the observer knowing in advance that a word and not a single letter is to be exposed. In this case there occur as before the coexcitations from the parts of the letter, knitting to an associative complex from habit and quite automatically, and tending to set off a recognition act for this letter. However, there occur simultaneously the other groups of coexcitations from the other letters, each tending to set off its own letter recognition, but tending also, when occurring in this particular combination of letter-groups, to function with them in setting off the recognition of the word. The context "set" for words tips the balance in favor of the unitary recognition of the word, which drafts to itself the energy and consciousness which would otherwise have been given to the letters as such. With very familiar words, the letter recognitions are checked in their incipiency. With new words, the recognition of certain letters may quite complete itself before the whole word is known.

With the familiar word, as with the letter, certain parts may be dominant parts, being first factors or more effective factors in setting off the word-recognition. And here we may, in part, accept the findings of Goldscheider and Müller, Zeitler, and Messmer as to what the dominant parts are, and that these are first factors in initiating the word-recognition, for most readers and for most words. That these dominant parts have apperception acts precedent to or distinct from the apperception of the words as wholes must be denied, it seems to me, for actual reading. Such separate apperception acts seem to occur mainly as artifacts of the experiments with short exposures and strained attention. That we may be conscious of the dominant parts *earlier* than of the other parts, inside the total recognition act, seems to be the real fact, and the greater *prominence* of the dominant parts, in consciousness, is verifiable by introspection.

Again, as to perceiving by total form: for some readers, and for all of us in the case of many familiar words, coexcitations from the various parts that make up a word's *total outline*, independently of their being parts of letters, mutually assist each other in acting as cues to touch off the recognition of the word. When this recognition occurs, we are conscious of the total form, as in the other case we were conscious of the dominant letters, earlier and more prominently than of the constituent letters of the word-form. Here again it seems that total form is not apperceived separately, but that, in one act of projection, the total form and the parts to fill it are placed, although this unitary act is not necessarily simultaneous any more than is the act of hitting a target.

The visual recognition of a familiar phrase, *as* a phrase, is but a repetition of the process described above, the recognitions of constituent words as well as of letters in this case being partially inhibited in favor of the total recognition of the larger unit. Total visual form seems to be a less important factor in mediating the recognitions as the unit grows larger. Unitary recognition of phrases is very common in reading, for mentally the words do not stand entirely apart. The exigencies of printing have brought about the division on the page of much that belongs together in speech, and again many of our words are logically phrases and might be printed as separate words. The psychological process of apperceiving these words or phrases would not change very greatly if they were printed differently. Very many compounds are written sometimes as separate words, sometimes as two words with a hyphen, again as a single word. Indeed, as we shall see elsewhere, the usual separation even of words upon the page, in Latin and Greek, came very late. In partial disregard, therefore, of the printer's divisions, there is naturally a gradual progress, with practice, toward recognition in larger units, for those who learn first the recognition of letters and words. Larger and larger unitary reactions are set off as familiarity makes this possible, the same excitations coming to serve as cues for the larger recognitions instead of for the smaller, while the earlier processes or recognition habits, even when they do not atrophy, are performed automatically, consciousness ever tending to leave them for higher levels.

We must remember, however, that there are continual reversions to older habits, consciousness descending to even the level of letter-recognitions, on occasion, and very often taking account of particular words. Here there seem to be very great individual differences, and these depend partly, although never wholly, on the methods by which the reader has learned to read. We are brought back to the conclusion of Goldscheider and Müller that we read by phrases, words, or letters as we may serve our purpose best. But we see, too, that the reader's acquirement of ease and power in reading comes through increasing ability to read in larger units.

We cannot complete our account of visual perception in reading until we have first taken account of the part played by inner speech and by the consciousness of meaning. These have an important function in conditioning recognitions in reading. Meaning, indeed, dominates and unitizes the perception of words and phrases, as indeed, according to such writers as Stout at least, it dominates all perceptions. Zeitler's remark will be remembered, that the word's form first gets anchored or established as the sense is filled into it. This appears in perceiving phrases in which words are "seen" which are not there, but which make sense. The excitations from the page act here as cues to a meaning which reacts in the projection of an equivalent expression. As for the inner vocalization of what is read, we shall find this, too, a powerful factor in welding together what is seen, and in keeping it together before the mind's eye until the full meaning dawns. It will be our next task to take account of this important constituent of the reading process.

CHAPTER VI

THE INNER SPEECH OF READING AND THE MENTAL AND PHYSICAL CHARACTERISTICS OF SPEECH

THE fact of inner speech forming a part of silent reading has not been disputed, so far as I am aware, by any one who has experimentally investigated the process of reading. Its presence has been established, for most readers, when adequate tests have been made. Its characteristics and functions have been variously described by many writers on general psychology and philosophy and on the psychology of language.

Purely visual reading is quite possible, theoretically; and Secor, in a study made at Cornell University, found that some readers could read visually while whistling or doing other motor tasks that would hinder inner speech. We might perhaps all have learned a sort of visual reading, and might yet require ourselves to read so in a measure. But although there is an occasional reader in whom the inner speech is not very noticeable, and although it is a foreshortened and incomplete speech in most of us, yet it is perfectly certain that the inner hearing or pronouncing, or both, of what is read, is a constituent part of the reading of by far the most of people, as they ordinarily and actually read. The evidence is cumulative from many sources, and cannot all be given here, but there is no doubt as to the fact. We shall here consider some of the experiments which throw light upon the presence and character of this inner speech.

In the writer's own experiments in which single unrelated words were exposed for four seconds each, the reader to state just what was suggested as he saw each, the words were usually "mentally pronounced" immediately after or accompanying the recognition of their visual form. When other words or phrases were suggested, as often occurred, these were almost always mentally pronounced. The conjunctive and relational words, definitive adjectives, etc., aroused few associations other than verbal ones, the latter usually being

phrases of which the words customarily form a part. The inner pronunciation of these words and of the suggested phrases constituted
much the most prominent part of the reader's consciousness of them.
When sense matter was exposed similarly, giving the reader four seconds for each consecutive word or phrase, the words and phrases
were almost always mentally pronounced, and usually with a strong
feeling that they belonged with a preceding pronunciation or were
to be followed by another, or both.

In another series of experiments, the readers read equivalent
pages from an interesting novel, by various methods assigned them.
Sometimes the instructions were to read "the way you like to read";
sometimes they were to "say it all to themselves"; again they "read
aloud"; then they thought of "how it would sound" as they read; and
sometimes they were directed to use lip-movement. Sometimes the
readings were at the ordinary and most comfortable speed, and again
they would be as fast as possible. The time required for the reading
of each page was carefully taken and will be referred to in discussing
the rate of reading. In many cases these experiments brought the
readers to an awareness of their inner speech in reading when this
had gone unnoticed before. When asked to say the words over to
themselves, they found that really this was what they had been doing all along in their ordinary reading, and was the one thing that
they could not escape doing when they tried. In such cases, the time
required for reading a page in the assigned way would be nearly the
same as when the page was read "the way you like to read." In the
same way the reader's habit of hearing the sound of what he read,
or of using lip-movement, etc., was often revealed. Of nearly thirty
adults who were thus tested, the large majority found inner speech
in some form to be a part of their ordinary reading. Purely visual
reading was not established for any of the readers, although the test
did not show that it was not present for a few. Motorizing with lips
closed at the "comfortable" speed gave nearly the same average rate
as when the reading was by the reader's "own method," 5.29 words
per second for the former and 5.35 for the latter, for twenty readers
tested. Of twenty post-graduate students who were tested, but two
or three used lip-movement when reading "as they liked." Many of
the others who "motorized" said that the pronunciation was "up in

the head," and it usually seemed to be without any very noticeable movements of the articulatory apparatus.

For the readers tested in these experiments it seemed that the inner speech was a combination of auditory and motor elements, with one or the other predominating according to the reader's habitual mode of imaging. Sometimes when the inner speech was very prominent it was difficult for the reader to say whether it was auditory or motor, although it seemed to him to be of but one kind. The fact is that what we say is always heard as well, and there comes to be an indissoluble union of the auditory and motor elements. Our hearing, too, has an active aspect which may go so far as to include an inner saying, or imitation, of what is heard. And so the auditory and motor types of readers are really apt to be audito-motor types, with one or the other aspect leading in many cases.

That the speech of silent reading is simpler than in reading aloud is indicated by the fact that it was faster for each of the readers tested, both when the reading was at normal speed and when it was as fast as possible. Reading aloud was 66 per cent slower than reading silently, at the normal rate, and 56 per cent slower at the maximal rate, on an average for twenty readers. In reading aloud, as in talking, generally, the words are practically all pronounced as the breath is expired, and there are pauses at the inspirations. The inner speech of reading, on the other hand, goes on during inspiration as well, and thus time is saved. Then, as Professor Dodge shows in his "Die Motorische Wortvorstellungen," the inner articulations do not call into play the chest and larynx muscles that are used in speaking aloud, and there is a shortening of the pronunciation, a slurring of the words, and indeed the omission of many for some readers. Professor Dodge states that in his own ordinary silent reading almost every word is pronounced, but that in his fastest silent reading only the beginnings of words are pronounced. In his fastest reading of very familiar matter only certain words were pronounced. His speed of reading seems to be determined by the speed with which his motor word-ideas can follow one another. He finds, as I have found, that auditory elements are present in the reading of those who motorize, and that those who auditize are apt to have more or less of the motor present.

Zeitler and Messmer did not investigate the inner speech of reading, but Messmer asserts that "in visual reading the auditory and motor centres work along," and that purely visual reading is normally not to be found.

Quantz found lip-movement, and consequently inner speech, to be universal in the early reading of children. The lip-movement decreases with practice and usually, although not always, disappears in the rapid and more intelligent readers. He found that "lip-movement in silent reading is not an acquired habit, but a reflex action, the physical tendency to which is inherited." "It is a specific manifestation of the general psycho-physical law of dynamogenesis by which every mental state tends to express itself in muscular movement." Reading without lip-movement is "an acquired habit," the natural thing being to use the lips, as almost all of us do in practice when we come to a difficult place requiring close attention.

My own observations indicate that the disappearance of the lip-movement is no indication of the absence of inner speech in reading. In my own case, the lips are seldom moved, but I can never escape the inner pronunciation that forms a part of all my reading.

It would be easy to quote authority almost endlessly for the presence of inner speech in reading and, indeed, in most thinking. The simple fact is that the inner saying or hearing of what is read seems to be the core of ordinary reading, the "thing in itself," so far as there is such a part of such a complex process. It is so in all use of language. The spoken language is the language *par excellence*, as Professor Whitney says in his "Life and Growth of Language," "gesture and writing being its subordinates and auxiliaries." The child comes to his first reader with his habits of spoken language fairly well formed, and these habits grow more deeply set with every year. His meanings inhere in this spoken language and belong but secondarily to the printed symbols; and always, for most readers, we can say with M. Egger that "to read is, in effect, to translate writing into speech." And while this inner speech is but an abbreviated and reduced form of the speech of everyday life, a shadow copy as it were, it nevertheless retains the essential characteristics of the original. In order, therefore, to understand the inner speech of reading and its relation to the interpretative processes, it will be necessary to examine briefly the nature of speech generally, and its relation to thought and meaning.

Language begins with the sentence, and this is the unit of language everywhere. A sentence is a unitary expression of a thought. A thought may be expressed in a word sometimes, and this is then a sentence-word, as when Preyer's child put his milk cup down quickly and said "Hot!" This single word was to signify, "This drink is too hot." It was "a whole proposition in a syllable," as Preyer says. The *meaning* that might have suggested "This drink is too hot" and that would have bathed every part of it as spoken, suggested only "Hot" as its expression, with this child who yet knew but little of language. But there was more than the articulated word. The pitch, accent, modulation of voice, which characterize a sentence-word's pronunciation, are important factors in expressing the particular unitary meaning that is felt. "Papa" may mean "Come here, papa," "Look out, papa," "Please do, papa," according to variations in the tone, etc., and according to the situation context. Often the modulation, accent, or rhythm are more expressive of the speaker's meaning than are the words as such, and the former factors belong to the sentence *as a whole*.

The child, the primitive man, and indeed any speaker, when he would form a sentence, begins with a *meaning*, a total idea, as Wundt calls it, which he would express. This total idea is at first little differentiated and may find expression in a gesture, a tone, or a word, as when the earnestly spoken "Hot" was all that came. With more experience this total idea or consciousness situation, of being burned with milk, falls apart somewhat into the sub-notions milk—this—hot—drink, and gets a correspondingly analyzed expression in these several words, these expressing still, however, one unitary meaning. The part of the total idea that is most prominent in consciousness is apt to be expressed first, and in child speech, as with many primitive tribes, the words may come in any order according as the various aspects of the total idea successively become prominent in the speaker's mind.

The child's language, however, is not an invention, but is learned by imitation; and he accepts, in English, certain fixed habits of breaking up the total ideas into parts that are expressed in parts of speech, such as nouns, verbs, adjectives, etc. Certain habitual sequences of these parts are also learned by imitation and his words come to fall into this habitual order. Thus, beginning with a total meaning and a total intention of expressing this meaning, the development is toward a more and more particular division of it into aspects or parts, and toward the expression of these parts in words that are arranged in grammatical sequence, this arranging and indeed the whole development being largely automatic, the result of associative habits learned gradually by experience and by imitation. But *meaning leads*, and the idea of the whole dominates the parts. The sentence is *not* naturally composed of words which originally existed independently, just as we shall find that the word is not a mere collection of syllables and letters.

In the ancient languages a single expression would often be word and sentence together. Wundt says in his "Völker-Psychologie"[1]: "The Latin *amavi* is both word and sentence. The Romance languages resolve this thought into three words, *ego habeo amatum, j'ai aimé.* Accordingly, if we compare, on the one hand, languages of an evidently more primitive development with those that are more developed, and if on the other hand we compare the earlier with the later stages of one and the same language, the differentiation of the parts of speech everywhere shows itself as the process of gradually resolving the word out of the whole to which it belongs; namely, the sentence, — the process which lends the word a relatively greater independence and fixes its grammatical form at the same time with its independent significance." There exist to-day languages in which the sentences are spoken without differentiation of either words or parts of speech, in a continuum of syllable sounds, or it might be said that the sentence is one long word. Our English and the kindred languages have made the analysis into parts of speech, words, etc., and our fashion of printing has made us very conscious of the results of this analysis. But in the living speech of conversation and thought these parts still inhere organically in the original sentence-wholes, and the actual structure is very different from the written or printed expression, as we shall presently see.

---

[1] Vol. I, p. 561.

Genetically, then, as we might go on to show, the growth of living speech both in the race and in the child has been from the protoplasm of total meanings expressed in sentence-wholes, through a progressive analysis to parts of speech and words, then to syllables and to elementary sounds. We shall later trace the analogous development of the written and printed characters from primitive picture-wholes to characters representative of word-meanings, word-sounds, and finally to symbols for syllables and for elementary sounds. Let us now look more nearly at the processes that go on as we speak our English sentences to-day.

In the first place it is certain that in ordinary speech some thought of the whole sentence pervades every part as the part is spoken, and the part is felt in a perspective of the whole. This is true of the sentence's beginning as well as of its other parts, and some consciousness of the whole usually precedes even the initial utterance. Says Wundt in the volume mentioned (p. 563): "At the moment in which I begin a sentence the whole of it stands already in my consciousness as a total idea." Wundt adds, however, that the sentence is then felt only in its main outlines, its constituent parts being at first dark, but coming out as the speaking goes on. "The process," he says, "is something like the sudden lighting of a complex picture, where one at first has only a general impression of the whole, and then successively of the particular parts, always seen in their relations to the whole." Only thus, Wundt thinks, can we explain the fact of a speaker going correctly through with a complex sentence without having reflected on it before.

The total idea of what is to be said thus exists in consciousness precedent to the utterance, and dominates the utterance throughout. This total idea is not a mere sum of associations, but is an apperceptive unity. This unity becomes differentiated in the manner and in the direction indicated in its sentence expression, and the sentence is, according to Wundt, "the analysis into its parts of a whole that is present in consciousness." Accordingly, he says, sentence formation is analytical, as it is a separation of the parts of a whole, but it is also synthetic in that it is an appearance of part after part in the focus of consciousness. "Above all, however," he adds, "it is an analytical process."[1]

---

[1] "Völker Psychologie," Vol. II, p. 236.

Again, Wundt considers the sentence to be a "voluntary act," willed as a whole. True, it is a complex act, but the constituent movements of articulation, etc., go off automatically like the constituent movements of any other unitary performance. We "give the direction to the thought" and "the requisite words stream to us of themselves"; that is, "they are awakened associatively from the first-excited word-ideas under the influence of the total idea that is present."

"Psychologically considered the sentence is therefore at the same time both a simultaneous and a successive whole — a simultaneous since in every moment of its formation it is in consciousness in its entire extent, although particular secondary elements may occasionally disappear from this; a successive, since the whole changes from moment to moment in its consciousness content while definite ideas one after the other appear in the focus and the others grow darker."[1]

Professor James bases his psychology of the sentence on his view of consciousness as a continuous stream of processes in which "breaks are produced by sudden contrasts in the quality of the successive segments." Consciousness makes us aware of things, and things, being discrete and discontinuous, "pass before us in a train or chain, making often explosive appearances and rending each other in twain." But these do not break the *flow of the thought that thinks them*, with its continuum of feelings, bodily sensations, etc. There are, however, the apparent breaks, which are really "transitive places," places of rapid flow, of flight from the perch of one substantive resting-place to that of another, — to a conclusion perhaps or to a place in which the thought may bask in sensorial imagery. The consciousness life is like a bird's life, made up of an alternation of flights and perchings. "The rhythm of language expresses this, where every thought is expressed in a sentence and every sentence closed by a period."

The places of flight are filled with thoughts of relations, static or dynamic, obtaining between the matters contemplated in the periods of comparative rest. Our thoughts and sentences are largely made up of these fugitive transitional processes, and are thus extremely hard to introspect. To attempt cutting such a sentence

---

[1] *Ibid.*, Vol. II, p. 236 ff.

in the middle to get a look at it is, in James' figure, like catching a snow-flake crystal in the warm hand. The flake is no longer a crystal, but a drop. "So, instead of catching the feeling of relation moving to its term, we find we have caught some substantive thing, usually the last word we were pronouncing, statically taken, and with its function, tendency, and particular meaning in the sentence quite evaporated." It is like "seizing a spinning top to catch its motion, or trying to turn up the gas quickly enough to see how the darkness looks." To these feelings of relation, expressed or named by such words as *and, if, but,* and the like, far oftener not named but felt as the sentence moves forward, we will return when discussing interpretative processes in reading.

According to Professor James, the speaker has "an intention of saying a thing before he has said it," "an entirely definite intention distinct from all other intentions, an absolutely distinct state of consciousness therefore, but with little sensorial imagery, — that welcomes right words as they come and rejects wrong ones." "One must admit that a good third of our psychic life consists in these rapid premonitory perspective views of schemes of thought not yet articulate. How comes it about that a man reading something aloud for the first time is able immediately to emphasize all his words aright, unless from the very first he have a sense of at least the form of the sentence yet to come, which sense is fused with his consciousness of the present word, and modifies its emphasis in his mind so as to make him give it the proper accent as he utters it? Emphasis of this kind is almost altogether a matter of grammatical construction. If we read *no more*, we expect presently to come upon a *than*; if we read *however* at the outset of a sentence, it is a *yet*, a *still*, or a *nevertheless*, that we expect. A noun in a certain position demands a verb in a certain mood and number, in another position it expects a relative pronoun. Adjectives call for nouns, verbs for adverbs, etc. And this foreboding of the coming grammatical scheme combined with each successive uttered word is so practically accurate that a reader incapable of understanding four ideas of the book he is reading aloud can nevertheless read it with the most delicately modulated expression of intelligence."[1]

---

[1] "Psychology," Vol. I, pp. 253-254.

In regarding the sentence as a total unity felt throughout as each part is uttered, and indeed in a measure existing in consciousness precedent to any utterance, James is in agreement with Wundt. "Even before we have opened our mouths to speak," James says, "the entire thought is present to our mind in the form of an intention to utter that sentence." Again, "after the last word of the sentence is spoken, all will admit that we again think its entire content as we inwardly realize its completed deliverance."

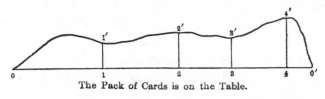

The Pack of Cards is on the Table.

Fig. 14

James' diagram, reproduced here, represents the progress of consciousness throughout the utterance of such a sentence as, "The pack of cards is on the table," the horizontal line representing time, the spaces above representing the consciousness content during this time. Not only is the total thought of the sentence present at its beginning and at its end, but "all vertical sections made through any other parts of the diagram will be respectively filled with other ways of feeling the sentence's meaning. Through 2, for example, the cards will be the part of the object most emphatically present to the mind; through 4, the table. The stream is made higher in the drawing at its end than at its beginning, because the final way of feeling the content is fuller and richer than the initial way. As Joubert says, 'we only know just what we meant to say, after we have said it.' And as M. V. Egger remarks, 'before speaking one barely knows what one intends to say, but afterward one is filled with admiration and surprise at having said and thought it so well." The same object of thought or total idea is "known everywhere now from the point of view, if we may so call it, of this word, now from the point of view of that. And in our feeling of each word there chimes an echo or foretaste of every other."

The total idea is "the overtone, halo, or fringe of the word *as spoken in that sentence. It is never absent; no word in an understood sentence comes to consciousness as a mere noise. We feel its meaning as it passes; and although our object differs from one moment to another as to its verbal kernel or nucleus, yet it is *similar* throughout the entire segment of the stream." Cut a thought in cross-section at any moment of its utterance, and "you will find, not the bald word in process of utterance, but that word suffused with the whole idea."[1]

I have quoted at length the words and figures of Professor James, as giving the most nearly correct and most graphic view that is yet obtainable of the organic unity of the sentence with its subordinated word-parts, on the side of consciousness and meaning. On the side of physical utterance the articulatory processes have been carefully analyzed and described, and here, too, the organic unity of the sentence-utterance and the subordination of the partial processes to this whole have been established beyond a doubt. The painstaking analysis made at Yale University, by Dr. Wallin and Professor Scripture, of sentences spoken into a graphophone arranged for the purpose, have given us an especially accurate account of what we do when we talk, and the studies of various eminent philologists corroborate their results. We shall therefore find it profitable to review the facts concerning speech as a mechanical process.

The utterance of even a single word requires the coordinated action of three distinct and very different groups of muscles. The breath is forced outward and regulated by the action of the large muscles of respiration of the chest and abdomen. The sound is produced by the action of the muscles of the larynx, tensing and controlling the two vocal cords or bands between whose edges the air passes. The particular character which the sound has when uttered as vowel or consonant, the articulation as it is called, is produced by the action of the muscles of the tongue and jaw and palate. Indeed, most of the other muscles of the body are involved in the movements of expression, gesture, posture, etc., which always form a constituent part of speech as it is actually spoken.

---

[1] "Psychology," Vol. I, p. 243 ff.

Professor Scripture, in his "Elements of Experimental Phonetics," finds that this complex machinery for vocal utterance is in continuous action throughout the utterance of any word or phrase, with no interruptions such as letters, syllables, or even words suggest. "The word *manly* represents continuous action of the breath organs, continuous action of the vocal cords, with a smooth rise and fall of pitch, continuous movement of the lips, tongue, and velum, through various positions." "In fact, the word is a continuous sound change, with no limits or minima of any noticeable kind." The word is to be considered as a fusion of a series of continuous changes, certain stages of which may be characterized as "*m-n-l-i*, etc. As far as the vocal movements are concerned the word is just as continuous as *manned*." "I do not believe a division of the flow of speech into separate blocks termed *syllables* has the slightest justification or the slightest phonetic meaning." "A word is a continuous series of an infinite number of sounds, and the letters indicate, in an incomplete fashion, nothing more than certain characteristic points of this series." Even single vowel sounds were found to vary constantly in pitch, in talking though not in singing.

It is true that, for the listener, there are really brief interruptions or moments of silence, not noticed as such, however; but "the motor activity of the speech organs goes on just as vigorously during the occlusion (silence) as before and after." The lips, tongue, etc., do not assume fixed positions at any moment, and "it seems therefore somewhat artificial to divide the words *who'll*," e.g., "into three or five sounds; we may preferably say that for the sake of discussion five stages in the changing sound may be picked out as typical of the whole process." Professor Scripture likens this to taking kinetoscope pictures of a runner, treating his whole movement as a series of positions in which the runner remains at rest. "This treatment has its advantages for certain cases, but we should never lose sight of the fact that the true movement occurs otherwise." Not only is the utterance of a single word found to be such a unitary and indivisible act, but the experimenters find that words are not separated as they are spoken in sentences. Indeed, Professor Scripture asserts that "speech is a flow of auditory and motor energy with no possibility of division into separate blocks such as letters, syllables, words, feet, etc., except in a purely arbitrary manner that does not represent the actual case."[1]

Professor Sweet, the English philologist, in his "Primer of Phonetics" says: "The only division actually made in language is that into 'breath-groups.' We are unable to utter more than a certain number of sounds in succession without renewing the stock of air in our lungs. These breath-groups correspond partially to the logical division into sentences; every sentence is necessarily a breath-group, but every breath-group need not be a complete sentence.

"Within each breath-group there is no pause whatever, notwith-standing the popular idea that we make a pause between every two words. Thus in such a sentence as *put on your hat*, we hear clearly the 'recoil' or final breath-glide which follows the final *t* of *hat*, but the *t* of *put* runs on to the following vowel without any recoil, exactly as in the single word *putting*. In *put back* there is no glide at all after the *t*."

The inhalation pauses afford momentary opportunity for rest, to both speaker and listener. The average number of syllables uttered between pauses was found by Wallin to be about six, for reading prose, with a "range" of 1.85 syllables. However, on an average about thirty-two times this average number of syllables *could* be uttered at one exhalation. Wallin found that in impassioned speech this maxi-mum was most nearly reached.

But if the spoken sentence is, except for inhalation pauses, an unbroken continuum as uttered, it is by no means an even or monot-onous continuum, in natural living speech. There is a continual rise and fall of pitch and energy and a variation in quantity, producing a rhythm and melody of speech that is as characteristic and constant for prose as for verse, but not so marked. Indeed, when Dr. Wallin had persons read prose printed as poetry and poetry printed as prose, in a large number of cases they were unable to distinguish the one from the other. The poems of Browning and Tennyson were called prose and the prose of Bacon was called poetry.

Certain variations in force or stress, in the continuous flow of speech, give the effect, as Sweet says, of its being broken up into

---

[1] "Experimental Phonetics," pp. 279-593.

syllables, even when there is not the slightest pause. The vowels are the more sonorous sounds and thus help to make the syllable divisions. A vowel is "voiced breath, modified by some definite configuration of the superglottal passages, but without audible friction which would make it a consonant." In other words, "a vowel is voice modified by a resonance chamber, to wit the mouth." "Consonants," Sweet continues, "are the result of audible friction or stopping of the breath in some part of the mouth or throat. The main distinction between vowels and consonants is that while in vowels the mouth configuration merely modifies the vocalized breath — which is therefore an essential element of them — in consonants the narrowing or stopping of the mouth passage is the foundation of the sound, and the state of the glottis is something secondary." "Consonants can therefore be breathed as well as voiced, the mouth configuration alone being enough to produce a distinction without the help of voice. All consonants can be whispered." Between the consonants and the vowels are glides, —"transitional sounds, produced during the transition from one sound to another," the written letters representing, as we have seen, but a portion of the sounds actually uttered.

So the ear "learns to divide a breath-group into groups of vowels (or vowel equivalents, as the sonorous *l* in *cattle*), each flanked by consonants (or consonant equivalents)," giving a division into syllables.

Sometimes variations in stress may suggest word-division, but often, and regularly in French, there is no such thing as word-stress or word-division. In French, says Sweet, the "sentences are cut up into syllables without any regard to the structure of the words they are made up of."[1]

The sound of any letter, therefore, and the movements necessary to produce it, depend partly upon the context in which the letter stands. The sound that occurs in context cannot usually be given in isolation, and in any case the vocal movements used for its isolated production are different, often very different, from the corresponding movements in the continuous utterance of a word or sentence.

---

[1] Sweet's "Primer of Phonetics," selections from various parts.

Similarly, a word sounded alone is somewhat different in sound and in the vocal movements required than when spoken as part of a sentence; and a sentence whose words are uttered each for itself has, as we all know, a sound that is very different from the sound of a sentence uttered as such.

Indeed the action in uttering a sentence is of the same kind as in skating, dancing, throwing a ball, or any such unitary complex of muscular movements. In throwing a ball, for instance, there is the sub-movement of grasping the ball, itself quite complex; there is the raising and poising of the arm, with all the coordination needed for this performance, and there is the complicated final act of throwing. Now the grasping and poising and throwing might each be performed separately, with full attention directed to itself. But who thinks of these separate movements as he aims and throws? The meaning of the total act, viz. the hitting of the mark, guides and controls and unitizes all, and renders each movement different from what it would be alone. Each subordinate movement is made in a perspective of the whole, just as, in perceiving, the consciousness of the part is profoundly modified by the consciousness of the whole. We have already seen how meaning welds the parts of a sentence into unity. We see now how the necessities of physical utterance contribute to the same end.

A main force tending to unitize the sentence both physically and psychically is the alternation of stresses, the rise and fall of pitch, and the variations in quantity, already referred to as factors in producing the rhythm, melody, and emphasis of speech. The total sentence-meaning inheres vitally and comes most to expression in these characteristic variations in the sentence-flow. They are the life of the sentence, and give it its character-stamp. And these variations belong to the sentence *as a whole*, those made in one part having reference to those made in another, and all having a unitary significance. The written or printed representations of speech make no record of these its vital parts, except for an occasional use of italics, underscoring, or mark of accent. They fail, as well, to record the transitional sounds between letters and words, and the variations in letter-sounds according to variations in context. But the expressional variations, with all these others, come to life again when the written or printed characters are rendered into living speech in reading. In actual reading the rise and fall of pitch and inflection, the hurrying here and slowing there, what we have called the melody of speech, appears in the inner speech even more prominently than does the articulation of the particular sounds, wherever there is appreciation of the meaning of what is read. The inner saying of many a word, in rapid reading, is but a slurred remnant of its full sound, a motor tally as it were. But it is a tally that has its place and its time in the inner rhythmic sequence. Certain words may be omitted entirely, but they are usually words of relative unimportance, or they are parts which would be unstressed in ordinary speech and whose omission will not affect the natural swing of the sentence. The expression shell or form is the most persistent and essential part of the inner speech, certainly in my own case at least.

I have thought it best to discuss rather fully the psychic and physical characteristics of speech and the relation of speech to meanings, both because I find these processes of speech, in their main lines, essential to reading as well, and because the pedagogy of phonetics and of reading methods generally needs the perspective which such a survey of the psycho-physics of speech can give, and needs it in this accessible form. We shall now, I hope, be better able to understand the part played by inner speech in the apperception of the printed sentence, and shall take up that discussion where we left it on an earlier page.

CHAPTER VII

THE FUNCTIONING OF INNER SPEECH IN THE PERCEPTION OF WHAT IS READ

IN so far as the cues from the printed page set off the recognition of phrases and sentences as wholes, they do this the more readily for the habits of sequence and expectation which exist among words according to grammatical and logical usages. We recall Professor James' account of how, in our English, the verb tends to follow its subject and precede its object, how the preposition tends to be followed by its related substantive, etc. Our words are thoroughly organized according to these general associative habits of our language, and when any given series has occurred in our reading, the sort of words and the sentence forms that belong in sequence with these are subexcited in advance of their appearance on the page, and need but slight cues from the page to cause them to spring into the perceptual consciousness. Indeed, hundreds of phrases and sentences have occurred so often in our speech that they have a place in mind as specific memory-wholes; and as slight a glimpse is needed to start the recognition of these as when the tap of a cane suffices to announce the approach of our grandfather. But though the phrase or sentence has never occurred in reading before, in exactly its present wording, the inner readiness for it is almost as complete; and it will inwardly complete itself almost as readily from a few visual cues, if it is cast in a familiar form, if its words and parts of speech stand in familiar grammatical sequences, so that each associatively helps the other to rise and remain in consciousness. It is unitarily perceived quite as truly as if it existed as a specific memory-whole.

All this would be true if the mechanism of perception in reading were purely visual, without the help of the inner speech. But the habits of inter-association and expectancy, which bind the units of our language into wholes that are ready to realize themselves when but a few of the constituent or context parts are suggested, are far most deeply founded in the audito-motor mechanism of speech. People ordinarily talk far more than they read, and the motor conditions which obtain in talking are much more conducive to the formation of lasting habits than those which obtain in reading. And even while people read, the talking habits are doubtless getting more effective practice in the inner speech than are the visual habits in visual perception, for all but persons who are strongly visual-minded. Even in silent thinking, clothed in a sort of language as the process always is, the organization of our speech habits goes on perfecting itself, and here again the more stably knitted if not indeed the more prominent language terms are motor and auditory.

While, then, the purely visual habits of inter-association and expectancy play an important part in enlarging our perceptive range and in unitizing our phrases and sentences, the visual range is itself enlarged and its content supported by the more stably organized inner utterance into which the visual percepts are constantly being translated. The carrying range or span of the inner speech is considerably larger than that of vision. No satisfactory measurements have been made of the amount of new "sense" matter that can be held in control at once by the psycho-physical mechanism of speech; but at least a couple of ordinary lines can be so held, and so perfectly that the relative stresses and melody of the original utterance can be faithfully reproduced. Indeed the rhythm and melody, by their binding the sentence together, become important factors in extending the *Sprach Umfang*, and the span is greater as the matter read is more rhythmical and more melodious in its composition. But of prime importance, of course, in making possible a large range of inner speech in reading is the existence of the inter-association habits which we have been discussing, and the range is larger as the reading matter follows more closely the associative habits of the language. We remember, of course, through the formation of associative links, and if these are ready formed for us in what is read, we can naturally carry more of it in memory at a single reading.

The inner utterance doubtless begins as the words are visually recognized, but the full utterance of the phrases and sentences as such follows at a considerable distance behind the eye, a variable distance that is greater as the reading is faster, but depends also on other factors than rate. The reader may observe this separation of eye and voice as he turns his eye to a new page, several words of the preceding page usually remaining to be uttered. Dr. Quantz measured the amount of this eye-voice separation by slipping a card over a reader's page, at certain places predetermined by the experimenter but not known to the reader, and recording the number of words spoken after the view was cut off. He found that much depended upon where in the line the view was intercepted. "When the reader is pronouncing a word at the beginning of a line, the eye is on an average 7.4 words in advance of the voice; in the middle, 5.1 words; and at the end, 3.8, giving an average of 5.4 words." The space between is thus "very elastic," as he says, "expanding and contracting with each line, but with a uniform regularity — except indeed where special conditions are introduced; an unfamiliar word, for instance, would decrease the distance to zero, or a familiar phrase might increase it to a dozen words. After the long pause which a period allows, the eye lengthens its lead of the voice."

Quantz found a close correlation between the increase of eye-voice separation and the increase of rate in reading, and states that the "rapid silent readers read farthest ahead of the voice in reading aloud," and thinks that "a certain considerable distance between eye and voice is a condition of intelligent and intelligible reading." He also made some indecisive experiments to determine whether the consciousness of meaning goes ahead with the eye, and states it as probable that it does not.

There seems to be a phase of inner utterance which follows the eye much more closely than this, but it is not the meaningful utterance of the sentence. It is true that further investigation has not justified Goldscheider and Müller's conclusion that the letter-sounds are immediately suggested by the visual letter-forms, in ordinary reading. The word-sound seems usually to be suggested as a whole. But this sound of the *word* seems to be dimly suggested immediately accompanying or following the word's visual appearance. This initial motorization, present in my own case at least, is of the words in isolation, is accompanied by a slight feeling of the word's meaning, and seems to help hold the word in consciousness until enough others are given to combine with it in touching off the unitary utterance of the sentence which they form, with the total sentence meaning which dominates the inner utterance of this sentence *as* a sentence. The full inner utterance seems, then, to be suggested partly by the individual word-sounds serving as cues, but the visual forms doubtless also serve directly as such cues. I have no doubt that the stability of the visual forms and their persistence in memory depend considerably on both the initial and final inner utterance.

The full inner utterance thus "hangs fire," as Quantz shows, behind the eye until there are present enough visual and motor data to suggest the total meaning and the corresponding sentence expression, and this utterance then occurs with an inter-dependence of meaning and word-expression such as Professors Wundt and James have described for speech in general. There can be little doubt that the main meaning comes to consciousness only with the beginning of the sentence-utterance, and the reader does not feel that he has the complete sense until he has spoken it. He is almost sure to deliberately say the passage over to himself if it is difficult, and persons who do not read very much must usually use an actual whisper, even in easy reading, if the meaning is to be obtained.

That the *general* meaning dawns upon the reader precedent to the full sentence-utterance is evidenced by the many cases in which variant words of equivalent meaning are read, and also by the comparative ease with which a reader may paraphrase the thought of what he reads. This is especially noticeable in the case of a person reading a foreign language which he does not pronounce easily but which he comprehends rather rapidly. Here the visual word and phrase percepts touch off total meanings which clothe themselves, as the meanings become articulate, in English sentences, and we have as a result the mongrel reading which passes for French or German in so many modern language classes.

It is of the greatest service to the reader or listener that at each moment a considerable amount of what is being read should hang suspended in the primary memory of the inner speech. It is doubtless true that without something of this there could be no comprehension of speech at all. When a considerable amount is thus suspended, the attention may wander backward and forward to get a fuller meaning where this is needed, with no fear of losing the minor parts, which are taken care of physiologically and may be taken into the focus of consciousness at will. Any careful introspection of actual reading will show that the main focus of attention is often far behind the eye, concerned perhaps with the sound of some word or phrase that is giving difficulty; and we know that the entire process of visually perceiving and inwardly pronouncing may go on, for even an entire paragraph sometimes, with but very little of even marginal consciousness, the attention being absorbed in some thought suggested earlier, or perhaps in some irrelevant imagery. Indeed, any part of the reading process or the whole of it may proceed automatically with but a minimum of consciousness, just as in walking, dancing, or other complex motor activity requiring adaptive reactions to stimuli. The attention, the concern of the self about what is going on, may be here or there as there is need of it, and again is often centered where there is no need of it. Some prominent letter or other form in a preceding or succeeding line may flash into the focus more prominently than the advancing stream of visual forms that the eye is just revealing. The movement of the attention may thus be backward or forward, but of course is usually forward. Doubtless its actual advance has little reference to the sequence of eye-movements and pauses. These are ordinarily indistinguishable to consciousness, and the attention has to do with an unbroken line. The crest of the advancing consciousness seems often to be double or even quadruple, composed of visual, motor, or any other content with which the reader is concerned. In so far as the attention is upon the visual forms, it is of course apt to note preferably the larger, the more characteristic, or the more meaningful of the letters, letter-groups, and word-shapes that appear. It is thus apt to be especially concerned with the so-called determining or dominant forms. But I consider that the better differentia of these latter forms is their greater effectiveness in neurally conditioning the perceptual reactions.

There has been much controversy as to whether there is a movement of the attention during a reading pause. Much of this controversy concerns the technique of making the brief exposures of reading matter in the various experiments, and would be difficult to make intelligible or profitable to the general reader, in any brief compass. The behavior of the attention in such experiments must at any rate be very different from what occurs in the pauses of reading.

And as to the proper length of the exposure, it is found in measuring the amounts that can be read during a reading-pause that exposure-times differing most widely and conditions of lighting, etc., that are most variant give much the same results. As to the question itself of whether the dawning of the visual forms in consciousness occurs simultaneously or successively over the given areas, careful intro-spection of actual reading, probably the sanest though still an imper-fect test, indicates that there is a successive coming to consciousness of the more striking forms at least. Doubtless the "forward push" of associative expectancy, on its visual side and supported, perhaps, by its auditomotor phase, would tend to pick up the prospective and just-appearing forms in a constant succession. Doubtless, too, these same conditions bring about the simultaneous appearance of many forms that go to make up expected phrases, etc.; but the general effect must be to bridge the chasm, if there is any to bridge, between the reading pauses, and to give a constantly but not uniformly for-ward movement of the visual consciousness.

Neurally, as I have elsewhere urged, it would seem that the cues from the various parts of the reading field work simultaneously, though doubtless with very unequal effectiveness, in conditioning the perceptual reaction. It may be, indeed, that here too we have to do with successive functionings as well as simultaneous, but the experiments have not proved that the stimulations are effective first at the left, or in succession. The automatic functioning of these neu-ral factors and habits, silent but effective workers behind the "stage-effects" which they arouse in consciousness, is worthy of a greater share of the attention in the discussion concerning how we perceive. Dr. F. Schumann illustrated this last year in his criticism of Erdmann and Dodge, rightly urging that when these experimenters read words at a distance at which the particular letters could not be made out, the letters might still be efficient factors, as his own experiments seemed to show, in neurally conditioning the appearance of the total form. Thus it will be seen that this experiment leaves unsettled the question as to whether total form or letter-shapes or still other fac-tors are mainly operative in arousing the perceptive reaction. The experiment deals with an effect and does not discover the cause.

CHAPTER VIII

THE INTERPRETATION OF WHAT IS READ, AND THE NATURE OF MEANING

WE shall now proceed to examine the processes concerned in the interpretation of what is read. How do we get the meaning of our reading, and in what does meaning consist? Our study of the relationship of speech to meaning has prepared the way for an understanding of this vital part of the reading process, but we have not yet considered the part that is played by imagery.

A series of experiments made by the writer gave data which throw some light upon this problem. The experiments were arranged as follows: Two printed articles of considerable interest and but moderate difficulty were selected, one an account of how a spider spins its web, the other a description of the arrangements made for the entertainment of Queen Elizabeth at Killingworth Castle. The words of both articles were first pasted singly each on a square of cardboard, were shuffled, and were then exposed to readers for four seconds each, the reader looking at the word exposed and allowing associations to play about it as they would, reporting what had occurred as soon as the four seconds had passed. Again, the lines of both articles were pasted consecutively end to end, on narrow slips of cardboard, and the successive words and phrases were exposed to readers, an additional word or phrase being presented at each exposure of four seconds, the preceding context being always in view as it is in ordinary reading. The reader again reported his associations, etc., as for the isolated words. The two series of experiments were separated in time sufficiently to prevent the memories of one from interfering seriously with those of the other.

With the isolated words there was first, usually, an indefinable recognition of the visual form of the word as familiar. Accompanying or very closely following this, probably the latter though the readers could not be explicit, the word was usually "mentally pronounced." After this there was apt to come a mental pronunciation of some phrase or other word that had been associatively connected, as when *by* gave *Sweet by-and-by*, *vertical* gave *vertical writing*, etc. Often there would be but a dim suggestion of some familiar line of poetry, leaving the reader with a vague and tantalizing feeling of something which he could not get. Quite often, especially with one of the readers, the characteristic *feeling* that belonged to such a suggested word or phrase was all that came, but this was vividly aroused. The words exposed tended to call up word-groups with which they had been rhythmically connected. Often the word that was exposed was pronounced "interesting," "agreeable," "full of meaning," etc., and occasionally these judgments seemed to refer to the sound or visual appearance of the word itself. More usually the feeling seemed traceable to some particular associations or uses of the word in past experience, though these latter would not appear above the threshold.

As to imagery, there was almost none suggested by the connective and relational words, the definite adjectives, etc., "the little words," as my readers called them. Because of this absence of imagery the exposure of these words was regarded with much displeasure, their isolated appearance seeming to be regarded as anomalous. They seldom aroused any ideas directly, and suggested few associations of any kind except verbal ones, usually phrases of which they constantly form a part. Occasionally they gave evidence of setting the readers' thoughts in some characteristic direction of expectancy, and doubtless the prepositions, especially, always had some very general influence in determining how the whole psycho-physical organism should face a coming related object.

The amount of imagery suggested by the other classes of words that were presented in isolation was several times as great with some readers as with others. In general the auditory and motor elements exceeded the visual even for these words, the two former being mainly verbal. Both the verbal associates and the other images suggested by the isolated words were of the most varied character, the word often being taken in several quite different senses in the course of the four seconds. There was a good deal of dawdling association, the words not taking much hold upon the mind. The readers were often surprised at the very different appearance and sound of the isolated word, suggesting how little the words had previously been thought of for themselves apart from the sentences in which they figure.

In the other series in which the words and phrases were exposed consecutively in context, the readers took a more active attitude, the associations were less varied but more numerous, and there were other very characteristic differences. A reader who had looked blankly at the word A when exposed singly, and had gotten no associations, had a rich content of associations when A appeared as the first word of a new paragraph. Besides, his feelings of expectancy, curiosity, strain, the "forward push" that was marked in all readers of the context exposures, were even more prominent than the definite associations. The mere statement that the word to be exposed is part of a sense passage limits the trend of association at the start. The limitation extends farther when the reader has caught the general topic discussed in the passage, and still farther when the exposed word is presented upon a verbal and ideational background formed by the complete preceding context. In the spider story, for example, after the mention of *web-weaving*, the word *top* no longer suggested *top of hill, flag-staff, spinning-tops*, etc., as when it was exposed in isolation, but now suggested the top of a post or gateway, with the spider-situation in mind.

The newly exposed word was usually mentally pronounced as before, and was "fitted into the preceding," as one reader very often put it, the new word seeming to contribute toward a notion of sentence unity to which each additional element added a needed part. Immediately following this there was usually a filling out of the sentence or phrase so as to make sense with what came before, and when this did not actually occur, there was usually the "forward push," "forward tendency," "tendency to fill out," as it has been variously described by the readers. All emphasized the strength and comparative constancy of this feeling, and mentioned it as perhaps the most striking thing observed in the experiments. It was usually not so strong at the beginning or end of sentences and paragraphs.

Beside this "forward" feeling, the "little words" gave few except verbal associations. They seemed, as one reader several times remarked, to be but "verbal counters" in the sentence. This reader showed comparatively little tendency to visualize, throughout the experiments. However, he did visualize some of the main objects and scenes referred to in the passages read, enough to form a vague background for the story, but in the main the story itself seemed to be thought in verbal terms.

The other readers, however, had more of the visual element. In the story of the spider's weaving, for instance, a visual picture of the spider was early formed and remained throughout, although it was more or less modified to suit the different references to it as the story progressed. The spider itself was seen in a visual background that had various components fused in a kaleidoscopic fashion into it, each time that the story gave additional data, but still without any violent transitions being made. While this fluctuating spider-scene would sometimes pass temporarily out of the attention field as some particular substantive called up scenes peculiar to itself, it constantly returned and remained as a factor controlling the course of association and expectation.

The visualization was almost always static. The spider jumping was visualized as the spider ready to jump or just alighted. The thought of motion, when mentioned at all, seemed to be a consciousness of tendency to movement in the reader's organism.

The agreement or disagreement of the exposed word with the trend of expectation produced by the preceding context was a matter of frequent remark by the readers, and was often a cause of considerable feeling on their part. The sequence was felt as right or wrong, giving fulfillment or disappointment of expectation. If particular words were expected, the ones that came, although different from the expected ones, were often called "all right," "still better," etc., showing that the real expectation was rather of the expression of a desired meaning than of any particular words.

The meanings of particular words were commented on from time to time, as when *vertical* gave an "up and down feeling," *distant* gave "a kind of feeling of what it meant," etc. *Starting* gave a dim thought of starting machinery, although of no particular machinery. *Distant*, for another reader, produced "a raising of eyes and looking off." *Swings* gave a "motion from left to right," with perhaps a slight head-movement. Many words gave a sense of location. *Tribal* gave a "sort of western location," and *dress*, *patronage*, *alien*, among others, were located in particular directions. Throughout much of the exposure-reading of the Queen Elizabeth story, one reader maintained an orientation of the events as occurring to the left and front of him.

On the whole, the meanings seemed usually to be felt as belonging to the larger wholes, to the sentences and other large units. The words were mainly "counters," felt as having a part in the total, but their function being mainly to help tide one over to a place where a new meaning would be suggested or completed. The reader seldom escaped feeling the particular words in a perspective of the before and after, and was often much puzzled, even baffled, to know how to deal with them as they stood with the total sense uncompleted. The absence of images, at least with the individual words, was rather marked.

These are my more important observations from a considerable amount of such experimentation. They agree in the main with the conclusions of Professor Ribot from an extended and somewhat similar series of experiments in which words (general terms) were pronounced to listeners. The listener was to state immediately whether the word called up anything or nothing to the mind, and if anything, to state what it was. Out of a large number of replies, the most frequent was "nothing," the only sensory image present in consciousness being the sound of the word. In other cases, some concrete example of the term was imaged, sometimes with a visual image of the printed or written word. Sometimes the printed or written word would appear without other image. These were results for isolated words. Ribot also presented whole sentences, "abstract statements," and these gave a similar scantiness of imagery. In the latter test he considered only the sentence as a whole and did not look also for imagery from particular component words, as in my own experiments.[1]

Professor Stout, in the chapter on "Implicit Apprehension" in his "Analytical Psychology," points out that many of the early English and Scotch philosophical writers, as Hobbes, Berkeley, Hume, Stewart, and Dr. Campbell, "bore unequivocal testimony to the fact that the flow of words is for the most part unattended by a parallel

---

[1] Ribot's experiments are reviewed in Stout's "Analytical Psychology," Vol. I, p. 82.

flow of mental imagery." Burke had held that "in the ordinary course of conversation we are sufficiently understood without raising any images of the things concerning which we speak." Professor Stout himself holds that the presence of sensorial imagery is neither usual nor essential in the apprehension of spoken or written language. He does not think that even fleeting and shadowy images necessarily accompany the use of words in ordinary discourse, or are even usually present. Even when the image does appear, according to Professor Stout, it is often unessential and almost irrelevant, as when I have the image of two persons talking when I hear the word *understanding*. The real meaning is not in this image, nor is the meaning of the word *wealth* in the image of a bale of goods that may be called up at the word's appearance. "In reality, imagery of this sort is part and parcel of the word itself considered as a sign rather than of the meaning which it signifies."

At any rate, Professor Stout is certain that the part that images play in consciousness has been overestimated. Consciousness is not a picture-gallery, or a magic lantern exhibition with slide displacing slide in rapid succession. We may suppose presentational states of consciousness not composed of sense imagery, but functioning analogously, just as revived images "have a representative value in some degree comparable to that of sense-perceptions, in spite of very great differences in respect of distinctness, vividness, and quality." Even in actual sense-perception, the meaning of the object is something quite other than the deliverance of the senses. According to Stout, "an imageless representation of the whole is conjoined with the sensible appearance as its psychic fringe." In this fringe lies the significance of the object, as of the image or the word.

Apparently, Stout holds that a feeling of the possibility of reviving the experiences that one has had or may have with the object forms the basis of this fringe, of this halo of meaning. He says that if we dwell on a word, we have a presentiment that images are coming, followed by them shortly. "It is as if the multiplicity were somehow wrapped up in the distinctionless unity and were struggling to unfold itself." So he suggests the name *implicit apprehension* for "that apprehension of a whole which takes place without the discernment of its parts." Nearly all words stand for concept-wholes which are

representative of many particulars. Even singular names are somewhat so, standing for a whole that represents varying phases in the
history of the individual. Stout's main point in the whole discussion
is that it is possible and usual to think such a representative whole
"in its unity and distinctness without discerning all or even any of its
component details." However, when a detail, say a sense image, does
form a part of our thought of a word that is read or heard, it may,
although irrelevant or unessential, help the word to hold the
attention on the real meaning, which, however, is not the image.
The image, Stout thinks, is a helpful instrument for fixing the
attention, as the sense-percept itself is. The name, however, is often
superior to the image, in that it calls up the generic core of the
concept, while an image is apt to be particular and thus comparatively unessential.

In general, language, aside from its function as a means of communication, is most important as a means of directing the attention. It is a mobile "movement of fixation." "A word," says Stout,[1]
"is an instrument for thinking about the meaning which it expresses."
There is more facile and accurate control over these articulatory
"movements of fixation" than over the various muscular adjustments
of the sense organs; hence their advantage in the manipulation of
meanings in our thinking. Stout finds that one "has almost as great
a control over the internal articulation as over the external. The
chief restriction appears to lie in the inability to make the represented sound as loud as the actual sensation, but, apart from this,
one may do almost as one likes with it." So we have come to think
mainly in words, as the most rapid and accurate means of handling
our meanings, of using our experiences. With children and unedu-
cated persons, as we have seen, actual articulation is very common
as they think or read. Older and educated persons resort to the inner articulation. The thinking may indeed be done in part with
images as signs of meanings, but is far more usually and advantageously done with words as the instruments.

So much for the part played by imagery in reading, a part that
is far larger in the reading of young children than in that of adults

---

[1] "Analytical Psychology," Vol. II, p. 194.

and that is far larger in some than in others, but a part that is always secondary or auxiliary to the suggestion and control of meanings themselves. The consciousness of meaning itself belongs in the main to that group of mental states, the feelings, which I regard with Wundt as unanalyzables, or at least as having a large unanalyzable core or body. Each meaning-feeling is very much itself and unlike every other. Of the meanings felt with particular words as we read, most are, as James suggests, those of relations felt as existing between the larger objects of thought, feelings of *and, if, but, by,* etc. These feelings, fleeting and slight as they often are, and named only by the words which call them forth, are yet perhaps as definite and as much themselves as anger, pity, and the like. The poverty of names substantively used for the subjective states makes us unduly oblivious of the real distinctions existing among these most meaningful of all consciousness conditions. Indeed the relational states themselves have usually escaped notice, as when M. Egger states that the word-sounds in speech make ten or twenty times more noise in consciousness than the other components of the consciousness. Careful observation, however, reveals the fact that words are seldom or never heard as mere sounds; what seems to be their sound is really mainly the meaning which we read into them, as indeed is the case when we hear a tolling bell, a tramp of horses, or a familiar hymn. When we are occasionally able to attend mainly to the raw sounds of a word divorced from word-associates and from meaning, the word sounds as strange and unlike itself as the isolated words appeared in my exposure experiments, or as any letter or figure appears when unduly stared at.

The fact is that meaning is part and parcel of word-sound and of word-utterance, as these ordinarily occur in reading and in thinking; that is, what we take for word-sound and word-utterance is largely word-meaning. And as meaning inheres in or is fused with the word's sound or utterance, so to get the meaning we naturally utter the word, incipiently for the most part, actually when the meaning is obscure. And not merely for the "little words," the words showing relationship, etc., do the meanings lie in the passing feelings which they rouse. These relational words lead to the substantive resting-places of the sentence, where some sensory imagery is apt to occur, and should occur usually, to harmonize with the imagery awakened at the earlier substantive parts. But as Stout rightly argues, the meaning even here is not mainly in the image, but is in the feeling which attaches to the image and the word together as the feeling's sign. Often, as has been noted in the account of my experiments, we get this meaning-feeling without the word or image, often it is all we possibly *can* get, in those tantalizing cases of remembering only what a name *is like*, how it feels to say it, what its deeper significance is. Here we approach the pure meaning-consciousness as detached from articulation.

So for reading as for thinking, we would agree with James when he says that "The definite images of traditional psychology form but the smallest part of our minds, as they actually live;" and with Floumoy,[1] who warns against supposing that the words and ideas suggested by a given word express the thought really contained in it. This he believes lies deeper. "The true psychological centre of the concept seems then to be not in the images called up, but in those confused feelings which serve them for a background, and which James has so well described under the names of fringe, suffusion, psychic overtones, etc." Feelings, and the motor reactions or tendencies from which feelings cannot be disjoined, are far more fundamental and usual than images, and these constitute the consciousness of meaning.

There is an underlying feeling of meaning-in-itself, as it were, in reading any sentence that makes grammatical sense, and this quite independently of anything that the sentence tells. As James puts it, "Certain kinds of verbal associate, certain grammatical expectations fulfilled, stand for a good part of our impression that a sentence has a meaning.... Nonsense in grammatical form sounds half rational; sense with grammatical sequence upset sounds nonsensical." Often in our reading we are content, for considerable stretches, with this sense-meaning feeling, like children who listen with rapt attention to half-understood things, asking the meaning of none. "Their thinking is in form just what ours is when it is rapid. Both of us make flying leaps over large portions of the sentences uttered, and

---

[1] L' Année Psychologique, 1895, pp. 45-53.

we give attention only to substantive starting-points, turning-points, and conclusions here and there."[1]

Of specific meanings beyond this general feeling of "making sense," everything in my own experiments indicates that they are usually total meanings belonging to sentences or to unitary parts of sentences, but felt differently as this or that particular word is being dealt with; or we can say that the particular word's meaning is felt in a perspective of the total meaning. A relation can hardly be felt apart from the terms or objects related, a particular manner or intensity of action or being can hardly be suggested by an adverb apart from the thought of the action or being itself. And likewise a substantive that is thought of naturally has, in this thought, something of the substantive's relationships. In short, it is *total* situations and performances that we think of and read of, and these often complex, always with various aspects and various relationships of parts. No single word names or describes the whole. When a single word is presented, therefore, it suggests but a part or an aspect of this total meaning and is felt as inadequate and artificial unless given in its sentence context. With meanings, as with vocal utterance, the sentence-meaning is the natural unit, and smaller divisions considered apart from this are felt as *disjecta membra*.

We may safely conclude, then, that meanings in reading are mainly feeling-reactions and motor attitudes attaching most intimately to or fused with the inner utterance of the words and especially of the sentences that are read. And with the utterance in which the meanings mainly inhere, we must include the movements of emphasis, of inflection, of gesture, and of expression generally. We have referred to the peculiarly important part that these latter play in the expression of meaning. The feeling of these bodily postures, attitudes, gestures, etc., may well furnish the very body of much that we call meaning, according to the principle which Professor James holds to be true for feelings generally. At any rate, they have a most intimate relationship with meanings, and deserve more careful observational study than has yet been given them by students who would know the intimate structure of language.

---

[1] James' "Psychology," Vol. I, pp. 255-265.

But we must also remember that meanings in reading are not reached solely through the inner utterance. The sentence-utterance, as we have seen, comes at some distance behind the eye. But we have seen that with the first incipient thought of the word's isolated utterance there is present a suggestion of its meaning. Indeed, so strong is this with some words that they are said to "look like their meaning." It is so in my own case with the words *venomous. God*, with many proper names, and with very many other words. There is doubtless with most words some feeling characteristic of their visual form as such. And more or less of the word's significance is apt to be felt with this or immediately after. Indeed there seems to be a flash of the relation of this meaning to the preceding context-meaning, and to this extent some sense of total meaning seems to keep pace with the eye. This is indicated in the action of any reader as he finishes a page or a paragraph that he is reading aloud. He seems to feel that his work is done as his eye sees the last word, although the utterance is half a line or more behind. The total meaning, although not fully realized as yet, has begun to realize itself, and the reader is satisfied as having its realization initiated and under control. The visual forms may often act as cues to touch off this total meaning immediately, this total meaning then guiding the succeeding utterance of the sentence, which is partly an expression of the total meaning thus previously suggested and felt, and is partly also a means of bringing this meaning to full consciousness in its various aspects.

CHAPTER IX

THE RATE OF READING

It remains finally for us to consider an aspect of the psychology of reading which is of the greatest importance practically and pedagogically, the rate of reading and the factors which condition speed.

Romanes early experimented upon the matter, having "practiced readers" read paragraphs in a book containing "simple statements of simple facts," and noting the time needed for the reading. The moment the reading ceased, the reader wrote down all that could be remembered of what was read. Romanes found "astonishing differences in the rate of reading." "The differences may amount to 4 to I; or otherwise stated, in a given time one individual may be able to read four times as fast as another. Moreover, it appeared that there was no relationship between slowness of reading and power of assimilation." On the contrary, "when all the efforts are directed to assimilating as much as possible in a given time, the rapid readers (as shown by their written notes) usually give a better account of the portion of the paragraph which has been compassed by the slow readers than the latter are able to give; and the most rapid reader whom I have found is also the best at assimilating."

"I shall further say that there is no relationship between rapidity of perception as thus tested and intellectual activity as tested by the general results of intellectual work; for I have tried the experiment with several highly distinguished men in science and literature, most of whom I found to be slow readers."[1]

Miss Adelaide M. Abell, in the *Educational Review* for October, 1894, reported experiments on the reading rate of forty Wellesley College girls, the work being done under the direction of Professor Calkins. The girls read a short story at a definite time not long before the class was to meet, and timed the reading, not knowing the aim of the experiment. When the class met, the readers wrote the story from memory, as nearly *verbatim* as possible.

---

[1] Romanes' "Mental Evolution in Animals," pp. 136–137.

The slowest reader was found to have used in her reading six times as much time as the fastest. The reproduction test followed but a few hours after the reading, and was therefore taken as a test of comprehension rather than of memory. The results indicate that most of the readers "gain by relative slowness," but "two subjects head the list both in rapidity and comprehension," and these readers agree that except where matter is obscure "they grasp the thought more readily by rapid reading." "Of all three classes of readers — fast, moderate, and slow — some comprehend well and others fairly or poorly," showing that "comprehension may be independent of the absolute rate of reading." Miss Abell found, however, that on the whole the swift reading saves time without necessarily decreasing comprehension. She believes that the rate will be increased by "increasing the rapidity of association, by repeating and multiplying associations, and by intensifying interest and attention." The actual or imagined pronunciation of the words read was found to be "a characteristic correlate" of the slow reading, and Miss Abell thinks this a hindrance when habitual, and a tendency that should be discouraged in children. "Another peculiarity," she adds, "of the slow readers among our subjects, is the reading of a word at a time, while the rapid readers grasp phrases, clauses, sometimes even sentences, at a glance." She concludes that although every individual probably has his maximum rate, "determined by his natural quickness of comprehension and association, it is yet possible and desirable to some extent to increase the ordinary rate."

Dr. J. O. Quantz tested fifty university students, juniors and seniors of the University of Wisconsin, to determine their normal and maximal rates in reading, and experimented upon them further to determine the factors and conditions upon which rate of reading depended. He found that his readers varied from 3.5 words per second for the slowest to 8.8 words per second for the fastest, when reading at normal speed. At maximal speed the rate ranged from 3.5 words per second to 12.2 words. This was for silent reading. In reading aloud at normal speed the rates were within a range of 2.6 to 3.9 words per second. Generally, those who read fast at normal speed excelled in the maximal tests, and the slow readers were generally slow in both.

In testing the ability to reproduce what was read, he found that the rapid readers were on an average about 37 per cent superior to the slow readers in the quality of their work. "The superiority of the rapid reader is also shown by the fact that his memory of the substance of his reading is more exact than that of the slow reader. He introduces only two-thirds as many thoughts not found in the original selections."

The use of lip-movement in reading was not found to help in comprehension or in concentration of the attention, although it often occurred as a *result* of concentrating the attention. In general, lip-movement was found to be a serious hindrance to speed of reading, and consequently to intelligence of reading. "The ten slowest readers show almost double the amount of lip-movement that the ten most rapid do," while "not one of those whose reading is widest is a lip-mover to any extent which can be observed." "Extent of reading works directly against movement of lips, and is practically the only thing which does so, except among the medium lip-movers."

Dr. Quantz found that persons who are of the visual type "are slightly more rapid readers than the auditory type." Quickness of visual perception, shown in rapid recognition of colors, words, geometrical forms such as circles, squares, diamonds, etc., was found to be "an important factor in deciding one's rate of reading." Considering all the factors which he found to contribute to rapid reading, they are, "in order of importance, visual perception, practice in reading from childhood on, power of concentration, mental alertness estimated by rapidity of original composition, scholarly ability as decided by college records." These results were found in general for the readers tested, and as a particular confirmation the person whose reading was by far the most rapid of all those tested excelled markedly in practically all of the above conditions of rapid reading. It is interesting to note that the judgments of readers about themselves, as to whether they are slow, medium, or fast readers, agreed very well with the results of Dr. Quantz' tests of speed as taken later.

I have carefully tested the reading rate of twenty-eight persons, and have tabulated the results for twenty of these who were graduate university students and whose reading, accordingly, had been pretty extensive. The reading was from an interesting novel, presenting no special difficulty, and the tests were made under conditions which approximated as nearly, as possible those of comfortable reading in one's own quiet room. The readers were found to range in rate from an average of 2.5 words per second for the slowest reader to an average of 9.8 words for the fastest, when reading silently at their ordinary rate. When the silent reading was at maximal speed, the rates ranged from 3.5 to 13.5 words per second. In reading aloud, the average of the slowest reader was 2.2 words per second and that of the fastest 4.7, at the ordinary rate, and at maximal speed the corresponding range was from 2.9 to 6.4 words per second. The average rate of the twenty students when reading silently was 5.63 words per second at their ordinary speed and 8.21 at their maximal, while in reading aloud they averaged 3.55 words per second at their ordinary speed and 4.58 at their maximal. Several of the readers averaged near the fastest rates given above, and the other readers were distributed somewhat evenly, as to rate, from the fastest rate to one somewhat above the slowest.

Lip-movement was usual with only two or three of these twenty readers, but one of the fastest readers tested was a lip-mover. However, when those who were unaccustomed to lip-movement were asked to move their lips while reading, their speed was evidently hindered. The readers showed a strong rhythmic tendency. Each would fall into a reading pace that seemed most natural to him, and would then read page after page in almost exactly the same time. Quite usually the differences from page to page would not be over three or four seconds. Some of the readers showed surprising regularity, reading several successive pages in almost exactly the same time, although they were quite unable to estimate the same time interval, failing by as much as twenty seconds in the attempt to estimate the time of reading the page. Habits of eye-movement are doubtless important factors in setting this pace. When the same number of words was printed in fewer lines, of the same length and the same size of type, they were read faster in just the proportion that the lines were fewer, suggesting that the eye has a habit of taking about so much time for a line of a given length. I found by experimenting upon lines marked here and there by crosses, etc., for fixation points, as below,

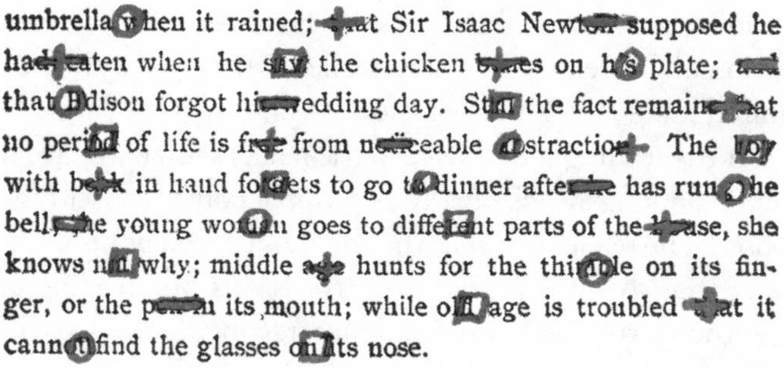

umbrella when it rained; that Sir Isaac Newton supposed he
had eaten when he saw the chicken bones on his plate; and
that Edison forgot his wedding day. Still the fact remains that
no period of life is free from noticeable distraction. The boy
with book in hand forgets to go to dinner after he has rung the
bell; the young woman goes to different parts of the house, she
knows not why; middle age hunts for the thimble on its finger, or the pen in its mouth; while old age is troubled that it
cannot find the glasses on its nose.

Fig. 15

that the eye readily falls into a very uniform rate of progress, corresponding more or less closely to its usual rate of reading, in traversing
the lines without reading.

Dr. Dearborn, as we have seen, finds that the eye falls into
a brief motor habit of making a certain fixed number of pauses per
line, or, sometimes, a certain succession of pauses for a given passage, independently of variations in the subject-matter from line to
line. The fast readers formed these "short-lived motor habits" much
oftener than the slow readers, and the moderately short lines of uniform length give the best conditions for forming these habits, which
seem to increase the speed of reading. We have already noted the
emphasis placed by Dearborn upon the establishment of "a regular
rhythmical movement" as a factor in increasing the reading rate.

Dearborn tested the reading rate of a considerable number
of readers, and found that for a given class of reading matter the
fastest reader read more than three times as fast as the slowest. He
also carefully tested the reading rates of three graduate students,
one a mathematician, one a teacher in a secondary school, and one
a psychologist, for various classes of reading matter selected from
literature and science. Each of these persons had quite different rates
for the different classes of matter read. However, the fastest reader
in his most interesting subject, in this case the mathematician, read
much the fastest in all the classes of matter, the secondary teacher
read much more slowly than the mathematician in all the classes,
and the psychologist read much more slowly still in all but one class.
Dearborn draws from this data the conclusion "that one who reads

rapidly in a given style and class of subject-matter will read somewhat proportionally faster than a slow reader, whatever, within certain recognized limits, the nature of the style and subject-matter."

After the reading of a passage in the reader's usual way, Dearborn had him read it again "as rapidly as possible consistent with getting the sense." The reader believed that he *usually* read at his maximum rate, and that this was particularly true of his first reading of this passage, the matter being especially interesting. It was found, however, that in the second reading nearly one-third of the total time was saved, the absolute time of nearly every pause being diminished, fewer pauses being made, and "the average distance of the eye's first pause from the left edge of the page noticeably increased." The length of the *initial* fixations in the lines was, however, even a little longer than before, permitting the preliminary general survey of the line which Dearborn finds to be needful for the more rapid reading. He finds, indeed, that "rapidity of reading is not necessarily correlated with regularity of movement," some of the fastest and slowest readers being found equally regular in movement. But "a wider 'spanning' of attention," shown in the frequency of long pauses at the line's beginning and in the fewer fixations per line, is found to be characteristic of the more rapid readers. "The slow readers have a narrower span or working extent of attention, and a greater total arc of movement."

Both my own experiments and those of Dr. Dearborn indicate that there can usually be much improvement in the rate of reading. There seems to be a rhythm into which each reader ordinarily falls in ordinary reading, and it seems doubtful whether ordinary practice changes this rhythm after it is well established. Doubtless many of us dawdle along in our reading at a plodding pace which was set and hardened in days of listless poring over uninteresting tasks, or in imitation of the slow reading aloud which was so usually going on either with ourselves or with others in the school. And indeed, for the later school period, I quite share Dr. Dearborn's opinion "that the careful dwelling upon each word and phrase, which is the daily method of the classical student throughout many years of study, helps not a little in fixing such a habit of slow assimilation." Bad form in reading is doubtless as distressingly common as bad form in swimming, skating, or tennis. And we know that the form once set is apt to remain for life in any of these activities, with all the correlated limitations in speed and in quality of performance. I have consider-ably increased my own speed in reading by waking up to the fact that my rate was unnecessarily slow, and then persistently reading as fast as possible with well-concentrated attention, taking care to stop short of fatigue until the new pace was somewhat established. I thus reached a speed of a page per minute for such books as Ellis' "The Criminal," of the Contemporary Science Series, maintaining this rate for a half-hour or so at a time, and with very good compre-hension of what was read, although after such reading a very hasty review of the leading points was the most satisfactory procedure. My earlier speed was not more than half as great.

It is especially desirable that the reading rate and the condi-tions affecting it should be carefully determined for the children of the various school grades, and for various classes of reading matter, taking into account the apperceptive relation of the reader to what is read. That fast reading may come quite early is indicated by a test which I made of an eleven-year-old schoolgirl who was said to be "a great reader," and whose rate was found to surpass that of almost all the university men both at normal and at maximal speed. On the other hand, it seems perfectly certain that there is, among children, a great deal of dead-level plodding, with little thought of varying the speed according to the importance of what is read; and investigation here, if carefully made and then acted upon pedagogically, may have the greatest value in lessening waste and in increasing effectiveness both in reading and thinking.

A university friend, a mathematician, informs me that he has read the whole of a standard novel of 320 pages in two and one-fourth hours. The occasional though very rare instances of such rapid reading suggest that we may be far within our possibilities in dealing with printed symbols. I am inclined to think that at any such speed the meanings suggested immediately by the visual forms suffice for all but the more important parts, and that these meanings are felt sufficiently, without inner utterance, to permit selection of what is more important, the more important places themselves having a fleeting inner utterance to vivify their meaning. We must indeed experiment further before we can conclude against the possibility of mainly visual reading at the very high speeds. The inner speech in such cases must at any rate suffer a foreshortening and atrophy of articulatory details which reduce it to little more than a slight motor tallying as the meanings are felt or dwelt upon.

In general, the question of individual differences in reading is a very important one, and merits careful study upon still other phases than rate. For instance, the natural characteristics of children's reading, at various stages, must be worked out carefully, and the normal range of variations must be determined. Differences in the extent of the perceptual span, in the size and nature of the units in terms of which reading matter is perceived; differences in the amount of attention given to total form, to letters, etc.; "legato" versus "staccato" reading, a very important and typical difference that is wisely taken account of by Principal Russell in his teaching of reading at the Worcester State Normal School; differences in phrasing, also made much of by Principal Russell, and important psychologically as well as pedagogically; I should consider all of these promising subjects for investigation, were I to continue the general study. Abnormalities of reading, typical or otherwise, are numerous and offer another rich field of study. Many of these abnormalities, to be found almost everywhere, are probably remediable or preventable in the light of careful analysis of normal reading, and the study of the cases may render much service to psychology as well as to education. The clinical method, following closely the fortunes of particular and significant cases, seems to have great advantages here, as indeed it seems to me to have for very many of the problems of general psychology.

Indeed, for all functions that are performed in reading, the determination of types, and of the normal as well as abnormal ranges of variation, becomes one of the important duties of a differential psychology which would render real service to education, and the returns to psychology itself will be well worth while. Messmer's suggestion of subjective and objective types of readers names only the first of important type-differences. For example, in what typical ways may we be conscious of *meaning*? Professor Titchener, in a letter of nearly three years ago from which he kindly permits me to quote, holds that while "the 'meaning' of a concept is," as indeed appeared in Dr. Bagley's thesis study with Professor Titchener, "always carried by the 'fringe' of consciousness," the constituents of this fringe have typical and important variations. These go back for their source to the division of men "into two great classes, according as they have or do not have a large amount of organic sensation in their general conscious make-up." For example, people for whom the organic sensations have practically disappeared "remember old events without any stir-up of feeling." "These are minds of cultivated and bookish people, like those that Galton found to be lacking in visual imagery." "These people are cold-blooded, as one says; they are intellectual and not emotional; they have no affective memory, but only an untoned reproductive memory; they are detached, impersonal, cool, reflective. That minds of this type exist I cannot have any doubt, although I myself belong to the former group. To say that these people do their conceptual thinking by means of felt organic attitudes simply goes against their own introspections. They find, in the extreme cases, that the fringe is verbal, just precisely as the center of consciousness is. They do not feel any attitude. It may possibly be (I say this hesitatingly) that their apprehension of meaning is purely physiological, — done by a not-felt attitude; at least, we have found cases of *recognition* in which neither felt attitude nor verbal fringe could be discovered by introspection, so that for all we could tell the act of recognition was a purely physiological, reflex matter: the organism fell into the recognitive attitude without any introspectively discoverable change in consciousness. This is uncertain ground; but of the existence of the verbal-fringe type I can, as I said, have no doubt. Doubtless, it is a development from the other; and doubtless there are all stages between the extremes."

I am glad that Professor Titchener has so ably stated these typical differences in this phase of the reading consciousness. Variations of great importance will be found in various other phases; but in view of the fact that there has been so little observational study of cases, any attempt to treat further the subject of individual differences in reading would scarcely be profitable at this time. Enough has been said to suggest the importance of such study. The conclusions stated in the present volume seem to hold for the great majority of readers; and the important contributions yet to be made by the study of individual differences are likely to be in the nature of additions rather than of contradictions.

We must rest here our survey of the psychology of reading, and attend to other aspects of the general topic. There yet remain to be written many most interesting chapters on the psycho-physiological phases of reading, which will be made possible as investigation proceeds further. The work that has already been done by many hands and in many lands illustrates well how the federated science of the world is making solid progress with specific problems, and bears promise of a day when education shall rest on foundations better grounded than were the individual and unverified opinions about "Reading," for instance, even twenty-five years ago.

PART II

THE HISTORY OF READING AND OF READING METHODS

CHAPTER X

THE BEGINNINGS OF READING, IN THE INTERPRETATION OF GESTURES AND PICTURES

WHEREVER there has been civilization there has been reading and writing, in the remote past as in the present. In North Babylonia, for example, written records have been discovered that are no less than six thousand years old, and these prove that writing and civilization were then by no means in their infancy. Clodd, in his "Story of the Alphabet," concludes that in Babylon writing had long passed the pictograph stage eight thousand years ago, and thinks that "Babylon carries the palm" in the age of writing. At least seven thousand years ago Egypt was reading a page that was at least partially alphabetic, showing that reading was even then an art that had been practiced for ages. In Crete, inscriptions are being unearthed that go back to the early part of the third millennium before the Christian Era. In all these cases, and especially in Egypt and Babylonia, there are abundant indications that reading and writing were already most ancient practices, with the story of their origin enshrouded, as we have seen, in mystery, and told only in myth and legend.

But the written records that have been preserved from these remote ages give sure signs of the true origin of the systems of writing used by these nations. They prove that in these early times reading and writing had much the same course of development that has been observed among later peoples and that is going on to-day among savage races so far as they are still uninterfered with. Various peoples and tribes on every continent have developed systems of writing, independently. Some of these systems have reached a high state of completeness, some have been arrested at one or another stage, some are still in their rude beginnings. Yet so far as each has gone it resembles almost every other in the general lines of its development. One finds most striking resemblances, even in details, in comparing such widely separated systems as the Maya of Yucatan with the Egyptian, or the Ojibwa of North America with the Babylonian.

Keeping in mind, then, this comparative agreement in the development of the different systems, I shall illustrate various phases of the evolution of reading and writing by citations from various systems, as each may best serve my purpose, emphasizing, perhaps, the Egyptian as being typical and best known.

Mankind began his reading with picture-books and his writing with picture-making, just as the child likes to begin. This seems to have been the case literally, when we recall that *book* probably once meant a piece of bark and that library (*liber*, bark) and letters (*lino*, to smear or paint) bring down with them the smell of the woods. The first pictures, however, were drawn in the air and were read as fast as drawn. They constituted a gesture-language. The spoken language and the gesture-language arose together as they do in the child, the words and the gestures being a joint means by which pre-historic man communicated with his fellows. So inseparable were these means of communicating, for some tribes, that they found it difficult or impossible to communicate in the dark when the gestures could not be read.

Primitive man became very expert in the use of gestures, and savages of to-day use them most effectively. Tylor, in his "Early History of Mankind" (p. 82), says that the natives of North America were as proficient in the use of the gesture-language as in that of picture-writing, much the same conditions having given rise to both. Professor Wundt believes that the languages of picture and of gesture grew up together, naturally influencing each other.

Even among certain modern civilized peoples, notably among the Neapolitans, the gesture-language still plays an important part in everyday communication. Indeed, Professor Ribot quotes with some approval Dugald Stewart's assertion that "If men had been deprived of the organs of voice or the sense of hearing, there is no doubt that they would have invented an alphabet of visible signs wherewith to express all their ideas and sentiments." It is to be hoped that the notable tendency of children to live over again the use that the race has made of gestures may soon be made the subject of careful obser-vational study.

The gesture-language is, in considerable part at least, a picture-language, a sort of drawing in the air. W. von Humboldt called it "a species of writing." Speaking of such a comparison, Tylor goes on to say (p. 82): "There is indeed a very close relation between these two ways of expressing and communicating thought. Gesture can set forth thought with far greater speed and fulness than picture-writing, but it is inferior to it in having to place the different elements of a sentence in succession, in single file, so to speak; while by a picture the whole of an event may be set in view at one glance, and that permanently, so as to serve as a message to a distant place or a record to a future time. But the imitation of visible qualities as a means of expressing ideas is common to both methods, and both belong to similar conditions of the human mind."

From drawing in the air to drawing in the sand, or on bark or stone or wood, would seem to be an easy transition. In Central Brazil the natives were found to fashion an explanatory design in the sand when their gestures proved insufficient for conveying an idea. Hirn, in his "Origins of Art" (p. 156), says of this that "these designs are only a projection on a different surface of the hand-movements with which in their pantomimic language they describe the outlines of the objects in the air. One is tempted, therefore, to find in these transferred gestures the origin of pictorial art." He adds that "in some tribes — particularly among the North American Indians — the picture-signs have evidently been derived from the corresponding gesture-signs." However, Professor Hirn and other authorities are uncertain whether the step was taken in this or in some other way. We cannot be sure whether the first pictures were made for purposes of communication or for the fun of the making, as when the child first scribbles.

Certain it is that from very early times primitive man made pictures in the greatest abundance, and that by their means he communicated with his fellows. He attained to this means of communication independently in the most diverse parts of the earth, though the pictures, like the gestures, are remarkably alike throughout the world. Of this Tylor says (p. 88): "As the gesture-language is substantially the same among savage tribes all over the world, and also among children who cannot speak, so the picture-writings of savages are not only similar to one another but are like what children make untaught even in civilized countries. Like the universal language of gestures, the art of picture-writing tends to prove that the mind of the uncultured man works in much the same way at all times and everywhere."

That the picture-writing is almost inconceivably ancient is shown by the many drawings that have been found of animals now extinct. Clodd, in the "Story of the Alphabet" (p. 22), writes of this: "On fragments of bone, horn, schist, and other materials, the savage hunter of the Reindeer Period, using a pointed flint-flake, depicted alike himself and the wild animals which he hunted. From cavern-floors of France, Belgium, and other parts of Western Europe, whose deposits date from the Old Stone Age, there have been unearthed rude etchings of naked hardy men brandishing spears at wild horses, or creeping along the ground to hurl their weapons at the urus, or wild ox, or at the woolly-haired elephant. A portrait of this last-named, showing the creature's shaggy ears, long hair, and upwardly curved tusks, its feet being hidden in the surrounding high grass, is one of the most famous examples of paleolithic art."

In these rude pictures of tens of thousands of years ago lay the germs of the alphabets which have made civilizations possible, and which have indeed slowly developed *pari passu* with these civilizations. We shall now sketch the typical features of this development.

1, a canoe. 2, man with hands outstretched, indicating "nothing." 3, the uplifted right hand means "food," or "to eat," and the left points to 4, the hut.

Fig. 16. — Record of starving hunter. (From Clodd.[1])

In the first stages pictography the drawings are made upon almost every conceivable material, and for the most varied purposes. Sometimes a hunter, out of food, would scratch upon a stick the picture-story of his destitution, and stick it in the ground on the trail nearest his dwelling. Sometimes upon some conspicuous rock his pictures indicated the game that was to be found in that locality. On grave-stones, the pictures told of the prowess of hunter and warrior. On some

---

[1] This and the other cuts and quotations from Clodd are reproduced, by permission, from Clodd's "The Story of the Alphabet," copyright 1900, by D. Appleton and Co.

great bowlder he would express his thought of his God, as, perhaps, on the "Indian God Rock" still to be seen on the bank of the Allegheny River south of Franklin, Pennsylvania. Again, the pictures scratched on the shoulder blade of a buffalo killed in the hunt tell of the efforts to track companions who had gone on in the chase.

And so on bark and wood and stone, on skulls and skins and bones and teeth, on surfaces formed of various fibers, and, with some tribes, on the human body in tattooing, the pictures were made according to the exigency of the case or the whim of the artist. The investigators of children to-day find here, too, a most interesting parallel in the pictures and symbols carved and scratched and chalked everywhere in and about the school-houses of our earlier days.

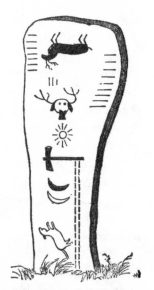

"His totem, the reindeer, is reversed, and his own name, which means the White Fisher, is not recorded. The seven strokes note the seven war parties whom he led; the three upright strokes as many wounds received in battle. The horned head tells of a desperate fight with a moose." — Clodd's "Story of the Alphabet," p. 49.

FIG. 17 .— Tomb-board of Indian Chief.

"The trail of the animals and pursuers is shown in the dotted lines. Of the three heads the lowest is that of the seeker, who is depicted shouting after his missing friends; then he is shown advancing and still shouting, till his call is returned from the spot where the hunters have camped."
— Clodd, p. 58.

FIG. 18. — Hidatsa pictograph on a buffalo shoulder blade.

The pictures of primitive man were at first sketches portraying directly objects to be found in the environment, and were rough sketches such as a child makes. Such lines and parts were drawn as stood for the object in the artist's thought, and imitative fidelity to the objective thing was not very essential. Of course this sketchiness is characteristic of the actual perception of objects, for savage and child alike, as indeed for all of us. A very few lines, angles, and other significant features make up the bulk of what we really note in casting a glance at any object. And perceptions, too, are full of things not really to be seen in the object, but standing for it in our thought. So the Indian drew the sound issuing from the mouth of the lost hunter. So the child makes the legs show through the clothing, etc.

There is found in the primitive drawings a happy "hitting off" of the core of the thing, of the general and essential, such as occurs in the race myths, in the child's imitations, etc. We shall later show how the pictures became conventionalized, gradually, in their continued use. But first let us note that they did not long remain simply representations of objects of sense, or pictographs proper. They came to represent ideas and feelings of most varied kinds, became ideographs, as this class of pictures has been called. Thus, by metonymy, combat was pictured as in Figure 19. Figure 20 shows a drawing placed for warning at the foot of a steep and rocky trail, intimating that a goat may be able to climb the cliff, though

FIG. 19. — Combat. (From Hoffman.[1])

at an angle of 45°, but that a horse would fall. By substitution of a part for the whole, various animals are represented by a drawing of the head, especially when horned. The wild turkey is represented by its three-toed imprint; the bear, by the outline of its paw, large claws indicating a grizzly bear, while the absence of claws, or small ones, denoted the black bear. By metaphor, the Egyptians represented the idea of mother by a vulture, this bird being supposed to nourish its young with its own blood. A king was pictured by a bee, the

FIG. 20. — Warning. New Mexico. (From Hoffman.)

latter having a monarchical government. Hoffman says, in his "Beginnings of Writing" (p. 50), that "ideographs representing abstract ideas, pictorially expressed, are more frequent in the pictography of some tribes than the mere portraiture of objects pure and simple."

FIG. 21. — Meat stored in a pit. (From Hoffman.)

Figure 21 shows the Dakota sign for abundance, the circle signifying the pit in which buffalo meat was

---

[1] This and the other cuts and quotations from Hoffman are reproduced, by permission, from Hoffman's "Beginnings of Writing," copyright, 1896, by D. Appleton & Co.

stored, as indicated by the outline of a buffalo head within, with a forked stick extending upward as used to support the drying pole.

Hunger was sometimes indicated by a man with a heavy bar across breast or abdomen, as the seat of suffering; or with prominent ribs, as from emaciation. Often the gesture-signs were drawn, representing the corresponding idea. The cross, representing trade or exchange (see Fig. 35), seems to have been an imitation of the gesture for the same, and so with drawings of the gesture-signs for eating, food, hunger, etc., among both Indians and Egyptians.

FIG. 22. — Eating (Easter Islands). (From Hoffman.)

The drawings tended to become mere conventionalized symbols or symbolic signs of the object or idea signified. Thus, for the Indians, a red tomahawk meant war; a pipe, or hand clasped, meant peace. The Ojibwa Indians represented spring by trees with faint signs of buds, and winter as in Figure 23, the curved line representing the sky, with snow descending in zigzags, the whole meaning the "season of snow." Sometimes autumn seems to have been represented by leaves flitting over the ground. A month was sometimes a crescent. A day was a sun, or a sleep, represented in the latter case by a man in a reclining position. Figure 24 shows the Ojibwa sign for morning, the curved line indicating the course of the sun, the short line signifying morning when at the left, midday when at the middle,

FIG. 23. Snow. (From Hoffman.)

evening when at the right. These latter signs seem to have been in imitation of the corresponding gestures. Another of the signs for morning was a radiant sun appearing above the horizon line. Figure 25 is a Mexican representation of *traveling*, the course in this case having led across a stream, as indicated by the paddles used in crossing it.

FIG. 24. Morning. (From Hoffman.)

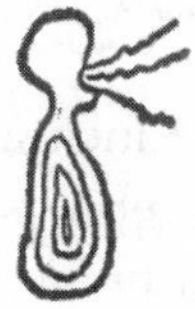

FIG. 26. — Singing (Ojibwa). (From Hoffman.)

Sound and speech were represented in various ways. Figure 26 shows the Ojibwa character for *singing*, the lines

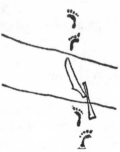

FIG. 25. — Traveling on foot and by water (Mexican). (From Hoffman.)

representing vocal utterance being repeated
about the heart to denote joyous emotion. The
Dakotas sometimes represent whooping-cough by a
number of lines issuing from the mouth as above,
but the lines were longer and more divergent.
Conversation was indicated by another tribe as
in Figure 27, the double voice lines signifying
"speech from both figures."

Fig. 27. —
Conversation.
(From Hoffman)

Primitive peoples have been thus versatile in representing
not only visual forms, but sounds, actions, feelings, and the
most abstract conceptions. The characters were more and
more conventionalized with continued use, especially among
the peoples who attained any degree of civilization. In many
cases the characters quite lost their original resemblance to
the thing signified and were mere arbitrary signs, to the writers, of an idea or its word-name, or both. The ancient Chinese

symbol for sun ⊙ thus became ⊟, some of the changes

being due to the greater ease of drawing straight lines with the

Chinese brush-pen. So ☽, the character for moon, became

⊟. So the Accadian character ▬▬▮, for sky, is a

simplified form of ✳, a star. The ideogram for Nineveh was

▰▰▰, which was derived from the archaic form ▰▰▰.

This older form was the ideographic picture of a house inclosing
the ideogram of a fish, and showing that "Imperial Nineveh was at
first, as its name implies, merely a collection of huts of fishermen."
(Taylor.)

The modern Chinese character for song, 卩臣, is conventionalized from ᵕ 🐦,, the characters for an ear and a bird. So their
character for light, 目月, is from ☉)), representing the sun and
moon. Other examples will be given in speaking of the derivation
of our alphabet.

The meanings of the characters also underwent gradual changes,
in many cases, as suggested in part in the illustrations already given.
This occurs, of course, with the words and concepts of any language,
as time goes on. But the comparatively limited number of available
picture-characters compelled a very great extension of their meanings, by metaphor, etc., as the number of ideas to be expressed increased. Among the Egyptians, for example, the ostrich feather,
besides its direct meaning, came to serve as the symbol for justice,
its feathers being supposed to be of equal length. A roll of papyrus
came to mean knowledge. The figure of a calf running toward water
meant thirst, a brandished whip was the symbol of power, and so
on. Of these extensions of meaning Clodd writes:[1] "Obviously, this
presentment of ideas through graphic designs into which metaphor,
often bordering on enigma, had to be read, implied good memories
and clear grasp of association on the part of the interpreter. Any
doubt or ambiguity, with resulting confusion, as to the meaning of a
symbol, rendered it worse than useless."

The additions of determinants, especially in the Egyptian and
Chinese languages, helped the matter considerably. Thus the addition of an ear to the character for bird gave the meaning of song to
the whole, as we have seen, and similarly with the succeeding figure for light. With the Chinese, repeating the character for woman
made it stand for "strife," and three women stood for "intrigue." An
ear between two doors gave the total meaning "to listen."

---

[1] "Story of the Alphabet," p. 122.

By the use of another class of determinants, referring to whole groups of words, a still larger number of total meanings could be added. Thus for the Chinese, says Clodd, the sign for white had, "with a tree prefixed, the meaning of 'cypress,' with the sign for man it means 'elder brother,' with the sign for 'manes' it means the vital principle that survives death." So the sign for tree had about nine hundred combinations, "to indicate various kinds of trees and wood, things made of wood, etc."

But all the devices and skill of the primitive pictographers, and all the keen insight with which primitive readers interpreted the picture-characters and picture-stories, could not and did not make the picture-languages suffice for the growing needs of the more progressive peoples. While picture-writing has certain advantages over the phonetic systems, as may be shown later, it has certain inherent limitations which are fatal to its exclusive use as a means of communication among civilized people. There comes a time when the ideas become too numerous for the "symbols to go round," and when there need to be divisions into parts of speech and arrangement into sentences. It may well be that had no phonetic system been found, the ingenuity of Egypt or Babylonia or of ancient Greece might have found some way of adapting a pictograph system to the needs of the changing times. With pictography, as with the gesture language, there were doubtless potentialities left unrealized, through displacement of the system by a convenient successor. Yet it is significant that, of the peoples who never attained to an alphabet, none developed their pictography or other system of writing beyond or even to the point of excellence which pictography reached among the nations which did develop an alphabet.

In the New World, only the peoples of Central America and Mexico seem to have passed the pictograph stage, and these did not attain to a true alphabet. In the Old World, only the Chinese and the various civilizations about the Mediterranean Sea seem to have reached any sort of phonetic system.

CHAPTER XI

THE EVOLUTION OF AN ALPHABET AND OF READING BY ALPHABETIC SYMBOLS

DURING the ages in which picture-writing was practically the sole means of written communication, the various *spoken* languages had been keeping pace in their development with the needs of the civilizations in which they were used. The further need was of some sort of "graphs" which would represent to the eye the *sounds* of these spoken languages, *as* sounds. This would solve for all time the problem of facile communication, in writing, of all that man had to communicate. But it was very long before it dawned upon men that all the words which men utter are expressed by a few sounds, and that all that was needed was "to select from the big and confused mass of ideograms, phonograms, and all their kin, a certain number of signs to denote, unvaryingly, certain sounds."[1] Such a step meant the birth of an alphabet, "one of the greatest and most momentous triumphs of the human mind." By the use of only twenty-six simple characters we may represent to the eye all that men say or have said, in languages whose vocabularies have enlarged until they number hundreds of thousands of words. Could the pre-phonetic scribe of Egypt have had a vision of such a system and its possibilities, he would have deemed it the miracle of miracles. His thousands of characters and his fertility of resource in their use were taxed to their utmost to produce results that were far inferior to the work of these simple letter-forms.

The alphabet came by degrees. There was no out-and-out invention of the forms or of their meanings. In the first place very many of the simplified picture-characters had naturally come to suggest, immediately, the spoken names of the ideas which they signified.

---

[1] Clodd, p. 124.

This name was often the same as another word of different meaning, as in the case of *sun* and *son*; and the character for the former came to stand also for the latter and was thus a true phonogram, or sound-picture, a "graph" symbolizing the word-sound as such. This use of the characters as phonograms did not help very much in itself, as, for the most part, the same number of characters would still be needed though each should represent a word-sound. But the thought thus came that a character might represent a sound as such, independent of the sound's meaning. From this the significant advance was made of representing a polysyllabic word by a succession of characters each representing the sound of one of its syllables, practically the rebus with which children puzzle each other to this day. So, says Taylor,[1] "Prior Burton's name is sculptured in St. Saviour's Church as a cask with a thistle on it, *burr-tun*. Indeed, the puzzles of this kind in children's books keep alive to our own day the great transition stage from picture-writing to word-writing, the highest intellectual effort of one period in our history coming down, as so often happens, to be the child's play of a later time." So, in Egyptian, a figure on a seat, *hes*, with the character for eye, *iri*, stood for Hesiri, their name for the God Osiris. The Aztecs had gone so far as to write their proper names in this rebus-fashion. Indeed Taylor[2] thinks it probable that the advance from ideograms to phonograms arose from the necessity of expressing proper names. In the Aztec pictographs the name of King Itzcoatl (Knife-Snake or Weapon-Snake) was sometimes written as in the first figure

FIG. 28.[3]

above, the stone knives on the back of the snake being named itz(tli) and the snake being named Coatl. Sometimes, however, the name was written as in the second figure. Here the first syllable, *itz*, is represented by a weapon, *itz(tli)*, the lower character. But above this appears, not the figure of a snake, but an earthen pot, *co(mitl)*, surmounted by the sign for water *a(tl)*. Thus the two latter pictures were used to suggest a total sound, the name of an object totally unlike either picture. So when the Spaniards came to Mexico, the Aztecs wrote the word

---

[1] "Early History of Mankind," p. 94.

[2] "The Alphabet," Vol. I, p. 22.

[3] From Tylor's "Early History of Mankind," reproduced by permission of Holt & Co.

Paternoster in their own characters as best they could, as shown in Figure 29, the characters in order being named *pan(tli)*, a flag, *te(tl)*, a stone, *noch(tli)*, a prickly pear, and again *le(tl)*, a stone.

This Mexican writing illustrates a still further and very important step, beyond the rebus, toward the formation of an alphabet. It will be noticed that some-times the character is used to stand, not

Fig. 29. — Pictographic title of Latin paternoster (Mexican).
(From Hoffman.)

for the sound of the whole word which it literally represents, but for that word's *initial* sound or syllable. By this principle of acrology, as it is called, first steps were taken in the breaking up of the word, and especially of the syllable, into constituent sounds. With the results of sound analysis constantly before us in the lettered words of our printed page, we have arrived at an over-consciousness of the elements, as we call them, of which words are composed. But for primitive man and for the young child the spoken word is a unit, without separable parts; as graphophone records, indeed, show that it is, as we have seen, for all of us. The analysis into syllables came late, came with difficulty, and came to but few nations at all.

Dr. Judd, in his "Genetic Psychology for Teachers" (p. 207), thinks the child makes for himself a beginning of such analysis when he says over words which contain similar sounds "with obvious delight at the similarity he has discovered. The pleasure which children get from such combinations as ding-dong, see-saw, is evidently due to the like sounds at the beginning of these syllables, and the interesting contrast in the later sounds." Some of my readers will recall with me the pleasure of using such "secret languages" of childhood as combined the initial sounds of our words with some absurd constant, — as when we mystified all but the initiated by shouting, "Igery wigery nogery gogery togery schoogery togery morgery," (I will not go to school to-morrow).

To return to the rebus-writing, we have here the use of signs for word-sounds independently of any reference to meanings.

The direct suggestiveness of the picture-characters was lost in favor of their secondary suggestion of a name. They were now pure phono-graphs, or sound-symbols. It seems probable that this transition step was taken regularly through the efforts to represent proper names, as with the Aztecs. The Mayas of Yucatan went further and used the rebus-principle with words generally. Of course, sentences as well as words could be written rebus-fashion; as in the old example cited by Taylor,[1] "I saw a boy swallow a goose-berry," represented by pictures of an eye, a saw, a boy, a swallow, a goose, and a berry.

Many characters came to represent homophones, or words of like sound but unlike meaning. As already mentioned, the character , sun, could be used to represent the word *son*. The picture of a pear could represent that fruit when used as a pictograph, or as a phonograph could represent any of the several words having the same sound, as *pair* or *pare*. So a pen might serve as an ideograph for *write*, or as a phonograph for *right*, *rite*, or *wright*, according to the context.

The Chinese have a great many of these homophones. Their lan-guage is confined to monosyllables, and there are but a few hundred of these. Naturally enough, therefore, each of these must serve for a great variety of totally different meanings. The distinctions can-not be made by variant spellings like our *write* and *right*, as they have never analyzed their words into letter-sounds. It might be thought that the context would suffice to give the clew to the meaning in-tended, as when *write* is heard in our spoken English. But the Chinese homophones are too numerous for this. So in speaking they use four varieties of tone or accent, practically increasing the number of spoken words to twelve hundred and three.[2] In writing, they place after the word phonograph an ideograph character as a determinative, giving the needed clew to the meaning intended. To take an example from Taylor, the word *pa* "has in Chinese eight distinct significations; that is, there are eight different words which are thus pronounced. The phonogram expressing *pa* is apparently a conventionalized pic-ture of the tail of some animal. This phonograph character, when

---

[1] I, p. 22.

[2] Taylor, "The Alphabet," Vol. I, pp. 28-30.

followed by the character for 'plants,' denotes a banana tree; with the key for 'iron' it denotes a 'war-chariot,' with the key for 'sickness' it means a 'scar,' with the key of 'mouth' it stands for a 'cry,' and so on. The Chinese written language practically requires but 1144 phonetic signs and 214 ideographic keys. And by means of these 1358 conventionalized pictures, taken in groups, two and two together, any one of the 40,000 words in the Chinese language can be written down without ambiguity."

Here in this rebus-phonograph stage, however, the Chinese have staid, "stuck," to use a colloquialism, for thousands of years. With all their acuteness it never occurred to them to analyze their monosyllables, acrologically or otherwise, and arrive at their A B C's. At any rate the usefulness of such a procedure never dawned upon them. As one of the baneful results, according to Taylor, it may fairly be said that with the Chinese method it takes twenty years instead of five to learn to read and write, and most people cannot be expected to attain to these arts.

The Chinese had thus gone so far as to construct a syllabary, a set of symbols for syllable sounds, each syllable constituting a word. The Aztecs, as we have seen, had by the use of the rebus broken up their proper names into syllables, as in the case of Itzcoatl; and, by the acrological use of a character to stand for the first syllable of its name, had analyzed into syllables words that were other than proper names. Further the Aztecs did not go. The Mayas of Yucatan, alone of all the peoples of the New World, went still further and analyzed syllables, as we shall see.

Syllabism is best illustrated perhaps, in the development of the Japanese writing from the Chinese. Unlike the Chinese, the Japanese language is polysyllabic. About the third century A.D., when Japan came in contact with the civilization and religion of China, she adopted the Chinese characters, or verbal phonograms, as terms in which to write her own language. A selection was made of the phonograms which conveniently approximated the sounds of the Japanese syllables, and the entire Japanese language was written in these syllable-characters, much as the Aztecs had written their proper names. According to Taylor, the Japanese have but five vowel sounds and fifteen consonantal sounds, or seventy-five possible syllabic combinations of a consonant followed by a vowel. As many of these possible combinations do not actually occur, less than fifty distinct syllabic signs suffice for the writing of all Japanese words.

The Japanese have two syllabaries, both derived independently from the Chinese before the end of the ninth century A.D. One has about three hundred signs and is rather cumbrous. The other "comprises only a single sign, written more or less cursively, for each of the forty-seven syllabic sounds in the Japanese language." The Chinese characters were much simplified, and all determinatives, homophones, etc., omitted; so that the Japanese is, according to Taylor, "one of the best syllabaries which has ever been constructed."[1] "Here, however," continues Taylor, "the development has stopped short. The fact that during more than a thousand years it should never have occurred to a people so ingenious and inventive as the Japanese to develop their syllabary into an alphabet may suffice to show that the discovery of the alphabetic principle of writing is not such an easy or obvious matter as might be supposed." The Japanese are at last just beginning, as it would seem, the adoption of the alphabet that we use.

The cuneiform writing of ancient Chaldea, Babylonia, and Assyria, as we have seen, went through the usual stages of pictograph and ideograph, and in very early times arrived at phonograms and a syllabary. Their language was polysyllabic, and it seems that sometimes a character which had come to denote the *name* of an object rather than the object itself, that is, had become a phonogram, was used further, by acrology, to denote simply the initial syllable of the word. Generally, however, the characters for certain dissyllables, which by phonetic decay had worn to monosyllables, came to be used as phonographs for these monosyllabic sounds; and these characters were then used, as by the Japanese, to write the syllables of the polysyllabic words. Thus, to write their word for "soul," pronounced *nap-sat*, they combined the syllabic sign ▬ ▬, *nap*, which originally meant "light," with the sign for *sat*, originally "mountain," giving the total character ▬▬ for "soul."

Their language had many homophones, and determinatives had to be employed as with the Chinese. In the Assyrian cuneiform

---

[1] "The Alphabet," Vol. I, p. 36.

the mixture of variants, homophones, ideograms, determinatives, etc., made the writing clumsy and difficult to read. In the eighth century B.C., according to Taylor, the Proto-Medic tribes borrowed the cuneiform characters and effected a simplification somewhat as when the Japanese syllabary was constructed from the Chinese ideograms. They thus reduced the Assyrian cuneiform to a "comparatively simple and certain syllabary of ninety-six characters," retaining only about half a dozen of the determinative ideograms. But here again there was arrest. And most if not all of the forms of the cuneiform writing, except the Persian, stopped short of the construction of a true alphabet, and were content with the use of characters for syllables only.

The Egyptian writing, it is certain from the evidence of the monuments, went through the usual stages of primitive pictographs and ideographs, had its homophones and determinatives like the Chinese, and went through its stages of rebus, acrology, and syllabic signs. Up to this point, as Taylor says,[1] it "offers a remarkable parallel to the development of other primitive methods of writing, such as the cuneiform or Chinese." But the Egyptians went further, and *analyzed the syllable*. Indeed, in the very oldest of all the Egyptian inscriptions, according to Taylor, the inscription of King Sent, which indeed he believes to be "the oldest written record in existence," three alphabetic characters are employed to spell the monarch's name, which

reads .[2] Two of our English letters," he thinks,

"*n* and *d*, are derived, in strict historical filiation, from two of the alphabetic signs, ᴡᴡᴡ and ⸗." These and some other originals of our letters he thus finds to be "older than the pyramids — older probably than any other existing monument of human civilization with the possible exception of the signs of the zodiac."[3]

---

[1] I, p. 60.

[2] These and the other cuts and quotations from Taylor are reproduced, by permission, from Taylor's "The Alphabet," copyright by Edward Arnold, London.

[3] I, p. 62.

Thus early had the Egyptians reached an ultimate analysis of the word and syllable into letter-sounds, into vowels and consonants. The difficulty of such analysis must indeed have been very great, as shown by the fact that astute peoples like the Babylonians, Assyrians, Medes, Chinese, and Japanese never succeeded in making it. "Symbols for vowel sounds are found in the syllabaries of some of these nations, but the more difficult conception of a consonant was not attained or even approached. Easy as it seems to ourselves who are familiar with it, the notion of a consonant, a sound that cannot be sounded except in conjunction with some other sound different from itself, is by no means so simple as it may appear. It involves the decomposition of the syllable into its ultimate phonetic elements — the mental isolation, for instance, of the unpronounceable sound *t*, which is common to the articulations *tea, tie, toe,* and *two,* and yet is not identical with any of them."[1]

Taylor thinks the Egyptians were aided in making this analysis by the nature of their vowel sounds. These seem to have been of a rather indeterminate character, like the italicized vowels in *a*bout, ass*e*rt, b*i*rd, b*u*t, d*o*uble. Their words were very often written without the vowel-signs, the vowel being perhaps regarded as inherent in the preceding consonant. So only initial and final vowels were necessarily written down, except for emphasis. For example, their character ✛ originally represented *ses*, a bolt, and came to stand for the syllable *se*. With ❙❙, a character used for the vowel *i*, the combination ✛❙❙ is read *si*, "the vowel sound of *e* being elided, so that the symbol ✛ has here the power of a pure consonant. It may be regarded as probable that it was in some such manner that the difficult conception of a consonant grew up, slowly and almost unconsciously."[2]

The principle of acrology helped constantly in the analysis. Almost any one of the four hundred Egyptian phonograms could be employed, it seems, to denote the initial sound of the corresponding word. Gradually, however, for any given alphabetic sound, one or two or three of the more easily written characters representing words beginning with this sound came to commonly stand for the sound. It is as though we should take seriously the rhyme, "A is an Archer who shot at a frog, B is

---

[1] Taylor, "The Alphabet," Vol. I, p. 62.
[2] Vol. I, p. 65.

a Butcher who has a big dog," and reversing the terms, make the picture of an archer stand for the letter A and that of a butcher for the letter B, ignoring all the other words and things that A and B might stand for.

So the Egyptians came to represent all their sounds by an alphabet of forty-five characters, having sometimes two or three characters for the same sound, as with *c* and *k*, *c* and *s*, etc., in our alphabet. There was a further simplification in practice until the Egyptian alphabet, as ordinarily used, consisted of but twenty-five letters. Figure 30 shows the Egyptian hieroglyphic alphabet with the letter-names and approximate equiv alents in our alphabet. The pictorial origin of the Egyptian letters is evident enough.

EGYPTIAN HIEROGLYPHIC ALPHABET.

	Values.	Name.	Normal Characters.	Variants.
1	a	eagle		
2	a	reed		
3	ā	arm		
4	i	parallels		
5	i	double reed		
6	u	chick		
7	k	bowl		
8	k	throne		
9	q	angle		
10	x	sieve		
11	h	mæander		
12	ḫ	knotted cord		
13	t	semicircle		
14	t	hand		
15	t	snake		
16	θ	tongs		
17	s	chairback		
18	š	inundated garden		
19	p	shutter		
20	b	leg		
21	f	cerastes		
22	r	mouth		
23	l	lioness		

FIG. 30. (From Taylor's "The Alphabet.")

Thus very early the Egyptians came to have this set of simple signs, sufficient in itself to express all that they thought and wrote. But they never realized its sufficiency, and continued to use their ideographs, syllabic signs, etc., side by side with their letters. As Taylor says, we "find a word spelt out alphabetically, a needless syllabic sign is then added, and this is followed by an unnecessary ideogram. So many crutches were thought necessary, that walking became an art of the utmost difficulty."[1] All that remained to be done was to reject the superfluous mass of ideograms, homophones, syllabics, and what not, and use the nearly perfect alphabet which had at last evolved itself. But the scribes clung to their ancient characters with a greater tenacity even than we do to our silent letters, and the writing of Egypt remained a confusion, their magnificent discovery going begging for a nation that could make use of it.

During the latter half of the nineteenth century it was generally supposed that the modified Egyptian alphabet had been borrowed by the Semites, and had been put into convenient form by that businesslike Semitic people, the Phœnicians. Thence transmitted to the Greeks in commercial intercourse, it had been further modified and handed on to the Romans; and thence, as we know, came our Latin script. Recent investigations, however, particularly the excavations in Crete reported by Sir Arthur Evans, render the theory of Egypto-Phœnician origin extremely doubtful, if not impossible. Greece is far older than has been thought. A flourishing civilization has been shown to have existed in the Ægean at least nearly 3000 B.C., with centers in Crete and probably later in Mycenæ. There was intimate intercourse between this civilization and that of Egypt about 2500 B.C. Works of art found at Mycenæ show that Greece and Assyria were in contact fifteen hundred years before Homer's time, though Greek art had even then its own characteristic features.[2] Mr. Hogarth, in his "Authority and Archæology" (p. 230), says: "Man in Hellas was more highly civilized before history than when history begins to record his state; and there existed human society in the Hellenic area, organized and productive, to a period so remote

---

[1] I, p. 68.

[2] See Clodd, "Story of the Alphabet," p. 187.

that its origins were more distant from the age of Pericles than that age is from our own. We have probably to deal with a total period of civilization in the Ægean not much shorter than in the Nile Valley." And these people possessed an indigenous system of picture-writing and a system of signs which were at least syllabic, perhaps in some degree alphabetic.

The Ægean script seems to have been in use long before Phœnicia existed. The Ægean civilization only fell when Mycenæ, its later center, though Crete was probably its place of origin, was overrun by the Dorians in the twelfth century B.C. Phœnician history, on the other hand, hardly goes back of 1600, and Phœnicia's chance for commercial importance seems only to have come with the fall of the Mycenæan civilization. Between this time and the rise of the later Greece that we know, Phœnicia was dominant in the Mediterranean, and seems to have taken the alphabetic material that was to be found and given it a more practical form. However, she used materials that were very much older than herself, and derived perhaps as much from Greece as from Egypt and from other sources. The Cretan signs have similarities with the Egyptian and with the Cypriote or Cyprus syllabary, and with the little-known Hittite. But while there are certain indications of a common origin, it cannot be said that one is derived from the other.

The busy Phœnicians adapted and unified the existing systems, changing and perhaps borrowing characters as needed, and the alphabet of later Greece was the result. Of some of the characters of this alphabet it seems possible to trace the actual pictorial origin. For example, the Egyptian hieroglyphic owl, *mulak*, becoming the sign for its initial letter *m*, was conventionalized successively by the Egyptian scribes to the second, third, and fourth forms shown in Figure 31. The first character on the lower line is from the Semitic; and, Taylor thinks, is a modification of the Egyptian form. Then follow three successive Greek forms of the same, reaching our capital M. The ears of the owl still show in the upper peaks of the M, and the beak shows in the angle between.

So the character ᴧᴧᴧᴧᴧ, originally a picture of a "water-line," became the Egyptian *n*; and it is said that our *n* has come from it. And so for D and others of our letters. Whether or not these particular lines

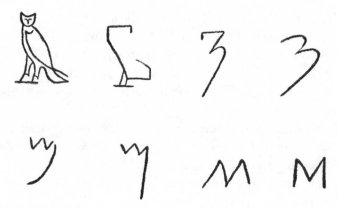

Fig. 31.[1] — Successive Forms of the Letter M.

of descent are the true ones, certain it is that our letters and all letters seem to have been the result of just such evolution from primitive pictures; and whether or not we are ever able to determine the particular ancestry of the whole Greek alphabet, we know that the development of writing, culminating in the production of alphabets, has proceeded practically everywhere through the stages already sketched as typical. The final stage, the analysis of the word to its elementary sounds and their representation by an alphabet, seems to have been reached by only a very few indeed of the world's peoples, these few dwelling in and about the Mediterranean; with the exception, perhaps, of the Mayas of Yucatan, who reached high-water mark in the New World by attaining, apparently, to the use of a few real alphabetic characters.

By borrowing and by derivation from these few sources, some two hundred and fifty alphabets have come into being, from first to last. Some fifty of these survive, says Clodd, about half being found in India, and the rest being mainly variations of the Roman, Arabic, and Chinese scripts, the Roman constantly taking a further lead.

The analysis into elementary sounds was made differently, and in different degrees of completeness, by the different peoples. A language may possess not more than a dozen consonants, as in

[1] This and the other cuts and quotations from Judd are reproduced, by permission, from Judd's "Genetic Psychology for Teachers," copyright, 1903, by D. Appleton & Co.

the case of the Finnic or Oeguese, "or it may have a delicate grada-
tion of sounds like the Sanskrit, which requires no less than thirty-
three consonants and fourteen vowels for its adequate expression.
Some languages are especially rich in sibilants, others in gutturals,
or nasals, or dentals, or liquids, or vowels. Hence either more or
fewer symbols of a particular class are required."[1]

The Semitic alphabet was mainly consonantal, and so are usually the scripts of Asia which are derived from it, the vowels being
only partially indicated. The Greeks made a further and better analysis, putting superfluous characters to new uses and using separate
letters to represent the vowels, "so that there might be a visible sign
for every audible sound of the human voice." But great as is our debt
to the Greeks for the improved alphabet which they bequeathed to

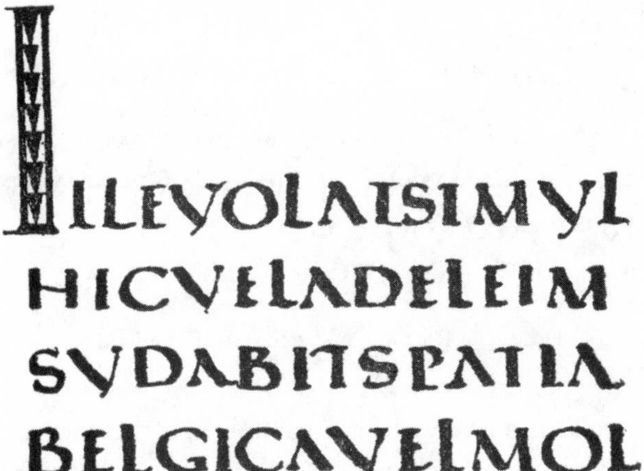

ILEVOLAISIMYL
HICVELADELEIM
SVDABITSPATIA
BELGICAYELMOL

FIG. 32. — Roman Capitals. (From Judd.)

us, we know that their ideal was only roughly approximated; and
our use to-day of a large number of diacritical marks attests the persistent deficiencies of our alphabet.

From the Greek alphabet to our own the steps are few and
well known. The Romans adopted a form of the Greek alphabet
in use among Greek colonists in Southern Italy; and after certain

---

[1] Taylor, Vol. II, p. 368.

modifications with use and as influenced by the contact with the later Greek, this alphabet became the vehicle of culture throughout Western Europe.

For inscriptions on monuments and for other writing demanding prominence, the Romans used the forms shown in Figure 32, practically our modern capital letters, which we use very similarly. These simple, sharp-angled letters were very legible, and could very readily be chiselled on hard materials, but could never be written rapidly. The Romans early developed another set of forms, a rapid, running hand used in business and in correspondence, a specimen of which is shown in Figure 33. Then, as now, greater speed seems to have meant decreased legibility.

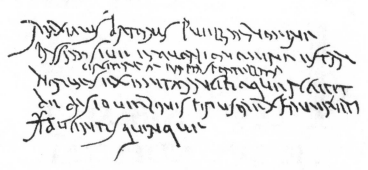

Fig. 33. — Roman Cursive Script. (From Judd.)

A compromise form between the capitals and the cursive, or running hand, was developed later in the uncials, as they were called, specimens of which are shown in Figure 34.

Through the many centuries in which letters were made only by hand, down to the invention of printing, the forms varied very greatly, according as legibility, beauty, or ease and speed of writing were desired. When printing came, the makers of types selected forms that pleased them from the handwritings of the time, and letters soon began to take stereotyped forms. The German printers made the unfortunate choice of a complicated and comparatively illegible Gothic script, and German readers still suffer the consequences. The English printers borrowed a beautiful running script

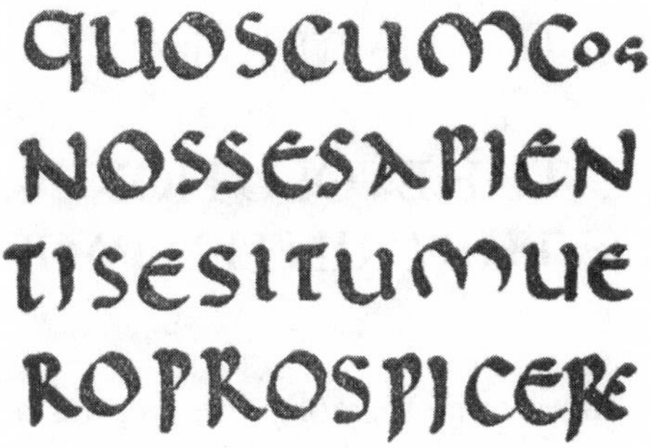

QUOSCUMCOS NOSSESAPIEN TISESITUMUE ROPROSPICERE

FIG. 34. — Roman Uncials. (From Judd.)

from the Italians. This was an imitation, by the fifteenth century Italian printers, of the beautiful minuscule letters, which were small, cursive forms of the large uncials, the "inch" letters or "crooked" letters shown above. By this happy chance of the early English printers, Anglo-Saxon readers have, in the present somewhat modified forms of this script, a set of symbols which are easier to read and more convenient to use than any other forms.

Thus by the slow processes of evolution, through variation and selection, the characters used in reading have developed through the ages,—from the rude pictures of the cave-dweller to the printed characters of the modern type-setting machine. It is remarkable how small a part conscious purpose has had in this development, how little rationalization there has been of the characters. They have been a growth, as language has been; and they have been allowed to carry down with them, from remote antiquity, useless but interesting marks of their origin, and rudiments of their stages of growth.

CHAPTER XII

THE EVOLUTION
OF THE PRINTED PAGE

In the earliest stages of pictography the pictures are arranged in almost every conceivable fashion. The reader's eye may traverse a page of picture-story with no constraint as to direction of movement or sequence of attention to the various symbols and parts. This is illustrated in the picture-letter shown in Figure 35, in which a

Fig. 35.[1] A Picture Letter.

Mandan Indian offers to a fur trader the skins of a buffalo, fish-otter, and fisher, in exchange (+) for a gun and thirty beaver skins. In Figure 36 I quote another example, with description, from Deniker's "Races of Man."

We go back to this protoplasmic free arrangement in our modern cartoons, and in certain advertisements. It is the all-at-once view that we take of objects and situations as directly experienced by the eye, or as we recall them in our imagery. This primitive lack of fixed order in picture-stories is paralleled by the young child's lack of fixed order in his speech. To him the order of words is nothing, at first. As Dr. Lukens says,[2] "He wants to say it all at once, anyhow,

---

[1] From Wundt's "Völker-Psychologie, Die Sprache," published by W. Englemann, Leipsig.
[2] Reproduced by permission of Walter Scott Pub. Co., Ltd.

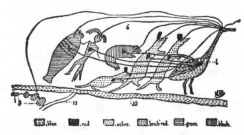

FIG. 36. (After Schoolcraft.[1]) — Petition of Chippeway Indians to the President of the United States. Example of pictography. "The petition is painted in symbolic colours (blue for water, white for the road, etc.) on a piece of bark. Figure 1 represents the principal petitioning chief, the totem of whose clan is an emblematic and ancestral animal (see Chapter VII.), the *crane*; the animals which follow are the totems of his co-petitioners. Their eyes are all connected with his to express unity of view (6), their hearts with his to express unity of feeling. The eye of the crane, symbol of the principal chief, is moreover the point of departure of two lines: one directed towards the President (claim) and the other towards the lakes (object of claim)."

FIG. 37.[2] The Story of Joseph.

---

[1] Pedagogical Seminary, Vol. III, p. 459.

[2] N.Y. Teachers Magazine, April, 1899.

just as he thinks it all at once." And so likewise does he draw. He is fond of making picture-stories, and they are of this go-as-you-please order, as in the "Story of Joseph and his Brethren," told in pictures to Professor Lukens by some children.

FIG. 38. Record of Departure (Innuit). (From Clodd.)

Even in the primitive picture-writing, however, there is evident a tendency to present the symbols serially. Figure 38, from Clodd, illustrates this serial arrangement. Figure 39 is a hunting story engraved by an Esquimau of Alaska on an ivory whip, and shows the same arrangement.

In making picture-narratives, this serial order would naturally suggest itself, expressing in a spatial sequence the temporal succession of ideas in the writer's mind. His story would often be more intelligible, too, when the order in which it was to be read was thus indicated. Very often, too, the material upon which the writing was done would favor the serial presentation, as in writing upon long strips of bark, or upon teeth, bones, or sticks.

FIG. 39. (After Mallery-Hoffman.[1]) — Journal of the Voyage of an Esquimau of Alaska. Example of pictography. The first figure (I) represents the story-teller himself, his right hand making the gesture which indicates "I," and his left, turned in the direction in which he is going, means "go." Continuing our translation, we read the subsequent figures as follows: —(2) "in a boat" (paddle raised); (3) "sleep" (hand on the head) "one night" (the left hand shows a finger); (4) "(on) an island with a hut in the middle" (the little point); (5) "I going (farther);" (6) "(arrive at) an (other) isle inhabited" (without a point); (7) "spend (there) two nights;" (8) "hunt with harpoon;" (9) "a seal;" (10) "hunt with bow;" (11) "return in canoe with another person" (two oars directed backward); (12) "(to) the hut of the encampment." (Deniker's "Races of Man," p. 138.)

[1] Reproduced by permission of Walter Scott Pub. Co., Ltd.

As the picture writing developed and became more definite, the characters came to be arranged almost exclusively in series, in more or less regular lines; and these lines came to have habitual directions which tended to become fixed for any given system. The Egyptian hieroglyphs were sometimes arranged in horizontal lines, sometimes in vertical columns. There was no fixed rule as to the direction in which they were to be written, but they were read in the opposite direction to that in which the animals' heads pointed. Thus in the first extract above, from Budge's "Egyptian Language" (p. 11), "we notice that the men, the chicken, the owl, the hawk, and the hares, all face to the left; to read these we must read from left to right, *i.e.*, *towards* them." In the second extract the arrangement is in vertical lines, to be read similarly in each line.

FIG. 40.[1] Egyptian Hieroglyphs.

The Hittites read from right to left and then returning, left to right, as the ox plows. According to Hoffman the groups of characters composing their words, on the other hand, were read from top

[1] Reproduced by permission of Kegan Paul, Trench, Trubner, & Co. London.

to bottom. With the Easter Islanders, the reading began in the lower left-hand comer and proceeded to the right, to the end of the line of picture-characters. Then, according to Hoffman, to read the next line above, the tablet was turned upside down and thus read again from left to right, to the end, when the reading of the third line began as the first. The Semitic writing, in general, was from right to left like the modern Hebrew. If we should collate the various ways of arranging the reading symbols, it would be seen that almost every conceivable arrangement has been used, but that the tendencies have been everywhere toward arrangement in vertical or horizontal lines.

Turning to the history of our own arrangement of characters, we find that the early Greek reading (not, however, that of the Mycenaean civilization, in respect to which there is uncertainty) was from right to left in each line, as with the Semites. Later, the reading came to be from right to left in the first line, from left to right in the second, etc. The characters faced, too, in the direction in which the reading was done, as in the inscription below, which read as printed in the third line, and which Taylor supposed was "the oldest Greek sentence in existence." Still later, the reading came to be from left to right in the first line, returning from right to left. This arrangement seemed to be more convenient for the scribe and was generally adopted in consequence. Finally, the still more convenient habit prevailed of writing and reading from left to right for all the lines, and this has continued to the present.

On ancient inscriptions the words were sometimes separated from each other by dots or points. The early practice in Greek and Latin literary texts, however, was usually to write continuously without spaces

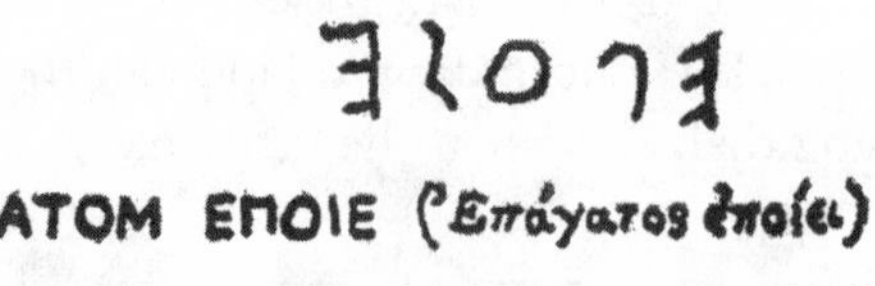

FIG. 41. Right to Left Reading in Early Greek.

or other divisions between the words. This, says Thompson, in his "Greek and Latin Palæography" (p. 67), "was certainly by far the more ordinary method, and in the uncial vellum manuscripts of the earlier Middle Ages it may be said to have been the only method that was followed. In the documents of ordinary life the distinction of words was, from early times, more frequently though still only partially observed." Even when separation of the words gradually appeared, the prepositions were still attached to their related word, and there was always a tendency to detach a final letter and to attach it to the following word. It was hardly before the eleventh century that a perfect system of separately written words was established in Latin manuscripts.

As early as Aristotle's time, according to Thompson, paragraphs were separated by a horizontal stroke or other mark drawn between the lines at their beginnings. Later the first letter of the new paragraph was placed farther to the left and also came to be enlarged, and thus the separation stroke came to be unnecessary and disappeared.

Division of words at the end of the line was often avoided by writing the last letters smaller, or by linking two or more letters in a monogrammatic form. When the word had to be divided, it was an ancient practice to break off with a complete syllable. This was continued in the later Greek and Latin manuscripts, though with many exceptions. The hyphen connecting parts thus divided did not appear until the eleventh century, although a point was used somewhat earlier, for the same purpose. The further breaking up of the written sentence by punctuation marks, quotation marks, etc., occurred gradually, principally during the earlier centuries of our era.[1]

The form of the modern book had its beginnings in the wooden, wax-coated tablets, something like our school slates, which were used from the earliest times in Greece and Rome. They were used for "literary composition, school exercises, accounts or rough memoranda." Two or more would be fastened together by ring hinges at the side, the raised margins of the tablet protecting the writing from being erased. Some such folded tablet seems to have existed even in Homer's day.[2] Little booklets of tablets, called codices, came into very general use by the Romans, for correspondence, legal documents,

---

[1] See Thompson's "Greek and Latin Palæography," pp. 67-71.

[2] "Iliad," VI, 169; referred to by Thompson, p. 20.

etc. The convenience of this form made it gradually supplant the roll form that had been generally used among them, and codices, or books composed of vellum sheets instead of waxed tablets, became common at Rome even in the earliest centuries of our era. As the book form became more general, papyrus was also used for the purpose, as well as vellum.

The arrangement of lines into two or more columns on the page was early adopted in these codices. Ordinarily a page had two columns, but three or four were also allowed. Thompson states that the three-column arrangement seems to have been "generally abandoned after the sixth century."

Paper proper, which of course is very different from papyrus, although known to the Chinese at a most remote period, was not introduced into Europe until the eighth century, and came from the Arabs. It does not seem to have been used to any great extent by Europeans until the twelfth and thirteenth centuries. In the fourteenth century, according to Thompson, it "began to rival vellum as a material for books and in the course of the fifteenth century it gradually superseded it." Manuscripts came to be composed, sometimes, of paper with a sheet of vellum forming the outer leaves of the quire.

And so, step by step, was evolved the modern book, with the present arrangement of pages and columns, and lines divided by spaces and marks into sentences, words, etc. The invention of printing stereotyped the forms that had up to that time found most favor or that were the most convenient for the mechanics of printing. This caused, to some extent, an arrest of the free development of forms of writing. At any rate, there resulted an immense limitation of the possibilities of variation, since very many had written where few could print. The history of the printed book and its adornment has been written elsewhere and cannot profitably be even sketched in this volume. Some references to the tendencies as to line-length, spacing, form of type, etc., will be found in a later chapter on present-day requirements of the printer.

It would be very interesting and suggestive if we could have a quantitative statement of the comparative amounts of actual reading done by the general population at various times in the world's history, and at various stages in the development of writing. Too little is known of culture history to furnish a safe basis for such estimates. The simpler forms of picture-writing could of course be read by all intelligent persons without special training; so that at this stage practically all were readers, just as all young children are picture-readers. With conventionalizing of the characters and transfer of meanings, special training became more and more necessary and reading tended to become limited to certain privileged classes, especially, as was noted in our introduction, to the priesthood. We have already referred to the difficulty of learning the Chinese syllabary; and in spite of the great reverence which the Chinese have for education, it is said that not more than one out of ten Chinamen can read. The Babylonian and Egyptian were also very difficult to learn, with their large number of characters and their many complicated features. Yet the Babylonians seem to have made education, including tablet-writing, compulsory on all free Chaldeans. Libraries were founded in all the chief cities of Babylonia. They had librarians, kept the books or tablets methodically arranged and numbered, took out books by handing the librarian a ticket inscribed with the requisite number, etc. The great number of their writings which have come down to us through so many thousands of years indicates that reading and writing must have been very general among them.

Egypt had an immense literature and great libraries, and manuscripts without number have been preserved to our own time. Among the upper classes of Greece and Rome, the power to read and write must have been almost as common as with ourselves, but the lower classes were illiterate.

During the Middle Ages readers were very few indeed, in proportion to the total population, and down to the invention of printing it can hardly be said that any very large proportion of the people were able to read, or did read habitually. Indeed it seems certain that there could hardly have been, in any of the older civilizations, any remote approach to the number of readers or to the amount of reading per capita found in these days of printed books and papers. The difficulty of learning the complicated systems of writing of the early times, which would necessarily prevent the mass of the people from ever learning more than the barest rudiments at most, did not of course apply to Greece and Rome. But the cost of the materials from which books were made, and the fact that every one must be hand-made, and by what one may call skilled labor, would necessarily preclude their possession or use by the great majority of the people, who were even far less able to have luxuries in that day than in our own. Even among the privileged classes, books and other manuscripts were, from their comparatively great expense, necessarily much less abundant than in our time.

The absence of inexpensive writing material was very important. The papyrus, made from an Egyptian rush or reed of that name, could not be produced cheaply; and although a sort of paper was made in early times from cotton, this material was very perishable and unsatisfactory. Forsyth, in his "History of Ancient Manuscripts" (pp. 25-27), says that the use of linen rags for the manufacture of paper "was wholly unknown to the ancients. Indeed, they did not understand the manufacture of flax at all, even if they possessed the plant." He quotes De Quincey as asserting that the ancients had repeatedly discovered the art of printing. "The art which multiplied the legends upon a coin or medal had, in effect, anticipated the art of printing. It was an art, this typographic mystery, which awoke and went to sleep many times over from mere defect of materials. Not the defect of typography as an art, but the defect of *paper* as a material for keeping this art in motion. There lies the reason, as Dr. Whately most truly observes, why printed books had no existence amongst the Greeks of Pericles or afterward amongst the Romans of Cicero. And why was there no paper? The common reason, applying to both countries, was the want of linen rags, and that want arose from the universal habit of wearing woolen garments…. How desperate," he continues, "must have been the bankruptcy at Athens in all materials for receiving the records of thoughts when we find a polished people having no better tickets or cards for conveying their sentiments to the public than shells." Hence, as we know, came our word *ostracize*, from the practice of marking upon shells (*ostraca*) the votes for civil banishment. A similar poverty of material was shown by the Romans, according to Forsyth, in their use of "tickets of admission to the gladiatorial shows just like tickets of admission to our own theatres," except that they were made of little oblong pieces of lead, some of which have come down to us and are now in the British Museum.

We find, in fact, that printing came very soon after paper had come into general use among the European nations; and the cheapening and increase of reading-matter through the two discoveries have been very great indeed. In consequence, as we have seen, reading and the reading habit have become practically universal, in all civilized countries. In later chapters we shall have to consider certain disquieting results that come from this tremendous modern development of reading.

CHAPTER XIII

THE HISTORY OF READING
METHODS AND TEXTS

WITH the development of syllabaries and alphabets came reading in the modern sense, and also methods of learning to read. Among the early peoples who used an alphabet each letter was used for a definite purpose to represent a definite sound, and this made the letters of much greater importance than at present, and tended to the practice of reading and learning to read by letters. The A B C method of learning to read became general among the Greeks and Romans, and persisted to recent times in the Western world, though here and there an ineffective protest was made by educational reformers. It was different in some parts, at least, of the Orient, where the method of teaching to read was to place a book in the hands of the child from which he repeated the words in concert with his comrades until he knew them by heart, learning by imitation, in word and sentence wholes. Renan, in his "Life of Jesus," thinks that Jesus was thus taught to read.

The Greeks and Romans, in teaching the child his letters, taught the combination of letters into syllables and words, and then of words into sentences. Various devices were used, at times, for getting the pupil over the difficult alphabet stage. In one case a Greek purchased twenty-four slaves as playmates for his stupid boy, giving to each the name of a letter in the Greek alphabet. Quintilian, A.D. 68, advised giving the young child blocks and tablets containing the letters, to play with, and that he should be allowed to trace with a pen the forms of the letters as engraved on ivory tablets. And so there were innumerable devices for teaching the alphabet. A popular method of a later century was the gingerbread method, described as follows by Matthew Prior:[1]—

---

[1] "Alma," Canto two, quoted from Reeder's "Development of School-Readers."

"To Master John the English maid
A horn book gives of gingerbread,
And that the child may learn the better,
As he can name he eats the letter.
Proceeding thus with vast delight
He spells and gnaws from left to right."

Basedow (1723-1790), who taught that the child should learn to read by playing, strongly advocated this gingerbread method. The school should have a special school baker. "The children must have breakfast, and it is not necessary for any child to eat the alphabet more than three weeks. The cost of shaping the dough into letters is less than one-half penny daily for each child. This makes three pence a week or for four weeks a groschen. The acquisition is entirely worth so much and is possible even to the poor children."[1]

Various mechanical devices were contrived to facilitate the manipulation of letters in script and print, in grouping them into syllables, words, and other combinations. Other devices were primarily to interest the child in the letters. The development of methods proper will be traced further after we have given an account of the development of primers and reading texts.

The early primers were all books of religious instruction, and their content was determined and limited by the authority of the Church. In the Abecedarien of the ninth century the alphabet and *ab, eb, ib* columns were followed by the Credo and Paternoster; later the Ave Maria and, soon after the thirteenth century, the Benedicite and Gratias were included.

From Charles the Great until Luther, no other material than the above appeared in school readers. The early primers of the Reformation were not only school books but manuals of church service. The German word for primer, *Fibel*, appeared in 1419, and signifies a little Bible. Henry the Eighth forbade the printing of unauthorized primers while a Catholic, and issued his "Reform Primers" in the interest of the true doctrine when he became a Protestant. "Alphabet and creed became united in one book which became the

---

[1] Kehr's "Geschichte des Leseunterrichts," p. 59.

forerunner on the one hand of the book of Common Prayer, and on the other of the modern school primer."[1]

The first Protestant primer, however, by Philip Melancthon, had no inconsiderable quantity of secular material. In addition to the usual Catholic content and some extracts from the New Testament, there were fourteen pages of the sayings of the wise men of Greece. Luther's primer followed the fashion of the Catholic primers of the time. The A B C book by Schulte, published in 1532, made one of the earliest attempts to adapt to the child's interests. The letters were presented with pictures and in rhymes, introducing the jingle in which the child soul revels. A form, that was much followed in the early English primers, ran as follows: —

"H h Hase   H h Hammer.
Gebratne Hasen sind nicht boes.
Der Hammer gibt Gar harte stoess.

K k Katze.   K k Kamm.
Die Schlaue Katze frisst die Maeus.
Der Kamm herunter dringt die Laues."[2]

The Puritans brought with them to America an A B C Catechism which was succeeded by the famous New England Primer, about 1690. "For more than one hundred years," says Reeder, "the New England Primer had the field in America against all comers, and for half a century longer it continued to be used in the schools." Its total sales are estimated to have been not less than three million copies. This primer was a Church book, but had enough of secular matter to make it "a step in the direction of a secularization of the course of study." It contained the alphabet, lists of the vowels and consonants, lists of syllables such as *ab*, *eb*, *ib*, etc., lists of words for spelling arranged according to the number of syllables; rhymes with illustrative wood-cuts for the letters in order, as in the cut; moral injunctions, prayers, catechisms, etc., for the children, including the "Now I lay me down to sleep," which was apparently written

---

[1] Reeder, "Development of School Readers," p. 10.

[2] *Ibid.*, p. 12.

for this primer and which has come to be "the dearest prayer of American childhood." This little book, present with the Bible in every home, had a profound influence on the moral and religious thought of the whole country. It is said to have been "the daily companion of President John Adams throughout his long career." When it went down, after more than a century of undisputed sway, it continued to exert "an abiding influence upon the quality of its numerous successors."

Beginning as early as 1450, the Horn Book, as it was called, came to be more and more the means by which the English child learned his first use of letters and words. It was used extensively in England down to the beginning of the nineteenth century, and in our schools as well. The cut below, from Johnson's "Old-Time Schools and School Books," shows all that there was of it. It was a paddle, with a card of printed matter tacked upon it under a protecting sheet of horn.

In England the Battledore paddles came to be transformed into wooden primers in a similar manner, and were used both for play and for lessons. In America the little girls of colonial times very often wrought out their own primers with needle and thread, in samplers containing the alphabet with vowels and consonants, bible quotations, prayers, verses, and sometimes illustrations, in various designs and styles of type.

As the New England Primer declined in America, the spelling-book took its place as the book for beginners. The spelling-book combined the alphabet, primer, speller, and reader in one book, and often included other subjects, as well. Webster's Spelling Book, published in 1783, soon displaced the few spellers previously introduced, and came to be used almost universally throughout the country. In 1785 five hundred copies a week were being sold, in 1818 the total number had reached five million, and to 1847 the total sales had amounted to forty-seven million. In 1889 Commissioner Harris stated that twelve hundred thousand copies were then being sold annually, and that it was "the most generally used of all school text-books." In 1900 it was still being sold at the rate of hundreds of thousands annually.

The book contained long lists of words arranged according to length, a large number of names of persons and places, illustrated fables for reading lessons, and short sentences for beginners in

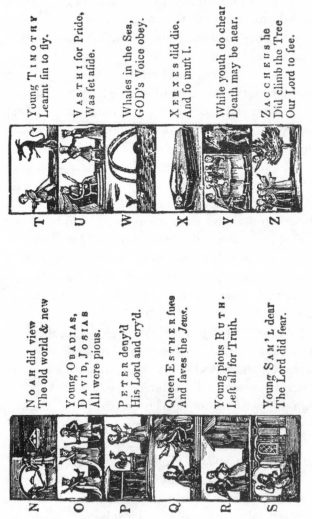

N O A H did view
The old world & new

Young O B A D I A S,
D A V I D, J O S I A S
All were pious.

P E T E R deny'd
His Lord and cry'd.

Queen E S T H E R fues
And faves the *Jews.*

Young pious R U T H.
Left all for Truth.

Young S A M ' L dear
The Lord did fear.

Young T I M O T H Y
Learnt fin to fly.

V A S T H I for Pride,
Was fet afide.

Whales in the Sea,
GOD's Voice obey.

X E R X E S did die,
And fo muft I.

While youth do chear
Death may be near.

Z A C C H E U S he
Did climb the Tree
Our Lord to fee.

FIG. 42. — Picture Alphabet from New England Primer.
(From "Old-Time School Books" by Clifton Johnson. This and the following illustrations
from Johnson are used by permission of The Macmillan Co.)

FIG. 43. — A Typical Horn Book.

reading. Supplementary matter, such as numbers, abbreviations, moral instructions, a catechism, etc., appeared variously in various editions. Artificial in its arrangement of words, thought, and vocabulary, most ill-adapted to the needs of its users and to the various ages of children, it yet served an important purpose in its earlier days, and through its universal use, in "reducing a dozen local dialects to one harmonious language," and bringing about "that remarkable uniformity of pronunciation in our country which is so often spoken of with surprise by English travellers."[1]

---

[1] Scudder, "Life of Noah Webster," pp. 38-39, quoted by Reeder.

Fig. 44. — A Sampler. (From Johnson.)

The list of geographical names below, quoted by Reeder from Webster's Spelling Book, illustrates the choice of words, arrangement, etc.:—

A bac' o	Cat a ra' qua	Schuy' ler	Wa que fa no' ga
A bit' i bis	Cat te hunk'	Scoo' duc	Win' ni pic
A ca' di a	Chab a quid' ic	Shen' brun	Win ni pis o' gy
A quac' nac	Chat a ho' chy	Sho' dack	Wy a lu' sing

Fig. 44½. — An Old Spelling Lesson.

Webster seems to have published the first American school reader, about the same time as his speller. Besides selections intended directly to instruct the youth in morals and religion, it contained dialogues, narratives, and many selections from American statesmen and patriots of those revolutionary times. Webster's reader was not so successful as his speller. Several rival readers, made on somewhat the same plan, divided the field with him. The preference of their makers for the productions of American genius "resulted in the selection of much that was commonplace and the omission of most that was really great."

Primers of various sorts seem to have abounded during the early part of the nineteenth century, but they took little account of method in teaching beginners to read. If they contained anything beyond the illustrated alphabet, it was the catechism or other moral or religious content. But by the end of the first quarter of the century, primer-makers began to attend to method and adaptation as well as to matter. For example, Keagy's Pestalozzian primer, of 1826, contained a series of "thinking lessons," a beginning of object-lessons. "The size, shape, color, number, origin, and use of common articles of the household, the street, and the field were to become rallying points for pleasing and useful thoughts. Exercising the pupils in handling the objects was recommended wherever practicable. It was probably the first primer published in this country in which there was a distinct purpose to make use of the child's environment in an educative manner."[1] The plan and arrangement, however, were exceedingly crude.

Early in the nineteenth century the readers began to be graded somewhat as to subject-matter, appearing in series of two and three books each. There would be an Introduction, a Middle Book, and a Sequel, a Primer and a Spelling Book completing the series.

In 1828 Putnam's series introduced a custom that has been much imitated, that of doing the work of a dictionary in defining the difficult words and phrases. Worcester's series of readers, published in 1828, contained a primer which seems to have been "the first American primer to advocate the word-method." Of this more further on. Pierpont's series of readers, beginning about 1823, omitted the usual treatises on inflection, emphasis, accent, punctuation, etc., as being little used, insisting that "reading, like conversation, is learned from example rather than by rule." The selections were taken mainly from the writings of Jefferson, Patrick Henry, Webster, Irving, etc., in the belief that our country had a "character of its own," physically and morally, which should be learned by the children while at

---

[1] Reeder, p. 43.

school. The series was long a popular one, and on its merits, with little pushing by publisher or author, and set an excellent example in its choice of "literature as the proper field for subject-matter."

The chief competitors of Webster's first American Reader had been Bingham's "Columbian Orator," Bingham's "American Preceptor," and the "English Reader" by Lindley Murray, an English author, with the Introduction and Sequel to the "English Reader." The "English Reader" continued to be very largely used in American schools during the first half of the nineteenth century. In literary worth it much surpassed its early American rivals. It had many selections from the best English poets, but still more of moral and didactic matter, proverbs, Bible stories, dissertations on Virtue, Friendship, Comforts of Religion, etc., pathetic pieces, public speeches, etc., with little adaptation to the needs of the young.

A series of readers by Cobb, begun about 1831, made some effort to interest the child by means of stories, information about animals, etc., and the author made a strong appeal to American patriotism in support of his readers as against the "English Reader," then so generally used. By 1844 more than six million copies of Cobb's Readers had been sold.

First Readers gradually took the place of spellers as introductory to reading, though the spellers remained in constant use. The readers came to give much instruction in correct articulation and in elocution generally. The various series that appeared each embodied some characteristic feature which publishers made the most of, as nowadays.

McGuffey's six-book series, which appeared in 1850, has, according to Reeder, "probably attained the largest sale and widest distribution of any series yet produced in America. In range of subject-matter it swept almost the entire field of human interest, morals, economics, politics, literature, history, science, and philosophy. Many a profound and lasting impression was made upon the lives of children and youths by the well-chosen selections of this series, and valuable lessons of industry, thrift, economy, kindness, generosity, honesty, courage, and duty found expressions in the after lives of millions of boys and girls who read and re-read these books, to the influence of which such lessons were directly traceable."

From 1860 to 1880 the character of school readers seems to have undergone little change, but changes in method were taking place. The word-method had again been advocated in the Bumstead Readers of 1843, and appeared again in 1860 as "new and original" in the "Word Builder," the first book of the National Series of readers.

Reading books had been taken into the service of the school subjects as early as 1824, in the "Agricultural Reader" by Daniel Adams. In 1827 appeared a "Historical Reader," by Rev. J. L. Blake, and reading was later taken into the service of the various sciences, notably in the Willson seven-book series of 1860. The latter seems to have marked the culmination of the tendency to utilitarian specialization in the choice of subject-matter for readers, as against the literary excellence shown in such readers as Pierpont's and in Murray's "English Reader." "In the new series and supplementary readers, which began to appear about 1880, literature took the field and since then has held it against all comers." It was the beginning of a new epoch in the development of school readers.[1] Science and the other departments of knowledge, while rather losing their place in the reading-books, have been given their own place in the present enriched elementary curriculum. Since 1880 the subject-matter of readers has been taken mainly from the field of literature, and the problem has been one of selection, arrangement, and adaptation within this field, the tendency being toward the use of literary wholes instead of the earlier selection of scraps. The scrap compilations of the school readers were scathingly denounced by Horace Mann as early as 1849, but with little effect. President Eliot forcibly renewed the criticism in his article in the *Educational Review* of July, 1891, arguing for the use of real literature and literary wholes in the readers as against the literary scraps and trash of most of the books. With the appearance of the supplementary readers, about 1880, came a tendency more and more to present literary wholes, condensations of such classics as "Hiawatha," "Robinson Crusoe," "Ivanhoe," etc. Most of the present-day series of readers are based on literature as the subject-matter, and the "Heart of Oak" series, a six-book series edited by Charles Eliot Norton, perhaps marks the

---

[1] Reeder, "Development of School Readers," p. 56.

extreme of this tendency to "read for literature's sake," as contrasted with the other extreme represented in the Willson books.

After this review of the contents of school readers, let us now return to the history of methods of learning to read. The alphabet method, in spite of occasional protest, was almost universally used from the Greek and Roman times until some thirty years ago, and of course has not been entirely discarded even yet. In this method the child learned first the names of the large and small letters, and their order in the alphabet. This was task enough, uninteresting as it was to many, to keep them employed for some months, or even in some cases for a year or more, Then the combinations like *ab*, *eb*, *ib*, were spelled out and pronounced, and then three-letter combinations like *glo*, *flo*, *pag*, etc., in all of which the early pages of the old spellers abounded. Then monosyllables and gradually longer and longer words were used. Spelling the word preceded its pronunciation, until it was known well. "It was assumed that there was a necessary connection between naming the letters of a word and pronouncing the word." "No other approach to the pronunciation of the printed symbol was imagined by the great majority of teachers."[1]

The alphabet method had early modifications in Europe on the side of phonetics. As early as 1534 Ickelsamer had a device of "placing the picture of an animal, its printed name, and the letter whose sound was most like the animal's voice or cry in parallel columns. Against the picture of a dog, for example, was placed the growling *r*, against a bird the twittering *z*," etc.[2] Later, A was associated with Apple, B with Boy, etc., and in this century we have seen various imitative picturings of the sounds of the letters, as of *m* by a cow lowing, *sch* by children driving away hens, etc.

The philanthropinists, in Germany, had their boys personate the letters by their dress and actions; for example, *f* by "dressing in helmet, big necktie, and stilts," *w* by twisting their bodies into its shape, etc. Such methods had, as one of their results, the lessening of attention to the letter's name, in favor of its sound or visual

---

[1] Reeder, "Development of School Readers," p. 63.

[2] Hall, "How to Teach Reading," p. 2.

form. Germany much earlier than America began to realize that spelling was not the only or the best approach to reading, but the spelling method held its ground there until well into the nineteenth century.

Outside of the illustrations of the alphabet which we have noticed, the first illustrated schoolbook seems to have been Comenius' "Visible World, or a Nomenclature, and pictures of all the chief things that are in the world, and of men's employments therein; in above an 150 Copper Cuts." This book, the "Orbis Pictus"

FIG. 45. — Part of an Illustrated Alphabet in the "Visible World."
(From Johnson.)

as it is usually known, published in Nuremberg in 1657 or 1658, was for more than a hundred years the most popular text-book in Europe. Reeder calls it "the first attempt at object-lesson instruction, and the beginning of the word-method in teaching reading. It was translated into ten European and four Asiatic languages" (p. 67).

In the "Orbis Pictus" each subject had its picture, with explanatory sentences below in Latin and in English or other language. In his preface Comenius says: "The very looking upon the thing pictured suggesting the name of the thing will tell the child how the title of the picture is to be read. And thus the whole book being gone over by the bare titles of the pictures, reading cannot but be learned — and indeed, too, without using any ordinary

The Barbers Shop. LXXV.   *Tonſtrina.*

The Barber, 1.
in the Barbers-ſhop, 2.
cutteth off the Hair
and the Beard
with a pair of Sizzars, 3.
or ſhaveth with a Razor,
which he taketh out of his
Caſe, 4.
    And he waſheth one
over a Baſon, 5.
with Suds *running*
out of a Laver, 6.
and alſo with Sope, 7.
and wipeth him
with a Towel, 8.
combeth him with a Comb, 9.
and curleth him
with a Criſping Iron, 10.
    Sometimes he cutteth a Vein
with a Pen-knife, 11.
where the Blood ſpirteth out, 12.

Tonſor, 1.
in *Tonſtrina,* 2.
tonder *Crines*
& *Barbam*
Forcipe, 3.
vel radit *Novacula,*
quam è *Theca,* 4. depromit.

    Et lavat
ſuper *Pelvim,* 5.
Lixivio defluente
è *Gutturnio,* 6.
ut & *Sapone,* 7.
& tergit
Linteo, 8.
pectit *Pectine,* 9.
criſpat
Calamiſtro, 10.
    Interdum Venam ſecat
Scalpello, 11.
ubi Sanguis propullulat, 12.

FIG. 46. — A Page showing the Method of Teaching in the "Visible World."
(From Johnson.)

tedious spelling — that most troublesome torture of wits." However, Comenius was far beyond his times, and his book was little used as such a method of learning to read.

There were glimpses of better things in the phonetic system of the Jansenists, and in the primer of Gedike, in 1791, which advised teaching words before letters, as the natural order is from the whole to the parts; but none of these had appreciable effect in changing current A B C practice until Jacotot (1770-1840) advocated the word-method as a part of his system, and set forth clearly the arguments for it.

In America, Worcester's Primer, in 1828, seems to have been the first beginners' book to recognize any other than the alphabet method. The author says in his preface: "It is not, perhaps, very important that a child should know the letters before it begins to read. It may learn first to read words by seeing them, hearing them pronounced, and having their meanings illustrated; and afterward it may learn to analyze them or name the letters of which they are composed." Bumstead, in the first book of his series of readers published in 1840-1843, stood stoutly for the word-method, and urged that a scholar be never required to spell a word "before he has so far learned it as to be able to read it." Horace Mann had already advocated the word-method for years, and ridiculed the en-o—no, pee-you-tee—put, tee-aitch-ee—the, way of beginning reading, as it was taught in Webster's Spelling Book. As early as 1790 Dr. Thornton, head of the Patent Office in Washington, had issued a pamphlet proposing that letters be named as they sound; and, as there are more sounds than letters, he introduced new letters to supply deficiencies, making a phonetic system such as we have seen much of in recent years. But the A B C method and the reading by spelling went on with little disturbance from these protests. Reeder calls attention to the fact that even in advanced reading "analysis played the leading rôle" (p. 78). Pupils would "spell and define the words, tell their synonyms and opposites, write and paraphrase the sentence or paragraph, analyze and reduce it to its simplest sentences," etc., sometimes spending twenty to thirty minutes on six or eight lines.

J. Russell Webb, author of the Normal Readers, did much to bring about the adoption of the word-method, and by 1870 it began to be adopted by progressive teachers in various parts of the country, and gradually grew in favor.

The phonic method, so early used by the Jansenists, helped also to displace the alphabet method. In the phonic method, the words are spelled by producing the succession of sounds forming them. As there are some forty-four sounds, new characters must be added to the usual twenty-six if the system is to be complete. If the child is able to successively reproduce the sounds of the letters as they stand in a word, he can learn for himself to pronounce new words as they appear, a great advantage of the phonic method over the word method. As for the alphabet method, it was easy to show that knowing or saying the letters' names gave no clew, necessarily, to a new word's sound. The phonic method was tried in various parts of the country, and met with great success for a time, developing into what came to be known as the phonetic method, notably in the "Pronouncing Orthography" system of Dr. Edwin Leigh, published in 1864 and patented four years later. In this system the letters were given various special forms to represent their different sounds, these forms being slight modifications of the ordinary form. Silent letters were printed, but in hair lines. The method is further described and illustrated on a later page.[1] This system was used in a series of readers by Leigh, and in several other series, including McGuffey's. It was introduced into the schools of St. Louis, New York, Washington, Boston, and other large cities. It met with great success, but only for a short time. The "pronouncing print" was hard on the eyes, requiring an unnaturally close inspection of each letter, in the beginning; besides, it made trouble for the printer, distracted from attention to the thought in reading, and caused confusion in the attempt to use two alphabets.

The sentence method was more or less used, here and there, as early as 1870, and indeed was advocated by occasional writers very much earlier, as we have noted. It was not very generally used until as late as 1885 or 1890. Since then there have appeared a very great variety of modifications and mixtures of all these methods, devices for making them interesting to the child, arrangements for correlating the beginnings of reading with writing, drawing, number work, etc. There has been development simultaneously along so many and so conflicting lines that historical treatment seems impossible in any brief compass. I shall, however, endeavor to briefly describe the methods that are now in most general use or that have much of promise or suggestion, and shall note the present trend of practice among the better teachers of reading.

---

[1] See Fig. 48.

PART III

THE PEDAGOGY
OF READING

CHAPTER XIV

PRESENT-DAY METHODS AND TEXTS IN ELEMENTARY READING

THE methods of learning to read that are in common use to-day may be classed as alphabetic, phonic, phonetic, word, sentence, and combination methods. The special systems of teaching to read, which now pass under the names of their authors, are usually but specially adapted means of using one or another of these standard methods. A brief account of these standards will therefore pave the way for an account of the concrete systems now in vogue.

The alphabet method, used almost universally in Greece and Rome, and in European countries generally until well into the nineteenth century, and which was nearly universal in America until about 1870, is now chiefly of historical interest. However, there are innumerable corners of our country, a little removed from the centers and thoroughfares of civilization, in which the alphabet method is still "the good old way." In this method, as we have seen, the names of the printed or written letters are first taught, and the order of the letters in the alphabet. Sometimes the sounds of the letters are also taught. Then nonsense syllables like *ab, ib, ob* are spelled and pronounced; then combinations of three letters, monosyllabic words, dissyllables, etc., follow, the word usually being spelled before it is pronounced. Just how naming the letters was supposed to assist in pronouncing the word it is difficult to see. The value of the practice in learning to spell doubtless had much to do with blinding centuries of teachers to its uselessness for the reading of words and sentences.

However, in dealing thus constantly with the letters and their combinations, the pupil necessarily acquired a familiarity with the sounds represented by each letter, whether purposely taught these or not. And thus this method always combined something of phonics as well.

The phonic method, used by the Jansenists in the Port Royal Schools, long neglected but advocated again by Thornton in 1790, began, as we have seen, to be extensively used as a special method in this country in the system of Leigh, about 1870-1873. It is a spelling method, but the word is spelled by its elementary sounds and not by the letter-names. The word is slowly pronounced until its constituent sounds come to consciousness, and these sounds are associated with the letters representing them. Drill in this sound analysis trains the articulation, trains the ear and the ability to sound the letters of any new word, and gives the power to pronounce it by blending the sounds suggested, — provided there are no silent letters and provided the sounded letters represent but one sound. This seldom occurs, and the reader of new words must be helped out by context or conjecture. Both Thornton and Leigh met the difficulty by contriving additional characters to represent the other sounds after one

2 And both Jesus was called, and his disci'-ples, to the marriage.

3 And when they wanted wine, the mother of Jesus saith unto him, They have no wine.

4 Jesus saith unto her, Woman, what have I to do with thee? mine hour is not yet come.

5 His mother saith unto the servants, What-soev'er he saith unto you, do it.

6 And there were set there six waterpots of stone, after the manner of the purifying of the Jews, contain ing two or three firkins apiece'.

7 Jesus saith unto them, Fill the water-pots with water. And they filled them up to the brim.

8 And he saith unto them, Draw out now, and bear unto the governor of the feast. And they bare it.

FIG. 47. — A Specimen of Leigh's Print.

sound each had been allowed to the twenty-six regular letters. The forty-four or more sounds used in English needed as many characters, and when these were furnished the method came to be known as the phonetic, to distinguish it from the simpler phonic. Leigh made the additional characters by slightly modifying the existing letter-forms, and silent letters were printed in hair lines, as shown in these extracts (Figs. 47 and 48) from his article in the Report of the National Educational Association, 1873.

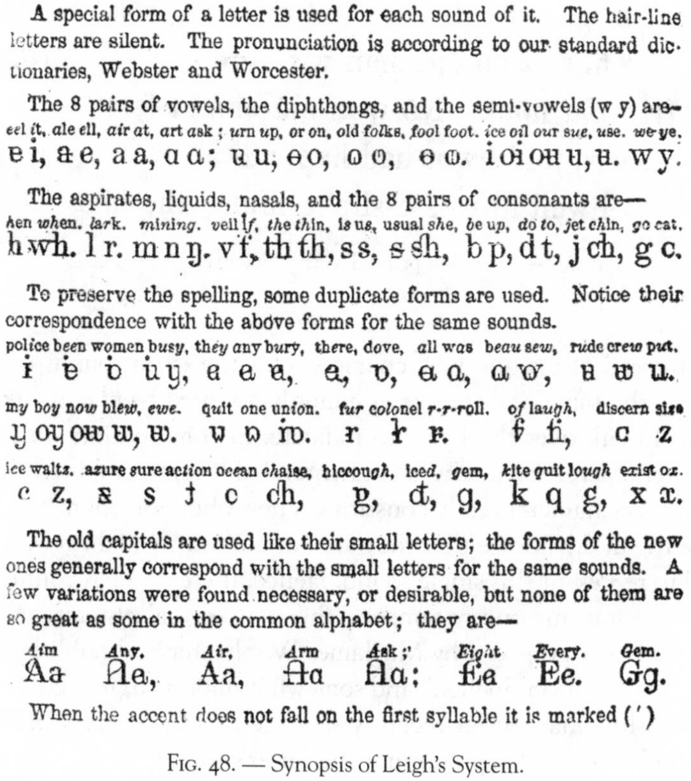

A special form of a letter is used for each sound of it. The hair-line letters are silent. The pronunciation is according to our standard dictionaries, Webster and Worcester.

The 8 pairs of vowels, the diphthongs, and the semi-vowels (w y) are—
eel it, ale ell, air at, art ask ; urn up, or on, old folks, fool foot. ice oil our sue, use. we-ye.
e i, a e, a a, a a; u u, ө o, o ω, ө ω. ioi ou u, u. w y.

The aspirates, liquids, nasals, and the 8 pairs of consonants are—
hen when. lark. mining. veil if, the thin, is us, usual she, be up, do to, jet chin, go cat.
h wh. l r. m n ŋ. v f, th th, s s, s sh, b p, d t, j ch, g c.

To preserve the spelling, some duplicate forms are used. Notice their correspondence with the above forms for the same sounds.
police been women busy, they any bury, there, dove, all was beau sew, rude crew put.
i e o u y, a a u, a, o, ө a, a w, u w u.

my boy now blew, ewe. quit one union. fur colonel r-r-roll. of laugh, discern sise
ŋ oy ow w, w. w o ro. r r r. f f, c z

ice walts. azure sure action ocean chaise, hiccough, iced, gem, kite quit lough exist ox.
c z, s s j c ch, g, d, g, k q g, x x.

The old capitals are used like their small letters; the forms of the new ones generally correspond with the small letters for the same sounds. A few variations were found necessary, or desirable, but none of them are so great as some in the common alphabet; they are—
Aim   Any.   Air,   Arm   Ask ;'   Eight   Every.   Gem.
Aa   Aa,   Aa,   Aa   Aa;   Ea   Ee.   Gg.
When the accent does not fall on the first syllable it is marked (')

FIG. 48. — Synopsis of Leigh's System.

The "Scientific Alphabet" used in the Standard Dictionary and, in part, in the Funk and Wagnalls series of readers, is a modification of this same method, the silent letters being omitted.

This is illustrated in the following extracts,[1] the first being from Funk and Wagnalls' "Standard First Reader," and the second from their "Standard Second Reader."

Wuns, Rip Van Wiṇ'-kl went up
   a-mung' thẹ hilz, hwār hî sō
   cwîr lit'-l men plê'-ing bōl.
Thê gêv Rip sum'-thing tū driṇk,
   hwich put him tū slîp.
Hî slept twen'-ti yîrz, and hwen hî wōk up
   hî wez an ōld man with grê hār and bîrd.
Hî went hōm.   Nō wun niū him at fẹrst.
Hî wez tōld hwet had hap'-nd
   hwail hî wez a-slîp' a-mung' thẹ hilz.

FIG. 49. — Selection printed in the "Scientific Alphabet."

Instead of making new characters for the extra sounds of the letters, the same end is more commonly attained by placing a diacritical mark over the letter to indicate, in combination with the letter-character itself, the sound intended.[2] The combined mark and letter-character really constitute a new phonetic character, but have the disadvantage that they are not constantly and exclusively used to represent this single sound. Hence, there is much confusion even in using any one system, and there are several systems.

A system proposed by Mr. James W. Shearer and published in his "Combination Speller," and somewhat improved, indeed, in an unpublished manuscript recently sent me by Mr. Shearer, has the great advantage of representing the letter's sound, where it might be equivocal, by a mark which constantly stands for that sound and

---

[1] These extracts are reproduced by permission of Funk and Wagnalls Co.
[2] See Fig. 54.

THE SCIENTIFIC ALPHABET.

LETTERS.	NAMES.	AS IN —	LETTERS.	NAMES.	AS IN —
ɑ, a, a	(ah)	ask, stär	O, o, ō	(oh)	obey, nō, bōat
A, a, ā	(ai(r))	fan, fãre	O, o, ŏ	(awe)	not, nŏr
B, b	(bee)	bat	P, p	(pee)	pet
C, c=k, q	(kee)	cat	[Q, q]=c	(cue)	(quit) cwit
Ch, ch	(chee)	church	R, r	(ar)	rat
D, d	(dee)	did	S, s	(ess)	so
Dh, dh	(thee)	then	Sh, sh	(ish)	she
E, e, ê	(ay)	met, thêy	T, t	(tee)	tell
F, f	(eff)	fit	Th, th	(ith)	thin
G, g	(ghee)	go	U, u, ū	(oo)	full, rūle
H, h	(hee)	he	U, u, ᴜ̄	(u(r))	bᴜt, būrn
I, i, ɪ	(ee)	it, caprɪce	V, v	(vee)	vat
J, j	(jay)	jet	W, w	(woo)	wo
[K, k]=c	(kay)	kin	[X, x]=cs	(ex)	wax
L, l	(el)	lo, noble	Y, y	(yee)	ye
M, m	(em)	me	Z, z	(zee)	zone
N, n	(en)	no	Zh, zh	(zhee)	azure
Ng, ng	(ing)	king			

Diphthongs: ɑi, ɑisle, I; ɑu, stɑut (stout); ɑi, cɑin (coin); iū, fiūd (feud), miūzic (music)."

FIG. 49½. — (See also Appendix of Standard Dictionary.)

for it only, irrespective of what the letter may be. Comparatively few marks are thus needed, and the constant value of the marks gives an easy guide to pronunciation and lessens the confusion. The silent letters are indicated by a dot. The system is illustrated in the extracts below: — [p. 180]

The word method, beginning with the "Orbis Pictus" of Comenius, 1657, and taught by various reformers, notably by Jacotot in France and Worcester and Horace Mann in America, was very little used in America until 1870, when progressive teachers began using it in various parts of the country. The pictures of the "Orbis Pictus" were intended to suggest the names printed below, "without using any ordinary tedious spelling." In the word method, the whole sound of the word is associated with the word's total visual appearance, and is suggested just as the name of any other object comes to mind on seeing the whole object. Children learn the name of a word about as quickly as that of a letter, and recognize the whole

I. ALPHABETIC NAMES, SOUNDS AND SYMBOLS.

KEY TO CONSONANT AND VOWEL SOUNDS.

p,	as	pĕt, tŏp.	sh, ch, ş,	as	show, chaişe, şŭrę.
b,	"	bĕt, rŏb.	ç, t,	"	ȧppreçiatę, ȧetĭŏn.
t,	"	tĕn, nĕt.	ş, z, g,	"	vĭşĭŏn, ȧzûrę, rôuzę.
d,	"	dĕn, ĕnd.	x,	"	ȧx, bŏx.
ch,	"	chĕss, whĭch.	x,	"	ĕxȧmplę.
j, g,	"	jĕt, gĭn.	wh,	"	whĕn, whăt.
k, e, q,	"	kĭt, eȧt, pīquę.	w,	"	wĕn, wăş.
g,	"	gŭn, pĕg.	h,	"	hȧt, hŏt.
f, ph, gh,	"	fŭn, phiz, tôugh.	y,	"	yŏn, yĕt.
v,	"	vinę, hȧvę.	l,	"	lĕt, tālę.
th,	"	thĭn, hȧth.	r,	"	rȧt, tȧr.
th,	"	thĕn, lāthę.	m,	"	măt, ȧm.
c, s,	"	cĕnt, sĕnt.	n,	"	nĕt, făn.
z, ç, ş, x,	"	zero, dĭşçẽrn, xebẽe.	n, ng,	"	sĭnk, rĭng.

—	as,	lātę, thĕy.
ı	"	lĕt, săḭd, (bŭrў).
ʃ	"	fȧr, (sẽrġeȧnt).
ʅ	"	fȧst.
⟨	"	fȧrę, thĕrę.
⟨	"	făt.
..	as,	fẽet, pīquę, (quăў).
:	"	fĭt, bĕęn, bŭşy, (wŏmĕn).
<	as,	nŏtę, sĕw, (hȧutboy).
Λ	"	eȧught, wȧll.
V	"	eŏt, wătch.

C	as,	prûnę, mŏve, mŏon, dręw.
)	"	fŭll, bŏok, wŏmàn.
C	"	bûrn, wŏrd, hẽrd, bĭrd, myrrh.
ᴗ	"	bŭn, sŏn.

DIPHTHONGS.

ʃ	as,	fīnę, tўpę.
ʃC	"	eow, loud.
Λ:	"	oil, boy.
C	"	fûşę, nęw.

II. A SAMPLE OF ALPHABETIC REFORM PRINT.

Bỳ the *phonĕtĭe ȧlphabĕt a child maỳ be tȧught the ȧrt ŏf reȧdĭng, nŏt fluĕntlỳ, bŭt wĕll, both ĭn phonĕtĭe ȧnd ĭn ŏrdĭnȧrỳ bŏoks, ĭn three mŏnths—aўe, ŏftęn ĭn twĕntỳ hourş ŏf thŏrough ĭnstrŭetĭŏn, a tȧsk whĭch ĭş rȧrelỳ ȧeeŏmplĭşhed ĭn three yęarş ŏf toĭl bỳ the old ȧlphabĕt. What făthẽr ŏr teȧchẽr wĭll nŏt glȧdlỳ haĭl ȧnd eȧrnĕstlỳ wŏrk fŏr thĭs great bŏon tŏ ĕdueatĭŏn —thĭs powĕrfŭl măchĭnę fŏr the dĭffŭşĭŏn ŏf knŏwlĕdġe.

*Dots above g and y, and below other letters indicate silent letters. The signs are omitted for the alphabetic sounds of a, e, i, o and u, except for exact representation.
As copyrighted, 1894, by Rev. James W. Shearer, St. Louis, Mo.

FIG. 50. — The Shearer System.

word about as quickly as they recognize a single letter. A word is not a sum of letter-names, anyway, nor even merely of letter-sounds. Its visual appearance, indeed, is not a sum of letter-appearances, but has a character of its own. So the word method short-circuits the whole process of word learning. The method is very generally, almost universally used at present, but usually in combination with the phonic or sentence methods, or both. It is argued that the method does not give the pupil power to pronounce for himself words that have not been met before, and that phonics is finally necessary for this purpose.

The sentence method, although suggested by Comenius, (vas scarcely used in America until popularized through the experiments of Farnham in the schools of Binghamon, New York, about 1870, and was not widely adopted until 1885-1890. Farnham's little pamphlet, "The Sentence Method of Reading," is still a very fair presentation of the method. The method urges that the sentence, and not the word or letter, is the true unit in language, expressing whole thoughts which are the units in thinking. If the sentence is the natural unit in language, it is the natural unit in reading as in speaking. As the word is not a mere sum of letter-sounds and letter-names, neither is the sentence merely a sequence of word-sounds and word-names. It has a distinctive total sound and appearance and meaning indicated plainly in the way it is spoken when its meaning is felt. It is read and spoken naturally only when this total meaning is prominent in the consciousness of the reader or the speaker. Hence the attention to letters, elementary sounds, words, and word-meanings — cultivated by the alphabet, phonic, and word methods — must be displaced by attention to sentence wholes and sentence meanings.

In using the sentence method, the teacher has come to make much use of the blackboard. A sketch of some object or scene interesting to the child suggests to the child a thought which he expresses in a sentence. The teacher writes this sentence and it is read, naturally with expression since the child's own thought here leads the expression. Other sentences are suggested, written, and read, until perhaps a little story of the picture is finished, all of which the child can soon "read" with natural expression. Sometimes the child's experiences on an excursion or at play or at work are thus written up as he tells them and made into a story which he soon can "read," although not at first knowing the place of a single word. But the frequent recurrence of certain word-forms, and sometimes substitutions, such as "I have a *dog*," "I have a *knife*," etc., bring these particular word-forms to his attention, and the sentence-wholes are gradually analyzed into their constituent words and these again, in time, into their constituent sounds and letters. The important thing is to begin with meaning wholes and sentence wholes, make thought lead, and thus secure natural expression, letting analysis follow in its own time. The method goes famously at first, like the word method, and naturally gives more "legato" reading than does the latter; but it breaks down when the child attempts to read new matter for himself, so the teachers commonly say. Hence the sentence method, too, is usually combined with or supplemented by phonics.

Perhaps we should catalogue still another, the imitative method. In the Orient, children bawl in concert over a book, imitating their fellows or their teacher until they come to know what the page says and to read it for themselves. Many an American child cannot remember when reading began, having by a similar method pored over the books and pictures of nursery jingles and fairy tales that were told to him, until he could read them for himself. Miss Everett, writing in the *New York Teachers' Monographs*, thinks that some day the débris and obtrusive technique of reading methods may melt away into the simplicity of some such practice as this.

These are the methods, about all that are to be found in use anywhere, although these are mixed in endless combinations, and the most various and often elaborate devices are invoked to make them interesting and effective. For instance, "reading machines" are used in Germany, but mainly to permit of quick combinations of printed letters into words or of words into sentences. The cut below represents a "machine" that has been much used. The apparatus consists of a large rectangular frame with rollers above and below. On these run strips of linen bearing letters and letter-groups as shown. The front of the machine is covered, except for a horizontal cleft to expose the words formed, as *lernen* in the cut. The rolls can be turned to form words as desired.

FIG. 51.[1] — A "Reading Machine."

<hr />

[1] From Fechner's "Grundriss der Geschichte der Wichtigsten Leselehrarten," by permission of Wiegandt and Grieben, Berlin.

The American teacher, however, prefers the blackboard and script. This is better for the teacher's own use, when supplemented by charts. For the pupil's practice in word and sentence making, however, the reading machines would doubtless be worth a trial.

Concerning texts, manuals, and specific systems for teaching children to read, the writer has recently examined with some care more than a hundred, representing the best that could be found in the modern literature of the subject. The leading publishers kindly sent in the texts that had their first recommendation, and teachers of reading in various quarters were consulted. In working over the primers and first readers, one is impressed with the fact that the artistic side has had far more attention and a far greater development than has the side of method and reading content. The books are often superbly illustrated, in colors or with fine photographs, and the covers and typography are most attractive. Of course these are the features which sell the books when, as too often occurs, the selection of texts is in the hands of persons who have no special familiarity with the methods and needs of the subject concerned. Competition has therefore forced the publishers to give special attention to the art side. It is a matter of gratification that we now have books that are so attractive and that set before the child high standards of beauty. It is an open question, however, whether the idealization of many of the pictures is not an adult one that is somewhat foreign to the child, and whether the use of the child kind of sketches, motivated as his own illustrative drawings are motivated, would not reach his real needs and interests better than these exquisite adult expressions. It is a question, anyway, how much reading owes to his æsthetic development, when pictures are needed rather to assist with natural child interpretation of what is read. The reading-books compiled by Jessie L. Smith, in which children's stories are illustrated by children's own illustrative drawings, suggest a very different ideal which is at least worth considering. A specimen illustration is shown [p. 185].

Next to the beauty of the primers, the most striking thing about at least three-fourths of them is the inanity and disjointedness of their reading content, especially in the earlier parts. No trouble has

FIG. 52. — The Bells. (Illustration from F. Lilian Taylor's First Reader.)

been taken to write what the child would naturally say about the subject in hand, nor indeed, usually, to say *anything* connectedly and continuously as even an adult would naturally talk about the subject. The language used often shows a patronizing attempt to "get down to the child's level," and results in a mongrel combination of points

FIG. 53. — George Goes Surveying.[1] (Philip Redmond — age, 12.)

of view and of expression that is natural neither to an adult nor to a child. The child avoids adults who try to play with him or talk with him in this manner, and down in his child heart he scorns such reading-matter, although he will often plod through it with some interest to please a beloved teacher. I quote some sentences from primers that are in common use and "highly recommended": —

"Is this a ball?"   "I do not like the tall grass."
"Is an apple round?"   "I am a kite."
"I can do many things."   "I am not a bird."
"It is a pear."   "How came you here?"
"You see my dog."   "Run, little squirrel, run."
"Can you see the rat?   It is a fat rat.   Does the cat see the rat?"
"I am a big boy.   Do you see me on the wall?   I will not fall."
"Will Fannie fill the can at the rill?"
"Fred is a boy.   Nell is a girl."

The primers contain hundreds of just such sentences, and yet one of the authors of these insists that all reading should be "like talking." How a child could talk such stuff naturally is beyond comprehension, and reading it can scarcely help developing that drawling, wooden monotone so generally found in reading classes.

---

[1] From Smith's "The Story of Washington," copyright by E. H. Harison, publisher, New York.

The early lessons are apt to be composed of sentences thrown together with little more than this of relation between them. Now the child, on the other hand, loves a story, loves to get somewhither in what is said, wants an outcome to the discussion, and has a persistence and continuity of thought that are constantly violated by such "sentence-hash." Better a thousand times that we have no primers than that we inflict such travesties on the child. No wonder that sometimes the authors withhold their names. The actual aim that has guided in the selection and arrangement of most of the early reading-matter has been the development of the power to recognize and pronounce words. Although the authors often disavow this and perhaps desired otherwise, the selections are such as to make reading a matter of word-pronouncing mainly. In some of the beginners' books, it is true, the lessons in word recognition and pronunciation are strictly separated from the reading exercises proper, and the child is supposed to already know all the words of a sentence before he attempts to read it. But very often this distinction is not even attempted. Most of the books teach phonics by one device or another, usually beginning after the child has had a little practice by the word or sentence method. Too often the line between phonics and reading is not drawn.

On the whole, the better classes of beginners' books have worked out with considerable care the successive steps in learning to pronounce words as they will meet the child in new reading matter. The lessons develop logically and easily until this power is acquired. They do this, however, by an adult method rather than by one natural to the child mind, and they do it at the expense of the child's formation of natural habits of reading, of using language generally, and of thinking.

A few of the systems of teaching reading deserve special mention, either from their prevalence in the schools, the care with which they have been worked out, or their having specially distinctive features. Of these the "Synthetic Method of Reading and Spelling," by Rebecca S. Pollard, has been very widely used, although its popularity is waning. This method is purely phonic, almost arrogantly so. The author states that "there must be no guesswork, no reference to pictures, no waiting for a story from the teacher to develop the thought;" and again, the "word and synthetic methods cannot be combined." The main business of the method is to make the child able to pronounce words for himself as he comes to them in reading new matter, and it accomplishes this result pretty effectually.

In its long "Johnny Story," which is told to the child section by section, Johnny goes to the country and hears the dog growl *rr*, the frog croak *ǧ*, the train puff *ch*, etc., seeing all sorts of performances and objects which suggest the elementary sounds and printed characters and which become associated with them. An interminable list of letter-sounds is thus woven into the story, with the diacritically marked characters representing each. The following extract[1] from the "Johnny Story" will illustrate the process: —

"But about this sound which Johnny calls 'a pant.' Here are the letters which stand for it, 'breath letters,' h = H. When you make these scales, breathe out in this way, h = H. Breathe very gently. Notice, too, that both teeth and lips are open. Now why is not this a voice letter?"

"Oh!" said Johnny, "because we just breathe out its sound."

"Yes, that is just the reason. Remember, you are not to sound *hŭ*, but just breathe out easily and run the sound into the next letter; as, *hit*, *hem*, *how*. You may think little *h* is the picture of the chair Bess sits in when she is very tired. As she sits down she breathes hard, *h*, *h*, *h*."

"How much this little fellow changed when he grew up! I should not suppose these were the same letters, h = H. Perhaps the large one stands for the tired *man's* pant and the small one for the *baby's*, or the little dog's hard breathing."

CHAPTER VIII

"There are pigeons at the barn, mamma. What letter stands for the sound they make?"

"This one: d = D. It is a sound made by young pigeons. You may outline these pigeons and sound as you print each d."

"This sound presses the tongue up, near its point, a little harder than *n*. Try the two together, *n*, *d*, *n*, *d*."

"I can scarcely hear that sound when you make it."

"No, you can not. It is, besides, a hard sound to make, but I think it sounds like the young pigeon's cry. As *d* stands for what the young pigeons say, you may just think how those two little fellows will talk when the eggs are hatched. It will be *d*, *d*, *d*, then."

---

[1] Reproduced by permission of American Book Company.

By songs, pictures, and all sorts of personifications, these associations are drilled in. The children diacritically mark the words in their spellers and readers; they form words from the letters, sometimes with a rotary machine; they learn the long families of words like *bake, cake, lake, take*, of the *-ake* family, *back, lack, hack*, of the *-ack* family, etc. There are many rules to be learned and more exceptions to rules. The pupil is to be kept constantly busy printing and marking letters, making words, learning the voice-letters, lip-letters, and what not else. The vocal organs are described to him and he learns the position of the articulatory organs for the various sounds. Everything is personified and suited to the child's imaginative interest so far as possible. The small letters are boys that grow to be men and become capital letters, sometimes changing their appearance entirely. Each letter is a non-talking baby and the child must be mamma and talk for him, interpreting what he wants to say. The *c* sound is such as when the fishbone troubled Johnny, and so on endlessly.

Granting the care and completeness with which the method has been worked out, and the success which it has met in the "mastery of word-structure and word-calling," it must be pronounced intensely artificial and adult in its conceptions, and destructive of right habits of reading and of using language generally. The phonic elements are made to precede the word, the word is made to precede the idea, and the sentence comes last of all, just the opposite of the natural procedure. Besides, to burden the young pupil with the cumbersome technique of such a method and to so fill his mind with the dead products of adult analysis is a crime against childhood which cannot long be suffered. Even in perfectly attaining its ideal it has not taught the child to *read*, and is most likely to permanently unfit him for intelligent, natural reading.

The "Rational Method," by Professor Ward of the Brooklyn schools, is perhaps the most increasingly and deservedly popular of the present-day methods. It is a combination of the word, sentence, and phonic methods, beginning as a pure word and sentence method until a small vocabulary of "sight-words" is known. The introductory sentences in its primer, it is to be regretted, are most inane and unnatural, and should certainly never be used, as indeed the author himself practically advises. Blackboard work is urged instead.

After a couple of months of the "sight work," the child is taught the sounds of certain easily sounded letters, and of some oft-recurring combinations (phonograms) like -ight, -ing, etc. He is drilled in blending letter sounds into words, and learns to do everything promptly at sight. The phonetic work is kept apart from reading, in the start, and the sentence is never supposed to be read until the child is sure of all its word-sounds. Training of the ear and of articulation go on separately from reading, by slow pronunciation of words and phonograms, thus analyzing them. When reading by phonetics begins, in the third month, phonograms that have been learned are underlined, as in "flight," "going, "and single letters are diacritically marked when this is needed. A larger and larger range of diacritical marks is introduced, and more and more phonograms, as -ick, qu-, -ness, -ful, etc. New sight-words, too, are continually introduced. The pupil thus gradually acquires power to read for himself anywhere, learning the words either as wholes (sight-words), or through knowing the sounds of their constituent phonograms and letters, at least when the letters are marked. The following extract[1] from the Ward First Reader (p. 119) shows the marking employed: —

> **1.** Once upon a tīmé there were twọ little dogs. They were nāméd Jịppȳ and Jimmȳ. They līvéd in a lŭmber yard. It was nēắr the rĭver by a dŏck.
>
> **2.** The mŏther of the pŭppĭés was an Īrish sĕtter. She was kĕpt in the yard, becạuṣé she was a good watch-dog. She was chāịnéd to her kĕnnél. This was a home for her and her childrĕn.
>
> **3.** The pŭppĭés playéd clōsé by. They nẹver thôụght of runnịng away. They had never seen anything but lŭmber. They did not knọẉ there was anything ĕlsé to see.

Fig. 54.

For the early reading the marks are retained, but the child comes to use them less and less as the words become familiar as wholes,

---

[1] Reproduced by permission of Silver, Burdett & Co.

and the mark crutches are gradually dropped during the latter half of the second year, supplementary readers beginning to be used by this time.

The Ward method uses script at first, changing later to print, the author finding that the transition can be made in a week or so of practice. The later reading-matter consists of simple and interesting stories, child conversations, etc., being a great improvement on the introductory matter. The method is well thought out and is comparatively effective. It is doubtless the most usable specific system that is available at present, though it is not in line with the changes to be urged for the elementary school. The criticisms to be made upon it will perhaps suggest themselves best in the later chapters on learning to read at home and at school.

The Comprehensive Method, by Emma K. Gordon, is becoming very popular in some parts of New England. It has much in common with the Ward method, but it begins with phonics. "Thorough work in phonics lies at the base of all rational teaching of reading," the author states. The letters and familiar combinations of letters (phonograms) are printed on card squares which the child can handle, and he is taught their sounds. The sounds are likened to those heard in Nature, as the dog's growl for *r*, etc., and stories are told which bring out these resemblances, somewhat as in the more comprehensive Johnny Story of the Pollard method. *Sh* is associated with the gesture of warning and with pictures of objects that make this sound. Personification is much used. There are the *-ack*, *-ing*, and other families familiar in the Pollard method. There is much practice in blending the sounds and phonograms into words, and much training of the ear and the articulation. Charts are much used for drill work.

So the power to read new words phonetically is developed. Words not phonetic in spelling are taught as sight-words, but are not allowed to appear at first, and sight-words are given sparingly for a good while. The phonic work is kept apart from reading, which does not begin until the second month. The child then reads whole thoughts from the start, and always from an unmarked page. The author manages to get along without using diacritical marks. She claims that after the first few months, "the child who has comprehended the drill

reads easily ten pages a day," and the publishers make startling assertions as to the number of primers that can be read in the second
year, after this drill. The reading-matter in the first book is of the
typical disjointed, unnatural, primer kind which the child should
never be permitted to see. As a phonic method the system has much
of excellent suggestion, but its use should certainly be deferred until
the child mind has grown measurably prepared to deal with these
phonic products of adult analysis.

Funk and Wagnalls have recently issued the "Standard First
and Second Reader," and a teacher's pocket manual for each. These
readers, besides being most beautifully illustrated, are distinctive
in their careful working out of a phonetic method, teaching pronunciation by the use, from the start, of the Scientific Alphabet
as now made familiar in the Standard Dictionary. By the help of
songs especially, and by teaching the position of the articulatory
organs for each sound, the child is trained to associate correct
sound values with the characters of this alphabet, and learns his
vocabularies through their use. The reading lessons themselves are
printed in the ordinary alphabet, without marks, but are sometimes duplicated in the Scientific Alphabet on the succeeding
page, as illustrated in the selection already given. At the end of
each reader is a vocabulary of its words in both alphabets, thus
showing the pronunciation of the words. The earlier reading lessons have a good deal of the disjointed, 'primer' kind of talk, re-
lieved, however, by frequent picture-reading and by short poems,
quotations, and songs. The Second Reader is made up of well-chosen selections from our best literature. These Readers mirror the
high ideals of their authors, and their use of the phonetic system
merits the attention, at least, of all teachers of reading; although
the writer would by no means make such a system introductory
to reading, not at all agreeing with the authors' assertion that "to
detect and produce each of the fifty-two sounds that make up the
spoken English language … should be a chief aim in the first two
years of a pupil's school life."

Reference will be made to some of the other more noteworthy
beginners' books in later chapters. We will now glance at the actual
procedure in teaching to read, in two institutions which may be

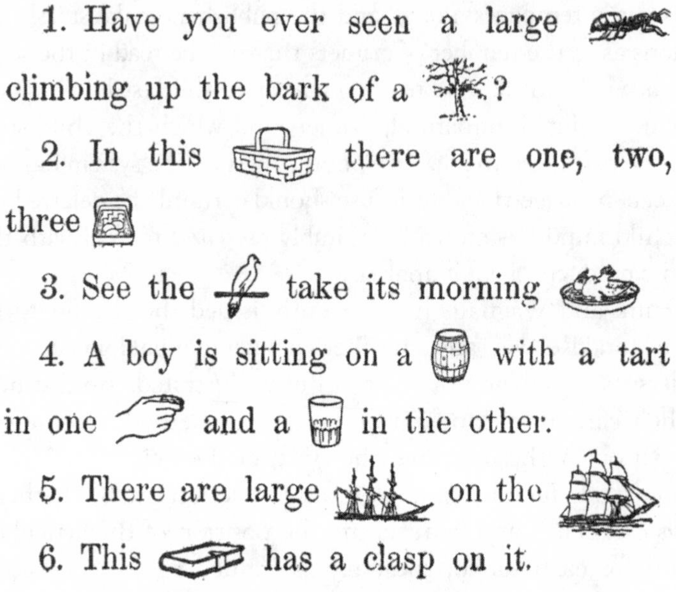

1. Have you ever seen a large 🦗 climbing up the bark of a 🌳?

2. In this 🧺 there are one, two, three 📦

3. See the 🐦 take its morning 🥧

4. A boy is sitting on a 🛢 with a tart in one ☞ and a 🥛 in the other.

5. There are large ⛵ on the 🚢

6. This 📖 has a clasp on it.

FIG. 55.[1] — Picture Readings.

taken to represent the better practice of American pedagogy. I have mainly used data which is accessible to all, descriptive of the work in reading in the Horace Mann School of Teachers College, Columbia University, and in the Chicago Institute, later incorporated as a part of the Department of Education in the University of Chicago. The quotations and other data concerning the Horace Mann School are from the articles by Edith C. Barnum in the *Teachers College Record* for January and September, 1906:—

First Year Work in the Horace Mann School.

"In the first grade in the Horace Mann School more time is devoted to reading than to any other subject, in order that the first steps may be mastered in this year." Professor Dewey's ideal is avowed, and the "first lessons are connected with the work on primitive life," — the cave man, etc. Stories from Stanley Waterloo's "Story of Ab" are printed in pamphlet form and given to each child to be put in his

---

[1] Reproduced from the Standard First Reader by permission of Funk & Wagnalls Co.

book-cover. In this way he makes his own collection of stories. The following is the first page of one of these pamphlets:—

HORACE MANN SCHOOL
FIRST GRADE READING No. 2.

One day Ab was swinging in a tree.

He was nine years old, now.

He saw something swinging in another tree.

It was another brown boy.

"Who are you?" asked Ab.

"I am Oak. Who are you?"

"I am Ab. I am not afraid of you."

"I am not afraid of you, either," said Oak.

"Let us throw stones into the river," said Ab.

"All right," said Oak.

They played for a long time.

Then they went home.

The next day, Ab went to see Oak.

The boys went to play in the woods.

They played for a long time.

"The child is not held responsible for knowing separately all of the words that appear in the lesson," and the vocabulary is "not limited to a very few words," the pupil gaining many words from the context.

"Usually about, three months are devoted to the stories about Ab, and during this time selections are also read from 'Stepping Stones to Literature' (First Reader), 'Child Life' (First Reader), and Cyr's Primer. After this the stories of 'Nino and Juanita' (connected with the work on primitive life), in Carroll's 'Around the World,' are read, also selections from Thompson's 'Fairy Tales and Fables' (Second Reader), and from Norvell's 'Second Book of Graded Classics.' About March the children begin to read Craik's 'Bow Wow and Mew Mew.'" The latter book appeals to the children's interest in animal life, and interests also by its conversational style and easily pictured situations. The children take their books home and read ahead to find what is to happen next. "Mothers often report that their children spend all of their spare moments in reading until the story is finished." In the latter part of the year poems are read "in connection with the literature," each child being given a typewritten copy of the poem, which he puts in his bookcover, making a collection of most of those studied during the year.

The lessons do not last longer than ten or fifteen minutes at first, gradually increasing to half an hour. At first there are two short lessons each day, but only one when the length of the period is increased. The class (of twenty-five) is divided into two groups, according to the readiness with which the children read.

From the first the child's attention is centered on the thought, by proper questioning, blackboard sketches, a limited use of pictures, brief dramatizations, and by using reading-matter that is related to the pupil's other studies. There is endeavor to have the pupil read fluently. Children are given a glance at familiar sentences pasted upon cards and are then asked to reproduce them; or the book is opened and quickly closed and the pupil reproduces what he sees. He is not allowed to point at the words when he reads, as "this habit results in reading word by word." The actual procedure in beginning with the children is as follows: —

Short sentences, in print, are introduced in the first lessons. These are printed on cards by a "Fulton Sign and Price Marker," and when the children can read the individual sentences, these are then arranged to tell a story and are printed upon a chart. Later, new sentences are presented in groups on the chart first, and are then read from the pamphlets; and still later the children "read new stories from the pamphlets without any preparatory chart work."

The first lesson is given on the third or fourth day after the children enter school, interest in the cave man and the conditions of his time having been first aroused. In the first lesson three sentences from the "Story of Ab" are generally learned from the board, the sentences telling part of the story to the children. The sentences are read as wholes at first, but "Soon the children begin to differentiate words, and some child will say 'this is Ab' or 'this is the cave,'" or some one is asked to find the "word that says 'Ab,'" etc.

The context is used to suggest what the new words are, or the new word is named for the child if he would lose the main thought in his anxiety about the word. "A new word is not given until it has been developed in the sentence." "Some drill on separate words is necessary," on words which will be used over and over, but "the best way for the child to become familiar with them is by much reading." The child need not know every word in the sentence before he tries to read it. Various devices and games are used to give the pupils drill on certain words such as *there, where, what,* etc., that need to be learned separately.

The children are likewise given daily practice in phonetics, but not as a part of the reading lessons, "for phonetics are of little value in reading until the child has gained some proficiency in getting separate words rapidly. If this method is used too soon, it results in word reading, as it takes so long to get the word that the thought is lost." When the children once know the sounds of the letters, they are "encouraged to use the initial sound together with the content of the sentence in getting new words."

The work in phonetics leads to clear and distinct enunciation. In the first lesson *f* is taught by pronouncing to the children words beginning with this sound. The children then give words beginning with the same sound, a card with the printed *f* is kept before them, and from time to time the children give its sound. So all the consonants are treated. After four or five have been taught they are combined with *an, at,* etc. The short vowel sounds are taught, then the long. The children find that such words as *mate,* ending in *e,* have the long sound, but that such words without the *e,* as *mat,* have the short sound. No diacritical marks are used. "By the end of the first year the child should be able to get by the sound words of one syllable, made up of regular long and short vowels, consonants, and simple combinations of consonants, as *th, sh, wh,* etc."

"It is apparent that no one method, as the sentence method, the word method, or the phonetic method, is followed. We believe that the teacher must use any method that seems to meet the needs of the child, and that one teacher may give her pupil the power of gaining thought and help him to form right habits in reading in one way, while another teacher may do the same thing by an entirely different method."

Second Year

In the second year the pupils read such books as Haliburton and Nowell's Graded Classics, Books II and III, or Baker and Carpenter's "Second Year Language Reader," or Baldwin's "Fairy Tales and Fables;" Wiley and Edick's "Children of the Cliff" and "Lodrix," Dutton's "In Field and Pasture." They read a great deal this year for the sake of practice. Much of the reading is easy, is read but once, and without much delay for comment. Favorite stories and poems are chosen by the children to be read several times. Children bring books from home to read to the others, or the teacher reads them parts of stories, leaving the children to finish for themselves.

In the second year phonetics deals principally "with the sounds of many combinations of letters, such as *oa, ea, ai, er, ir, ur, or, ar, ay, ight, kn, wr, sc, tch, ow, on,* and *th*." For instance, the teacher pronounces *thick, thin, think,* etc., and the children listen to the first sound. Then words containing it are written on the board and pronounced.

Phonetics is still kept apart from reading, though there is often phonetic practice on the new words of the day's reading lesson. The danger of reading words rather than ideas is especially great in this year, and to prevent this "a child must be fairly sure of the words and the thought in a paragraph before attempting to read it aloud." Silent reading is encouraged, and there is much reading *to* the children, and some dramatization. Many poems are memorized.

Third Year

In the third year the child's interest is best held by the "long story," or by a series of stories in which the same characters appear. Easy reading need not be sought, as "a child who is plunged in an interesting tale reads on in his eagerness to find out what happens next." Correlation with other subjects is now of "secondary importance," as this results in inferior literature when carried to an extreme. "Hiawatha," "Alice in Wonderland," and "Through the Looking Glass," Cook's "Story of Ulysses," and Brown's "In the Days of Giants," are read in this grade. There is much reading from a number of other books and poems. "No time is taken from the reading in developing difficult words, in the so-called preparation for the lesson.

The pupil gets the new word from the context, or it is pronounced for him and briefly commented upon in passing." "Sometimes a preliminary talk is necessary in order that the children may feel the atmosphere of the story, but the less analysis the better."

"In this year's work, the apparent gain in reading may not be as great as in preceding years, but the pupils have definitely formed a habit of reading, so that they voluntarily read at home." They have learned to give pleasure in the home-circle by reading aloud, and their tastes have been directed toward making a conscious distinction between good and poor literature.

Reading in The Chicago Institute and in the Francis W. Parker School

The work of the Chicago Institute, representing also, in the main, the present practice of the Francis W. Parker School in Chicago, is well presented in the articles by Miss Flora Cooke in the *Elementary School Teacher* for October, 1900, and April, 1904. In this Chicago work the children learn to read as they learned to talk, "from a desire to find out or tell something." From the child's point of view, learning to read will be incidental to other things in which he is interested. Willing effort is what makes him learn to read fast. After performing some experiment, or perhaps after working in the garden or observing things in nature, the children gather to tell what has been done, and the teacher writes their statements on the board. They read and correct their own statements, and often these are printed by some of the older children and returned as a printed story of what has happened. The child can read these, knowing the gist of it already, and takes the printed account, perhaps, to read to his parents at home. Below is a selection from one of these children's stories of a trip to a farm, the story being illustrated by photographs taken during the trip: —

READING LESSON ON THE FARM AT THORNTON

October 2, 1897, we went to visit a farm.

It was a beautiful day.

There was a deep blue sky above us, with not a cloud in it, and cool, fresh air around us.

We had bright sunshine all day long.

"The nicest day of all the year!" said Fritz.

The farm we visited is 15 miles from our school.

It is on Halsted Street.

We might have gone all the way in wagons, but that was too slow for us.

It only took us 42 minutes to go on the train.

Then we were only one mile and a half from the farm.

Big hay-wagons were waiting for us at the station.

Oh, what fun we had going to the farm!

We passed a big limestone quarry.

We wanted to see it, but we could not stop for that.

We passed some beautiful oak woods.

We wanted to gather leaves, but we could not stop for that.

We passed a great yard full of horses and colts.

The story goes on relating the adventures of the day, with photographs of the barn, stacks, cattle, pigs; of the children themselves in the wood, of chopping down trees, of stacked wheat, etc. Along with this story of their own trip, the teacher and children read printed accounts of other farm visits made by earlier grades, and compare their experiences. The knowledge that other children are to read their own account gives a stimulus to good expression. The children draw or suggest illustrations for making the story clearer to readers. The motive in reading the lesson when printed is to live over the day's experiences again, to see if anything important has been left out, and to see if the account is such as will interest mamma or absent children.

The child's reading vocabulary is allowed to grow with his experience. As a new word is used in a discussion about garden soils, the word is written on the board and is pointed to, but not spoken, when used later. Its visual form is thus impressed by use. The child may make a little index dictionary of these new words. Diacritical marks are not used appreciably until the third grade, and they are learned then to permit the use of the dictionary. Some work is done in phonics, but this is entirely distinct from reading. The purpose in phonics is to teach the child to associate certain sounds with certain forms, and

also "to strengthen his vocal organs," and so to lead "to clear enunciation and good pronunciation." The work is usually done in games
which involve slow pronunciation, and in using Mother Goose ditties
and other rhymes. As reading power develops, such stories as that of
the Pilgrims are printed on leaflets and partially told, the new words
being written on the board, until a very interesting place is reached,
when the teacher sometimes says: "The rest of that story is here on this
leaflet; find out what it says and tell us on the blackboard." Miss Cooke
adds, "It has been our experience that when a real desire for reading
has been awakened, the children have not been willing to stop until
they have read the entire leaflet for themselves."

Thus reading and writing and drawing are learned in the service
of what the children are doing as a social community. Reading is not
made an end in itself, and does not gather the mannerisms and the
débris of technique that accompany reading done for its own sake
and by "Reading's" own special methods.

In a recent letter concerning this work in reading, Miss Cooke,
now of the Francis W. Parker School, says: "I can vouch, after nearly
twenty years' experience, that the method is a success when carried
out by a thoughtful teacher.... . I think the third grade children are
good testimony on the subject, as they read, with ease, fluency, and
pleasure, almost anything one can put into their hands."

CHAPTER XV

THE VIEWS OF REPRESENTATIVE EDUCATORS CONCERNING EARLY READING

A SURVEY of the views of some of our foremost and soundest educators reveals the fact that the men of our time who are most competent to judge are profoundly dissatisfied with reading as it is now carried on in the elementary school. The objections are made from widely different points of view and for correspondingly various reasons; but they are most serious, and they merit the careful attention, if not the immediate and radical action, of those who have the keeping of our schools.

The immense amount of *time* given to the purely formal use of printed and written English has been a prime source of irritation. It seems a great waste to devote, as at present, the main part of a number of school years to the mere mechanics of reading and spelling. The unreasoned and unreasonable devotion to our irrational English spelling in itself robs the child of probably two whole years of school life, and makes him and all of us read an extra book for every five or six that are necessary. This is well shown in the pamphlet on "Spelling Reform," by Professor Francis A. March, issued by Commissioner Harris in 1893; also in the recent literature issued by the Simplified Spelling Board, New York. But even with spelling as it is, there is a general feeling that there is much time-waste that might be eliminated.

Again, notwithstanding all the time and effort given to the subject, the results too often show only mechanical, stumbling, expressionless readers, and poor thought-getters from what is read. The mechanical reading is thought to come from learning reading as mere word-pronouncing; the stumbling and hesitation, from the over-attention to form as against content, especially from the early and too constant analysis of the reading process in phonics — just as one sways and falls from a log when he attends to how he is walking it.

The poor thought-getting may be supposed to come from the simple want of continued practice in reading for thought. Colonel Parker insisted that oral reading was over-emphasized as compared with thought-getting, and that "saying it over" was the reader's ideal. Practice in abstracting meanings, in grasping the essentials of a page's thought, has been little thought of in the reading lesson.

Along with these conditions there have come premature reverence for books, a blindness to objective realities, and a neglect of own thinking which has atrophied the naïve originality of the children and made them slaves to "what is written." And then there has come the immense increase of near-sightedness and of other degenerative tendencies due to near work and to bad positions in dealing with books and written matter; and there has come, too, the nerve strain from the untimely use of the finer muscles of eye and hand, and from the overworking of the associative mechanism concerned in reading.

Besides, as child nature is being systematically studied, the feeling grows that these golden years of childhood, like the Golden Age of our race, belong naturally to quite other subjects and performances than reading, and to quite other objects than books; and that reading is a "Fetich of Primary Education" which only holds its place by the power of tradition and the stifling of questions asked concerning it. It is believed that much that is now strenuously struggled for and methodized over in these early years of primary reading will come of themselves with *growth*, and when the child's sense organs and nervous system are stronger; and that in the meantime he should be acquiring own experiences and developing wants that will in time make reading a natural demand and a meaningful process, with form and book always secondary to own thought.

Such views take form in assertions that reading, except at least as an exercise entirely incidental to other activities and interests, should usually be deferred until the age of eight, or as some put it, until the age of nine or ten. Such expressions have been made by many representative educators and scientists, among whom I may mention especially President Hall and Professor Burnham of Clark University, Professor Dewey of Columbia University, Professor Patrick of the University of Iowa, and Professor Mosso, the world's greatest specialist on Fatigue. I shall sketch in some detail the opinions of Professors Dewey and Patrick, especially since these are given in conveniently accessible form in recent articles on the subject.

In the New York Teachers' Monographs, November, 1898, Professor Dewey says that while there are exceptions, "present physio logical knowledge points to the age of about eight years as early enough for anything more than an incidental attention to visual and written language-form." In an article on "The Primary Education Fetich" in the Forum, Vol. XXV, he gives his reasons for such a conclusion. While the fetich of Greek is passing, there remains, he says, the fetich of English, that the first three years of school are to be given largely to reading and a little number work. This traditional place was given to reading in an early century, when the child had not the present environment of art gallery, music, and industrial development, but when reading was the main means of rising and was the only key to culture. Reading has maintained this traditional place in the face of changed social, industrial, and intellectual conditions which make the problem wholly different.

Against using the period from six to eight years for learning to read and write, Professor Dewey accepts the opinion of physiologists that the sense-organs and nervous system are not adapted then to such confining work, that such work violates the principle of exercising the fundamental before the accessory, that the cramped positions leave their mark, that writing to ruled line forms is wrong, etc. Besides, he finds that a certain mental enfeeblement comes from too early an appeal to interest in the abstractions of reading.

Again, Professor Dewey believes that the prevalent methods of teaching reading are such as cultivate wrong habits and attitudes concerning books. One can pick out the children who learned to read at home. They read naturally. One cannot read naturally when he reads for reading's sake. Speaking of the "utter triviality of the contents of our school primers and first readers," he suggests taking up the first half dozen such books you meet and asking yourself "how much there is in the ideas presented worthy of respect from any intelligent child of six years." Methods come and go, but all "lack the essentials of any well-grounded method, viz. relevancy to the child's mental needs. No scheme for learning to read can supply this want.

Only a new motive, putting the child into a vital relation to the materials to be read, can be of service here." Drill on form "benumbs" by its monotony and repetition. The child does not want to learn reading as a mechanical tool. He must have a "personal hunger" for what is read. He must come, too, to his reading with personal experience with which to appreciate it.

Slavish dependence upon books, with real inability to use them effectively, "is one of the results of the present ideal. Students can't see for themselves, accordingly. They ask for a book at once, if told to study an object. It shows enfeeblement from the 'book habit.'" And yet, with all the dependence upon books, we find that students cannot *use* books effectively, cannot get the point, cannot make synopses, get the characteristic, etc. Students that are considered good students are deficient here, and wrong habits of reading are at the bottom of it.

Reading must be postponed. The child is motor at the period when we teach him to read, and must not do this passive thing so much. There are writing, drawing, music, painting, modeling, etc., for the earlier years, and nature study. Manual training and work belong here. However, Professor Dewey thinks that suddenly to "throw out" the language work from the early grades would be a mistake. Present educational ways must be a compromise. The schools generally cannot completely change until experiment schools, now on the frontier, work out best ways. The hope of the educational world is for such work from experiment schools.

Professor Patrick reviews the situation in an article in the *Popular Science Monthly*, January, 1899, under the title "Should Children under Ten learn to Read and Write?" He raises the question whether reading and writing, any more than logic, are studies for the young child. Most States admit children to school at six years, more than one-third admit them at five. In a general way, during the first four years, the principal subjects are reading, writing, and arithmetic. In the first and second grades of the Chicago schools, for instance, of 1350 minutes of school work per week, reading gets just half, writing gets 75, mathematics gets 225. Seventy-two per cent of the total time goes to these three subjects, and the same percentage holds for the third grade. In the fourth grade the per cent is over fifty. Other cities usually give still more time to the three R's. Country schools are still worse, giving nearly all.

Now we do this, Professor Patrick thinks, because our grandfathers did it. There is no psychological basis for the course of study as yet. The Committee of Fifteen concluded that "learning to read and write should be the leading study of the pupil in his first four years of school." The Committee expressed present general opinion. With the Greeks, on the other hand, music and gymnastics were the principal subjects instead, and their system gave excellent results. The nervous and muscular systems of the child indicate that he should not read and write so early. The fine movements of eyes and fingers are for later times. Confinement to a seat and desk is bad for the child. His brain activity is sensory and motor but not central. So he should learn to sense and perceive objects, real things, not dealing mainly with symbols. Nature study is wanted. The child has retentiveness and may study history, but from the lips of a narrator. History taught in this way may begin here with profit.

From five to ten is the "habit-forming epoch," "the time to teach the child to do easily and habitually a large number of useful things," the time to teach "habits of conduct, various bodily activities, and correct habits of speech, expression, and singing." The fine coördinations should not be put before the coarser ones. "There are, at any rate, three subjects which are strikingly adapted to this period; namely natural science, history, and morals," using the terms with latitude and restriction. Mathematics in every form, he thinks, is a subject "conspicuously ill-fitted to the child mind."

There are great truths in the recapitulation theory, and reflection, reading, writing, reasoning, voluntary attention, etc., came late to the race and should not be hurried in the child. To make him read and write first is like insisting that he walk before he creep.

"The language of the child, like that of the primitive man, is the language of the ear and tongue. The child is a talking and hearing animal. He is ear-minded. There has been in the history of civilization a steady development toward the preponderating use of the higher senses, culminating with the eye." "An adult civilized man is now strongly eye-minded." The Greeks had a "decided relative ear-mindedness." Laboratory researches tend to confirm the recapitulation theory here. "It is the spoken language which belongs to the elementary school." "The ear is the natural medium of instruction for young children." All second-hand knowledge should come to the child "from the living words of the living teacher or parent, not through the cold medium of the printed book." In the elementary school, the child may be instructed "in language as it relates to the ear and the tongue, and this is the real language." Teach him to speak accurately and elegantly and to listen and remember. Study the best literature of the mother-tongue and get living sympathetic knowledge of it, "such as can never come through the indirect medium of the book."

"There is no other age when a child may, with so great economy of effort, gain a lasting knowledge of a foreign language as when he is from seven to eleven years old." Reading will be learned fast when the time comes. Valuable time is wasted on it in the early years. Better mental habits would come from banishing books from the primary and elementary schools. Children left at their seats to "study" at an age when voluntary attention is undeveloped "acquire habits of listlessness and mind-wandering" that are difficult to overcome afterward. "They read over many times that which does not hold their attention and is not remembered. Lax habits of study are thus acquired, with the serious incidental result of weakening the retentive power, which depends so much upon interest and concentration. With the substitution of the oral for the book method, reliance upon the memory during the memory period will permanently strengthen the child's power of retention." In conclusion, Professor Patrick thinks that "To teach him to speak and listen, to observe and to remember, to know something of the world about him and instinctively to do the right thing, will furnish more than enough material for the most ambitious elementary school curriculum."

I have given at such length the opinions of these two well-known writers, because they seem to me to be representative of the best modern thought upon the whole matter. Whatever the elementary school course is to be, when worked out for our times, it seems certain that reading and writing are not to be taught for their own sake in the earlier years; that the work of the new curriculum will gradually develop a natural desire to read, and to read for meanings; that it will give own experiences which will furnish the material for natural interpretation of suitable reading-matter; that habits of spoken language being well formed before much reading is attempted, there will be less likelihood of producing mechanical habits of expression, and less danger to speech habits from the self-dissection of phonics, which, after all, will be given thoroughly in its own time.

However, while agreeing with Professors Dewey and Patrick in their belief that, eventually, there will be little loss and often much gain if the child does not read much until his eighth year or later, the fact remains that at present he is expected to know the rudiments of the art of reading by that time. It is also a fact that most children will by that time learn to read tolerably, of themselves, without set lessons or formidable methods, if parents and teachers are only shown how to assist, by suggestion and coöperation, in the plays, games, and other natural activities of the children. Where children have good homes, reading will thus be learned independently of school. Where parents have not the time or intelligence to assist in this way, the school may similarly develop the power to read, while making it entirely incidental to other activities. In the following chapters on learning to read at home and at school, the writer gathers the best thought on the subject that has come to him from the study of the psychology and history of reading and from his review of earlier methods and the present-day practice and theory. The initial cue is taken from the statement so often made by observing teachers that the best readers learned to read at home. The school of the future will have as one of its important duties the instruction of parents in the means of assisting the child's natural learning in the home. The school struggles strenuously with many tasks that parents can accomplish far more naturally and effectively, if assisted a little. The reaction, too, upon the parents themselves will be of the greatest benefit. I believe that all this is peculiarly true of the subject of reading. In the belief that there are thousands of American homes in which the parents will delight to live over again with their children the experiences of learning to read, and that such parents will welcome some guidance from a student of the subject, the writer's own pedagogical conclusions will be given first for the benefit of parents.

CHAPTER XVI

LEARNING TO READ AT HOME

PARENTS who recall their own primer experiences naturally think first of the A B C's; but having heard so much of modern word and sentence methods they are confused as to whether familiarizing the child with the letters will interfere with his reading later. It may safely be said that it will not. A knowledge of the letter-names will of course not be needed for reading. Indeed, one may read very well without knowing even what *sounds* the individual letters represent. However, a knowledge of the names of the letters, and indeed of the fixed order in which they stand in our alphabet, becomes necessary on various accounts, for using dictionaries, directories, catalogues, and for dozens of other purposes. There is no reason why the child should not learn the alphabet, therefore, first as last, but let him do it only in his play, and as it interests him.

The familiar alphabet blocks, with the letters in colors if preferred, still make capital playthings. Tell him the names as he asks, and help him to arrange them in A B C order to match old primer pages that may be about. Let him arrange his blocks into words, if this gives him pleasure, and don't discourage his arranging them into "Gone to Dinner," "Evening Times," and other phrases that he sees and knows and wants to imitate. A few centuries ago, as we have seen, mothers baked gingerbread in the shapes of letters, and the child might eat all he could name. Perhaps even now pedagogy would not suffer so much as stomachs from this practice. Some little ones sing "Yankee Doodle," etc., with the letters in order for words. Such plays, and better ones that will occur to many a mother, give the child his alphabet, once the terror of many a child's early months in school, and give him lots of fun besides.

The child makes endless questionings about the names of things, as every mother knows. He is concerned also about the printed notices, signs, titles, visiting cards, etc., that come in his way, and should be told what these "say" when he makes inquiry. It is surprising how large a stock of printed or written words a child will gradually come to recognize in this way. He should simply be told what the whole word or phrase or sentence "says," with no attention to spelling it or dividing it into words even, when composed of several. Of course he should be shown what the meaning is, if he does not know. He will come to recognize the name of his street when he sees it posted on a comer, and the name of his trolley line, grocery firm, candy dealer, etc. It delights him to find his own name printed or written, and that of papa or mamma or sister; and he will play endless games finding the names he knows among the advertisements, in assortments of cards, on packages from familiar firms, etc. He delights in distributing the mail to the various members of the family, and thus learns all these names and the home address.

A friend whose children know the common birds has charts containing pictures of these birds, in colors, in the children's room, with the name of each bird printed large below it. The children soon know these words, even though nothing be said about it. The Germans print very large pictures of such familiar objects as a turkey gobbler, rooster, horse, etc., each picture occupying a full page, with the name printed large just below. An atlas of some thirty such pages presents words having all the German elementary sounds, and the child soon knows all these words, from seeing them constantly with the interesting pictures. This is the basis of the popular German "Normal Word Method," in which the child is taught, after learning the word as a whole in this way, to analyze it into its elementary sounds and letters, to recombine these, etc. This analysis, however, should not be attempted so early, but the home should certainly have such picture atlases.

Another practice, adapted from the Chinese and Japanese, and used, with the help of raised-letter labels, in teaching Laura Bridgman to read, is described in a most interesting way in an article in the *Outlook*,[1] by Mrs. E. W. Scripture, who used the method successfully in teaching her own child to read. The nursery bed, door, windows, chairs, etc., had labels bearing their names gummed on them, making the nursery look as though it had an attack of measles. The child soon knew the names and wanted to make them. She was given

---

[1] See Bibliography.

a Japanese brush with bamboo handle, ten inches long, and made ink with an India ink stick in the Oriental way. She printed the words large, one word often filling a whole sheet, but soon came to imitate the neatness of the printed names. The use of the brush instead of the pen or pencil allowed perfect play to all muscles of the arm, the movements being free from the shoulder. The child should always be encouraged to use these larger, more fundamental muscles, in the earlier years, in preference to the smaller muscles that involve fine coördinations.

When the names of the first labeling were pretty familiar, these labels were removed, and other objects, implements, etc., were labeled and their names thus learned. Then these were removed and all the labels were mixed together and given to the child to be placed on the object whose name they bore. This was great fun, and the child was soon familiar with a goodly number of printed words whose meanings she knew vividly, and could write them as well. Of course all this was not reading, it was word learning. But it was a preparation which made reading far easier when it did begin later in ways that were just as interesting and natural.

Mrs. Scripture printed the words and had the child print them. The child, however, should be accustomed to the written forms, and these are somewhat easier to make; but the early writing should be much like printing, and in any case it is found that the child very soon learns to recognize in print any words that he knows when in plain script. Since the transition is so easy, it has become the more usual and more convenient practice to use the script first.

And so there are many natural ways in which the child may become familiar with letters, words, and a good many phrases and sentences, with their meanings. The child *will* be busy all the day long, and this is a sort of business that he likes, for part of the time; and if the mother will only help him a little in these ways, and play with him, he will accumulate a stock of words larger than the school would teach him in the same time, and they are apt to be better learned and more useful ones.

Real reading, of course, begins only with the child's getting the meaning of whole sentences. Saying over individual words and recognizing their separate meaning, even when they stand in a sentence, does not imply that he has gotten the *sentence's* meaning. The latter is always some whole thought, different from the sum of the meanings of particular words. *Sying* the words, too, each for itself, is very different from saying the sentence for its meaning's sake, and sounds very different, too; sounds wooden, monotonous, unnatural. It is very important that the child should never practice merely pronouncing words as they occur in sentences; too often he mistakes this for reading, and often reads in this unnatural, wooden fashion all his life. He should always know what the whole sentence means or is likely to mean before attempting to say it, or should at least be *trying* to get or express a whole thought when he pronounces its words.

Many printed or written sentences will be used in his plays and will thus be read, especially if mamma will assist a little. He may have "Keep off the Grass" notices for his play-yard. He will soon help visitors read his "Look out for the Dog" sign, though he may know no single word or letter of it. "Not at Home To-Day," or "Gone to Dinner," will soon be familiar, if a part of his play. Play visiting cards, invitation forms, and various beginnings of written communication will be demanded by the exigencies of the playhouse and nursery, and letter-writing will often be learned just as fast as mamma can take time to help about it. Mrs. Scripture wrote letters to her little girl, which were delivered by the postman and "read" with avidity. The child is usually anxious to help other members of the family read their letters, if he cannot have his own, and gradually comes to know what the sentences and words mean. A successful superintendent recently stated that letter-writing was the best way to begin reading, even in school.

Mothers will be certain to ask whether a primer is to be used, and what primer. Unless especially advised about a choice, the primer should be avoided, except when it is to be used merely as a picture book or for practice in recognizing words. It is important that the child avoid attempting to *read* the sentences of even the most modern primers, except in the case of a very few indeed. Almost all the sentences are foreign to the child's natural thought and expression, and he can scarcely help reading them in a mechanical fashion that comes to make reading mere word-pronouncing. I shall venture to mention a few books that in one way or another will be helpful. Of course some equally good are to be found.

Besides the large picture atlases already mentioned, such books as the "Illustrated Primer" by Sarah Fuller, used in the Horace Mann School for the Deaf, give a large number of pictures of familiar objects, with the names just below each. These familiarize with words, and other pictures show the meaning of sentences placed below each. The pictures, being easy outline sketches, will suggest drawings that a mother may make to call forth children's own sentences about the drawings, these sentences being then written and read. Spears and Augsburg's "Preparing to Read" is a primer which is especially rich in very easy outline sketches.

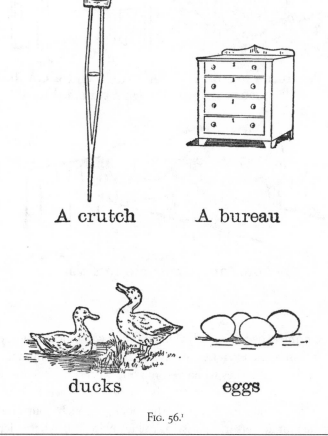

A crutch   A bureau

ducks   eggs

Fig. 56.[1]

---

[1] This and the following illustration are reproduced, by permission, from Fuller's "Illustrated Primer." Copyright, 1898, by D. C. Heath and Co.

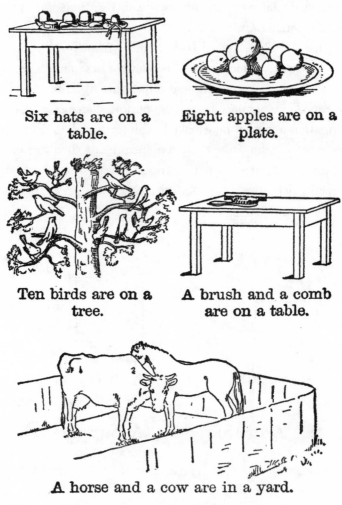

Six hats are on a
table.

Eight apples are on a
plate.

Ten birds are on a
tree.

A brush and a comb
are on a table.

A horse and a cow are in a yard.

FIG. 57.

The primers by F. Lilian Taylor are full of good suggestions, especially for games and exercises involving the reading of sentences. For instance, the child likes to have some one write him directions for some performance which can only be carried out when he can read the directions; such as "Point to the clock," "Touch your cheeks," "Bring me four flowers in a glass," as in Fig. 59 [p. 214], where pictures are substituted for some of the words.

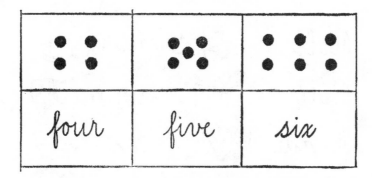

FIG. 58. — (From Taylor.)

As the child supplies the words for which the pictures stand, these words may be written over the pictures and thus learned. Sometimes an envelope containing pictures and another with the corresponding names of the pictures are given the child, to match them in a row. Names of numbers also may be used, as in Fig. 58.

The great value of showing illustrative pictures with sentences, aside from the interest aroused, is in their making the child feel the sentence's *meaning* as he reads it, thus habituating him to reading with expression from the start.

The following cuts illustrate this use of pictures, the first for single sentences [p. 215], the second for whole stories [p. 216].

"The Thought Reader," Book I, by Maud Summers, will be found a helpful one, and there are many others that will be found suggestive without being used for actual reading. The directions about phonics should all be ignored, ordinarily, until the child is much older. The child should of course be taught to articulate distinctly and to pronounce correctly, but entirely by imitation of others; and it is not necessary that he should know the sounds of the individual letters, in his earlier reading. Analysis should not be urged upon him, and he will seldom ask it, for sounds, until a later period.

A book that is useful in a somewhat different way is Frank Beard's "Bible Symbols, or the Bible in Pictures." It is made up of Bible texts and stories with some of the words printed and very many of them replaced by pictures, large and small, that suggest the omitted words [p. 217]. The pictures usually suggest enough of meaning to help the child guess the meaning of the printed words, and his knowledge of

NOTE.—This page shows how the use of outline drawings may furnish a variety of sentences at the time in the progress of the child when he can recognize but few words. Encourage the children to read each sentence as they would speak. Thus: "Roll a red ball on a chair."

FIG. 59.[1]

words grows apace, while the fact that he must always attend to the meanings to get the words develops reading for thought. The older "Book of Puzzles," by Robert Merry, also has much rebus-writing. Such books of picture-stories and rebuses represent the adult writings of the early times, in Egypt and indeed in most countries. It is a stage of reading and writing that is a natural one for the child, and he will make much use of it if encouraged a little.

---

[1] From "The Werner Primer." This and the other cuts and quotations from "The Werner Primer" and Taylor's "First Reader" are reproduced by permission of the American Book Company.

Five flowers
are in a cup.

One spider
is in a web.

Four flies are
on a leaf.

Two pencils
are on a book.

Fig. 60. — (From Taylor's "The Werner Primer.")

I have alluded to the child's early coming to demand some simple way of communicating in writing, as he plays imitative games with his little companions, and to his early interest in letters that come to the family. Picture-letters are his natural resource, and if mamma or nurse will join in the pictograph correspondence, he will soon come to make much of its possibilities. If the boy has been to the country, let him make a picture-story of his experiences, to show the family; or he may want to tell, in pictures, an interesting story that has been read to him. Objects that are pictured often in these picture-letters, such as cat, horse, man, house, etc., will soon be conventionalized, as occurred with the drawings of primitive man, into very simple figures that are quickly drawn with very few lines. For objects that will not simplify readily give him a sign, the written word, that may stand for them. Propose inventing a sign I that will always stand for himself, and other word-signs that are to stand for their pictures and be a sort

Fig. 61. — (From Taylor's "The Werner Primer.") Once a fly flying in the sunshine was caught in a spider's web. The cruel spider, who was watching, started to eat him. A pretty bird was singing on a tree near by. She saw the poor fly and flew to help him out. Some time after a hunter was trying to catch this bird in a net. The tired bird was almost caught when the fly buzzed in the man's eyes. In brushing away the fly, he dropped the net and the bird flew away. This fable teaches that if we help others they will help us.

of secret language that other playmates may not understand, for the child takes a delight in any sort of secret way of talking or writing. More and more written words will be needed for the ideas that he cannot picture, and these words will be made out as they appear in letters that come to him. Sometimes a picture dictionary, Chinese fashion, may be given him, having the written words opposite the pictures that his letters and stories are apt to require, thus permitting him to use the word or drawing as is most convenient. The history of reading and writing shows that some of the early peoples, notably the Egyptians, long made use of this mixed writing in pictures and words.

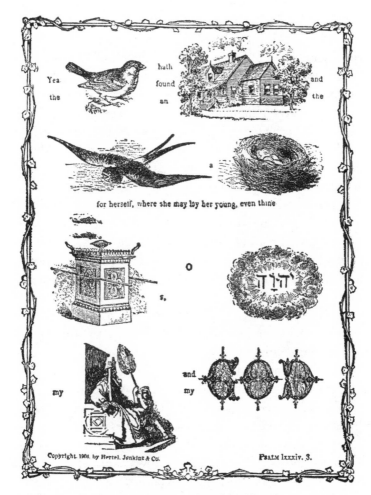

FIG. 62. — A Page from Beard's "The Bible in Pictures."

Such writing and reading as is suggested above will grow gradually and naturally into main or exclusive use of written words, as the child comes, in various ways, to know more of the latter. It is a natural method, too, of beginning to draw, and a method that I am inclined to think will be more and more used in beginning to read.

Thus far I have said little about the child's use of *books*, because I think we should be in no hurry to have him use them. The age is over-bookish, and bright children, at least, are all too soon possessed with a notion which never leaves them that all knowledge lies within the covers of books. Reading, writing, drawing, may be learned and practiced in such ways as I have suggested and in others that will suggest themselves, and may supply all the child's needs for years, without the use of books. Languages, arithmetic, geography, nature, may all be studied effectively, in the early stages, with no books other than such as the children and teacher may make for themselves. In the schools of the future books will surely be but little used before the child's eighth or ninth year. In the home at present the child should be taught to read them only as early and as fast as his spontaneous interest calls for them.

But this interest in learning to read books does come, and comes rather early and strongly to many bright children. It comes sooner or later to almost all natural children who see books being used about them. And here, I would repeat, we have a valuable suggestion as to right method given us by those children to be found now and then who learn to read for themselves, no one knows how or when. They grow into it as they learned to talk, with no special instruction or purposed method. And usually such readers are the best and most natural readers of all.

The natural method of learning to read is just the same as that of learning to talk. It is the method of imitation. Consider for a moment how speech is learned. The infant is born into an environment of spoken language. He long hears the sentences without grasping their meanings, and babbles forth all the sounds of letters and syllables without *expressing* any meanings. But gradually and with no confusion, without "special methods and devices," he catches glimpses of meaning in what is said, a little here and there, and not troubling about the still obscure parts, — getting the general drift of what is said first and the finer distinctions as time goes on. He repeats continually what he hears, and uses it with the meanings which seemed to attach to it from the speaker's tones and actions and the attendant circumstances. So with little friction or trouble he comes to understand all that is said to him and to say all that he has to say. Spoken language is not inherited, and he learns it all for himself in this simple fashion.

Just so, a few years later, he finds that he is in an environment of books, papers, notices, printed language, as omnipresent as was the spoken language. All of it has, at first, as little meaning as had the spoken sentences, and his scribbling is as little like writing or printing as his early babble was like speech. But he begins to be interested in these printed and written things, and to imitate; and the steps from this to facile reading and writing are as certain and as natural as were the earlier ones for spoken language.

Note what happens in the case of the child who goes about naturally in a library where there are books suitable to his age. There is a natural growth in his acquaintance with them. He first comes to know the books or periodicals that have pictures or stories in them. He distinguishes these from the others by their size, shape, color of cover, etc., and brings the right one. Then, as father reads to him from the favorite book, he looks on at the pictures and comes to know the parts of the book that contain special ones. He gets to know, too, the parts in which the most delightful stories are found, and turns to these and begs to have them read. The very page of certain favorite starting-points comes to be accurately located. Thus he gradually comes to a familiarity, in the large, with some books and their contents. When no one will read to him, he often takes one of his books to a corner and "reads," improvising a story, or perhaps only babbling, but "taking off," the best he can, the reading that he has heard.

Some of the jingles and stories read to him become so familiar that he knows them throughout. He will often ask, "Where does it say Jack," and "Where is Mother Hubbard;" and looking on as mamma points, he learns where various sentences and words occur on the page. He wants to know what it "says" here and what there, and comes to point, with mamma, to the right place as the reading goes on.[1] So, almost as naturally as the sun shines, in these sittings on the parent's knee, he comes to feel and to say the right parts of the story or rhyme as his eye and finger travel over the printed lines, and all the earlier and more certainly if illustrative pictures are placed hard by to serve as landmarks.

---

[1] This method has already been stated, in essentials, by Miss Iredell, in an article in "Education," Vol. XIX, pp. 233-238, entitled, "How Eleanor Learns to Read."

The secret of it all lies in parents' reading aloud to and with the child. To illustrate, the writer recalls a recent holiday experience with a little four-year-old boy who had never tried to read, but who had a new pictured storybook which contained lines about Old Mother Hubbard. He knew the story already, but had me read it aloud over and over again, following my finger over the lines and also keeping the place by the pictures. He would then "read" it by turns with me, and actually came to keep his finger "on the place" throughout, at the first sitting. All that is needed is books of good old jingles and rhymes and folk stories and fairy tales, with illustrative pictures, and a mother or father or friend who cares enough for children to play this way and to read aloud to them. The child will keep it up by the hour and the week and the month, and his natural learning to read is only a question of time. He comes to know from memory a great many jingles and songs and stories, and reading comes the more easily for these. Miss Taylor and others of the best primer writers advise much of such memorizing, though of course it is best done involuntarily, by listening to the readings and imitating. The child likes to hear good things repeated over and over again, and when but a part is read to him he will read the rest for himself. He likes, too, to sing his favorite songs along with mamma, from the printed page, and learns to read these readily in this way.

It may be said that in all this he is but learning to read that with which he is already familiar, and has acquired but little power to read new matter. But after such practice has gone on for some time mothers will be surprised to find how many new jingles and stories he makes out for himself, with the help of the pictures and stray suggestions that he picks up, and how interested he is in making them out. He has acquired familiarity with most of the printed words used in child language, and he meets these in the new story; they help him conjecture what the new words must be, and he enlarges his vocabulary for himself by the use of the context, just as he did earlier in learning spoken language. None of us need hear or see more than half or two-thirds of what is spoken or printed in order to get the general meaning of nearly all. Just so the acquisition of power over new reading-matter comes naturally, by this method, provided the new matter be well within the child's natural comprehension and interest; and he should not be encouraged or expected to read matter that is not.

Of course there comes a time when *phonics* should be taught, and carefully taught, but that task may well be left to the school. Besides, the child should long continue to hear far more reading than he does for himself. The ear and not the eye is the nearest gateway to the child-soul, if not indeed to the man-soul. Oral work is certain to displace much of the present written work in the school of the future, at least in the earlier years; and at home there is scarcely a more commendable and useful practice than that of reading much of good things aloud to the children. Scudder, in his "Childhood in Literature and Art," says there is no academy on earth that can compare with this practice. Thinking the same subject together gives a bond of union which binds the family together; and the most blessed memories of many of us cluster about the spell which held us as we listened time and again to mother or father or grandparent reading in the dear familiar voice.

As to choice of reading matter, there is no better guide than the perennial interest of childhood itself, which has voted its preference for Mother Goose and other such old and well-tried jingles and rhymes, to start with. These and the great old myths and folk tales. Teuton and Greek, are the rightful heritage of every child; likewise the Old Testament Bible stories, or such adaptations of them as are given, for example, by Felix Adier in his "Moral Instruction of Children." The old songs and ballads, and later the tales of heroes and adventurers, the best collections of animal stories told by writers who know their animals, even poems and stories that are somewhat beyond the child's full comprehension, provided he likes them and calls for them, — there is a wealth of this material which our librarians will advise with mothers about. Care should be taken to give the children the very best, and from the start. The tons of trash that are annually sold, on the theory that it doesn't matter what the young child reads, are robbing the children of the chastening influence of real child classics; which after all he himself prefers even in the start, and which do much to lay in him the foundations of correct literary taste as well as of right ideals of life and conduct.

CHAPTER XVII

LEARNING TO READ AT SCHOOL.
THE EARLY PERIOD

MOST children will doubtless continue to be started to school at the age of six, although a good home is usually a better place for them until eight years of age, provided parents can give them a little time every day and can have proper instructions about assisting with home learning. But many parents do not have the time or the intelligence, and the schools are not yet prepared to assist them effectively.

In any case, whether at school or at home, the young child is to be occupied mainly with quite other matters than formal exercises in learning to read, until his eighth year at least. The articles by Professors Patrick and Dewey suggest the natural bases of a school course for this early period, dominated as it should be by oral rather than by printed and written work, full of good literature and history suited to this early age, but given fresh from the lips of the enthusiastic teacher and talked over with the children, as the best means of forming right habits of English expression while deepening the culture value of the context. Real acquaintanceship with outdoor nature without too much of adult sentiment, well-directed muscular development in free play and in manual work, singing, illustrative drawing, picture-writing, perhaps some conversational work in a foreign language, these and other activities suited to this stage of the child's development will make the school session a wholesome delight instead of a burden, to child and teacher alike.

The child has not at this stage developed the logical and ideational habits that most printed language demands, any more than had primitive man when he used pictographs and gestures. Let the child linger then in the oral stage, and let him use the primitive means of expression and communication as he likes to do; this at least until we have developed a body of genuine child reading-matter. He must not, by reading adult grammatical and logical forms, be exercised in mental habits that will violate his childhood and make him, at the best, a prig. Doubtless this early primary course of study should vary much, according to the community and the station in life of the children. It presents a problem to be worked out in part, then, by each city and region, for itself. Helpful suggestions will be found in various writings by the authors just mentioned, also in articles appearing from time to time in the *Elementary School Teacher*, in the article by Professor E. B. Bryan on "Nascent Stages," published in the *Pedagogical Seminary*, Vol. VII, in Professor Search's book on "The Ideal School," etc.

However, as quite incidental to the main activities of the school, I believe that reading may gradually be learned during these early years without harm to the child and with better results than when made an end in itself. Most of the means suggested as available for his learning to read at home are also possible in his school life. His ability to recognize printed words will grow steadily as he deals with notices, signs, labels, and names printed with pictures that interest him, in charts and books. The written names of all schoolmates and teachers will soon be familiar if used in the school activities. Letter-writing, as advised by Professor Chadwick in the *New York Teachers' Monographs* for June, 1902, will be much enjoyed, using pictures where the words fail, and will gradually familiarize with sentences. Indeed drawing, used as a means of relating the child's experiences and thoughts, becomes a language which most naturally leads to writing and to reading, by gradual substitution of the more convenient word-forms, as already suggested. It is necessary, of course, for this early drawing, that the child have entire freedom in the choice of what he shall draw and indeed of how he shall draw it, although good taste and good execution may be encouraged from the first.

The history of the languages in which picture-writing was long the main means of written communication has here a wealth of suggestion for the framers of the new primary course. It is not from mere perversity that the boy chalks or carves his records on book and desk and walls of all-absorbing interest. There is here a correspondence with, if not a direct recapitulation of, the life of the race; and we owe it to the child to encourage his living through the best there is in this pictograph stage as a means both of expression and impression, before we pass on to the race's late acquirements of written speech and phonic analysis.

The activities of the school life will naturally create a need for making certain records of what is done, and a need for reading these records. Records of the weather, of the growth of plants, of attendance and proficiency, if made with the assistance of the children, will soon be read and used by them. In such ways, reading and writing may be made to grow as naturally and as fast as the other experiences of the child, and will only be used as needed. The articles by Miss Cooke are more lucid than any further directions that I could give concerning the use of this method. It is a perfectly proper and natural method, and one that has shown itself entirely feasible in the practice of schools in Chicago. The children readily learn to read such records of their own experience, without any particular "method"; and if the accounts, whether written or printed, are preserved and bound together, they make excellent "Readers" which the children read with natural expression and with much interest.

Miss Jessie R. Smith, of the Santa Rosa, California, Schools, has published two little volumes of such children's Readers, "practically written by children." I quote from Professor Burk's preface to one of these Readers, "The Story of Washington," and reproduce part of the first story. An illustration of this story, by one of the older children, has been shown on an earlier page.[1]

> "The method of the book's production has been as follows: she first related to her pupils, who were from seven to nine years of age, the story of the hero in the best form her instincts could dictate. Some days later, after the story, its form of presentation, and language have somewhat "settled" in the children's minds, she has called for reproductions, both oral and in written form, allowing the pupils also to illustrate their written work in any way they pleased. She has then made these reproductions the material for most careful study as to essential elements of plot, salient points of interest, and especially the words and forms of expression used by the children. By this means the story has been reconstructed. Portions over which the children love to linger are brought out to the fullest extent. Their words and forms of language, within the limit of grammatical usage, are followed scrupulously. Much care has been used to keep the stories within a limited vocabulary. Less than 750 different words are used in the entire series, and these, excepting the necessary geographical names are all of the commonest use among children."

---

[1] The selections and illustration are reproduced by permission of E. H. Harison, publisher, New York.

THE STORY OF WASHINGTON.
WASHINGTON AS A BOY.

When George Washington was a little boy, he lived in Virginia. His home was near the Potomac River.

George had a big brother named Laurence.

Laurence was a soldier, and he told George fine stories. George wanted to be soldier, too. But Laurence said: "You are too small. You must wait until you are a man."

George did not like that. He said: "I want to be a soldier right now."

So he played with the boys at school. At recess, he would get his sword and call: "Fall in! Fall in!"

Then the boys would run and get in line. They would march up and down the road.

The boys thought this was great fun.

Sometimes they would have a battle. One side had cornstalks and the other side had broomsticks for guns. George was the best captain, and his side always won.

The following selection is from "Old Time Stories Retold by Children," a Reader compiled somewhat similarly by E. Louise Smith, of the Santa Rosa Schools.

THE APPLES OF IDUN.[1]

Once upon a time three of the gods went on a journey.

One was Thor and one was Loki. Loki was ugly and mean.

The gods liked to walk over the hills and rocks. They could go very fast for they were so big.

The gods walked on and on.

At last they got very hungry. Then they came to a field with cattle.

Thor killed a big ox and put the pieces into a pot.

They made a big fire but the meat would not cook. They made the fire bigger and bigger, but the meat would not cook.

Then the gods were very cross.

The children's reproductions of the stories were at first type-written or mimeographed, and were read in this form. They are, of course, all the more pleased to read their stories when printed.

It is, of course, just as natural to discuss with the children an interesting drawing upon the blackboard, and to write and read with

---

[1] Reproduced by permission of American Book Company.

them the statements that they make about the objects drawn. This blackboard sentence method is always enjoyed by the children, and fast increases their vocabulary and their familiarity with phrases and sentences that are in common use. Miss Margaret Wheaton describes and illustrates this method in a very intelligible fashion in the *New York Teachers' Monographs* for November, 1898.

Miss Maud Summers, in her suggestive beginners' book, "The Thought Reader," Book I, emphasizes the importance of children's doing much of this early blackboard-reading *silently*, and urges that when there is reproduction aloud, it should not necessarily be in the exact words that are upon the board. Thus the children in the very beginning of reading come to think of it as the getting or giving of *thought* from what is written, rather than as the naming of certain written words. Miss Summers argues that silent reading, in any case, is the "necessity, oral reading a desirable accomplishment." Colonel Parker, in his "Talks on Pedagogics," argues that "the custom of making oral reading the principal and almost the only means of teaching reading has led to the many errors prevalent to-day." "Oral reading," he considers, "is a mode of expression, and comes under the head of speech." "The serious fault in the teaching of reading consists in making oral reading an end in itself." Instead of this, the aim should be "to enhance thought" in the mind of the reader, for "reading is thinking." We should of course keep in mind that most of the child's thinking is in speech or in actions, and that he will not inhibit these for very long if left to himself. But the practice of trying to get the meaning before stating it, and of stating it in the reader's own way and even in his own words, is most valuable in throwing the emphasis upon thought-getting, and is fundamental to securing natural expression in oral reading.

Sarah Louise Arnold, in her "Waymarks for Teachers," also emphasizes the importance of much silent reading, considering it a most helpful exercise, for instance, to question the children upon the subject-matter in such a way as to necessitate their reading silently before replying. She opposes concert-reading, as tending away from the naturalness of silent or individual reading. "The bright child or the loud-voiced boy leads, the others waiting to follow. The result is a dragging chant which has in it neither life nor thought, and which effectually prevents the natural and easy expression which should be cultivated in all the lessons."

Miss Summers would have the children sometimes read by *acting* the thought of what is written, as in reading such sentences as "Hop, skip, and jump;" "Hop to me;" "Sing;" "Run around the room;" "Toss the branbag;" "Form a circle," etc. "The Primer of Work and Play," by Edith G. Alger, also suggests much of this reading by actions.

Miss Taylor finds that the "silent reading and obeying of written directions ... holds the attention of a primary school," and her primers suggest much of this work, especially games and plays that involve silent reading, as in the example below. She also suggests making picture accounts of what is read, and this interpretative drawing is

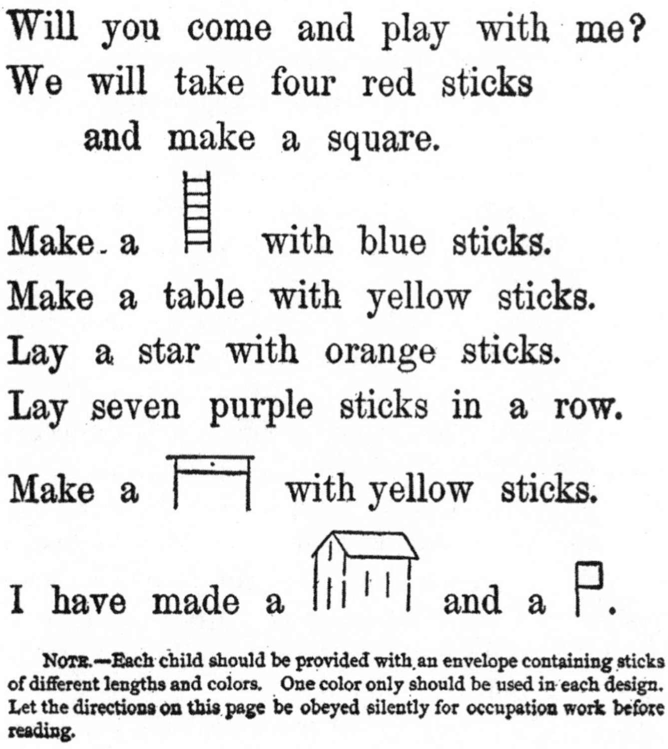

Will you come and play with me?
We will take four red sticks
and make a square.

Make a ⊞ with blue sticks.
Make a table with yellow sticks.
Lay a star with orange sticks.
Lay seven purple sticks in a row.

Make a ⌐─┐ with yellow sticks.

I have made a 🏠 and a P.

NOTE.—Each child should be provided with an envelope containing sticks of different lengths and colors. One color only should be used in each design. Let the directions on this page be obeyed silently for occupation work before reading.

FIG. 63. — (From F. Lilian Taylor's "The Werner Primer." By permission of American Book Company.)

commended by many good teachers and writers. The Werner Primer has much of suggestion on correlating early thought-reading with drawing and with the general school activities, and the book aims at developing silent reading before oral.

In these various ways, the power to read what the child really has need of reading, in the actual life at school, will be gaining steadily, without any forcing or technique of method. He will pronounce correctly what he reads because he will read the speech of everyday life, his abundant conversation lessons having habituated him to correct use of such a vocabulary. New words will first be used orally and will be written as used, giving acquaintance with their forms as wholes. No phonics will then be needed to suggest them, nor to correct mispronunciations; for when the meaning is mainly thought of in reading, the correct pronunciation of everyday speech will always prevail.

But the power to read will be growing, during all this time, in a somewhat different way, through the school exercises in literature. The study of literature should certainly begin with the pupil's first day in school, and his inability to read will be rather in favor of successful introductory work in this subject. The rhymes, jingles, and classic child poems and stories presented in such books as Williams' "Choice Literature," or the "Heart of Oak" introductory reader, will be listened to with wonder and rapt attention when told or read aloud by the teacher, and will bear repeating many times until many of them will be known throughout by all the children. There need be no hurry to have them read for themselves, as the teacher's story-telling and reading to them will long continue to be the more effective medium for teaching the literature, just as it was in the old Greek days. However, if the children are supplied with the books, they will delight to follow along with the teacher in the readings, especially if abundant illustrations help them to keep the place. Sometimes the teacher's copy is a chart which all can see, following the pointer or pictures as the reading progresses, thus becoming familiar with the printed sentences, phrases, and words.

Once children *know* a poem or a story, it is surprising how quickly they can locate its parts on the printed page, and read it. Accordingly, in the books by Miss Taylor, Miss Arnold, and other

successful primer writers, teachers are urged to make much of memorizing poems, especially, as an excellent means of learning to read.
Songs are readily learned and read in this way. There is no need,
usually, of assigning such learning as a special task. If the oral work is
well done, and if there is as much of it as there should be, the choicest
things in the classics for children will work their own way into their
memories; and the intrinsic pleasure of recognition is well illustrated
in the delight which children take in matching these memories with
what they can find in the selection as printed. Miss Mary E. Burt's
recent book, "Poems that Every Child Should Know," contains an
admirable selection of these classics. The children will often like to
read their favorite pieces aloud, largely from memory at first, but using
more and more cues from the printed page. These readings aloud
should always be from what is already quite familiar. Miss Arnold
rightly insists on the reading of much that is easy at first, rather than
hurrying on to the unfamiliar with the stumbling and hesitation and
mechanical procedure that come from the latter practice.

It should constantly be remembered that there is no need of hurrying the young child into the ability to read every kind of printed
matter at sight. The premature possession of this power is in itself a
temptation to use it with matter that is wholly unnatural and unfitted for the child, and sprouts the insidious thought of reading as
a formal end in itself. His reading vocabulary should grow mainly
from his daily varying and developing needs of self-expression, in the
social activities of the school. Whatever the children write for each
other's use, either in pictures or words, will be quickly read; and new
matter, whether a story of bear-hunting or directions about making
the new kind of kite, will be pretty promptly made out if it appeals
to an actual own interest, and the new written forms will be added
to the child's vocabulary. Matter which does *not* make such appeal
will long be read with difficulty and will demand phonics and special
methods. But the remedy is simple, for such matter should not be
read, its very difficulty being the child's natural protection against
what he is as yet unfitted for.

In any case new words are best learned by hearing or seeing them
used in a context that suggests their meaning, and not by focusing
the attention upon their isolated form or sound or meaning. It should

constantly be remembered that words are functional, and that their main function is to help express a total meaning which always requires or implies their association together with other words. If the word must be learned in isolation, it should always be thought of as saying something of a total thought. But their most natural and real meanings dawn upon the reader as he feels the part that is left for them to take in the various contexts in which they occur. The best way to get a reading vocabulary is just the way that the child gets his spoken vocabulary, by having the new words keep coming in a context environment that is familiar and interesting, and by trying to use them as they will serve his purposes. It is contrary to all natural processes of learning to insist on precise and focalized knowledge of meanings and functions before the more general use-knowledge has paved the way and given the material for reflection.

It is not indeed necessary that the child should be able to pronounce correctly or pronounce at all, at first, the new words that appear in his reading, any more than that he should spell or write all the new words that he hears spoken. If he grasps, approximately, the total meaning of the sentence in which the new word stands, he has read the sentence. Usually this total meaning will suggest what to call the new word, and the word's correct articulation will usually have been learned in conversation, if the proper amount of oral practice shall have preceded reading. And even if the child substitutes words of his own for some that are on the page, provided that these express the meaning, it is an encouraging sign that the reading has been real, and recognition of details will come as it is needed. The shock that such a statement will give to many a practical teacher of reading is but an accurate measure of the hold that a false ideal has taken of us, viz., that to read is to say just what is upon the page, instead of to *think*, each in his own way, the meaning that the page suggests. Inner saying there will doubtless always be, of some sort; but not a saying that is, especially in the early reading, exactly parallel to the forms upon the page. It may even be *necessary*, if the reader is to really tell what the page suggests, to tell it in words that are somewhat variant; for reading is always of the nature of translation and, to be truthful, must be free. Both the inner utterance and reading aloud are natural in the early years and are to be encouraged, but only when left thus free, to be dominated only by the purpose of getting and expressing meanings; and until the insidious thought of reading as word-pronouncing is well worked out of our heads, it is well to place the emphasis strongly where it really belongs, on reading as *thought-getting*, independently of expression.

It is wise that reading should be rather rapid from the first, — that is, that the particular sentences should be thought at the child's ordinary rate of thinking and feeling. Much halting over the meaning and utterance of particular forms prevents this natural movement of thought and feeling and injures the habits of thinking as well as of reading. It is encouraging to find Professor Ward and others of our influential teachers of reading insisting on the maintenance of a natural rate in the early reading; though many of the teachers to whom Professor James' appellation of "bottled lightning" seems apt need to learn, on the other hand, that the child's natural rate of thinking and reading is not that into which he can be confusedly hypnotized by an over-strenuous teacher.

In this connection, I am inclined to think that diacritical marks should rarely be used upon a page that is to be read by young children; and of course this is the period when their use is most urged, the practiced reader seldom needing them in actual reading. If the child must stop to make the letter-sounds focal, he must necessarily interrupt the natural rate of thinking sentence-meanings, to say nothing of his forgetting all about meanings of any sort in his concern about the sounds as such. If the words of the page are not already familiar and their meaning cannot be suggested by their context or by an illustration, it is simply obstructive of habits of natural reading and speaking to interrupt the reading with thoughts of letter-sounds, which are never normally and focally present in actual reading. If the recognition of the word must be learned by the use of marks, let it be done before the reading is attempted, and with the word in isolation, so that the child will not come to think of such learning as "reading." I am glad to find that the present practice of the better teachers is increasingly in harmony with this view.

Of course there will be times when the new word cannot be inferred from the context, and when it is important for the pupil to know what particular word it is and just how it should be pronounced. In such cases, if he cannot have it pronounced for him, which is always the most reliable way of getting new pronunciations, his resource must be the dictionary or special vocabulary, and a knowledge of certain marks is indispensable for their use. To ask *what* marks raises the whole question of phonics and phonetics.

It is usually stated that phonics has the double purpose of forming correct habits of articulation and of permitting the mastery of new words, either in the dictionary or in the reading-matter. There is no doubt that phonics may serve this double purpose, but neither is there any doubt that it should accomplish its purposes quite apart from early reading. Indeed the studies in the psychology and physiology of speech indicate that any but the most incidental analysis of spoken language, such as phonics implies, is dangerous before the age of eight or nine, and in my opinion the necessities of reading do not demand it before the latter age at the earliest. We know that the first year or two of school, about the time of the second dentition, is one of the times most liable to speech disturbance. And when we know, as we shall see in later chapters, that at least seven out of every thousand Boston children are found to stutter, to say nothing of the many others who are otherwise abnormal or backward in speech; when authorities like A. Melville Bell call schools the "nurseries of stuttering"; when the Director of Physical Training in the Boston Public Schools, after careful investigations, tells us that the elementary schools are "the breeding ground" of the stuttering habit, that stuttering "is largely due to faulty or misguided methods of instruction in speaking and reading," we are forced to say "Hands off" to those who would tamper with the speech habits of the little ones in any way that tends to increase the consciousness of the mechanism of speech.

Nor is it at all necessary that there should be the early analysis of speech into elementary sounds, for the purposes of correct articulation. Those who articulate most correctly form the habits by unanalytical imitation of the word and sentence wholes which are correctly spoken by those about them. Children who have not had such fortunate speech environment still find their best corrective in the copy set for imitation in the oral practice of the school. The elementary school should give endless opportunity for practice in the correct use of the mother-tongue, and particular faulty articulations may well be brought to consciousness until corrected by imitation of the correct form. But we have seen how intensely artificial and adult is the analysis of living speech into so-called elementary sounds, and how unnatural is even the word-sound apart from its place in the sentence whole; and it is evidently still more important for speech habits than for reading habits that the early emphasis should be placed upon meaning wholes, with the thought of the particular utterance always subordinate to the thought of the total meaning. If we would have our pupils taught the correct and effective use of English, we must have them practice, practice, in actual speech, under the school's favorable conditions of speech environment. Over-analysis has been the bane of our English teaching throughout, and it would seem that at least the child's earlier years might be spared for natural synthetic use of the mother-tongue.

It is probable that with any language so nearly phonetic as is the German, for example, the letter-sounds, once thoroughly learned, always play at least a minor function in mediating perception in reading; although I believe that Goldscheider and Müller go too far when they make a consciousness of the sounds of the determining letters a necessary intermediate in perception. But at any rate it does not seem to be so in our unphonetic English, and therefore a knowledge of the elementary sounds and of the characters which represent them is not necessary in the actual reading of what is familiar. However, the wider reading and the use of the dictionary, that may fairly begin after the age of nine, require the systematic learning of the sound-equivalents of all letters, and the learning as well of some system of diacritical marking or other phonetic writing, since the letters themselves indicate pronunciation but partially.

The word-sound may best be analyzed first, by speaking it slowly and in various other ways that teachers of phonics have worked out. The association of the particular sounds with the letter-characters is also readily attained by innumerable devices described in the primer literature. The matter would be simple enough if we could have a character for each elementary sound, but often there are several characters for the same sound, and again the same character may have several sounds. The ordinary recourse is to use diacritical marks, but the systems that are in prevalent use are very confusing. For the present, it is probably necessary that the child should know something of the Webster system, but only the more obvious distinctions should be attempted at first. The early use of the marks should be to call up a sufficient number of well-known letter-sounds to *suggest* the total word-sound, not to accurately *represent* that sound. Accurate representation of the word-sound is not possible in any case, and even provisional accuracy is not to be attempted at this time, by any use of marks. Untimely insistence upon the finer distinctions both as to letter-sounds and marks and as to punctuation and capitalization, use of the hyphen, etc., has often stood grievously in the way of the child's grasping of meanings in reading and of his free expression of meanings in writing or talking.

For the purpose of dictionary reference at least, the "Scientific Alphabet," used in the Standard Dictionary and promulgated by the American Philological Association and the American Spelling Reform Association, should at one time or another be made familiar to all children. The extracts already given from the Funk and Wagnalls Standard Reader illustrate it sufficiently. It should be remembered that this alphabet, in spite of imperfections on the side of legibility and on the side of pedagogical adaptability, is the best system of writing English phonetically that has yet been made accessible, and that it alone has the officially expressed authority and commendation of competent English-speaking philologists. Besides giving control of pronunciations in what seems likely to be the most generally used dictionary in America, a knowledge of the Scientific Alphabet familiarizes the child with the possibilities and with the great advantages of a consistent system of phonetic spelling. Such familiarity attained in the formative period forestalls prejudices; and it can therefore do much more for a reform of spelling than can any propaganda among adults whose habits have set and whose prejudices are naturally strongly in favor of the continued use of the only forms that they have known.

It is perfectly certain, however, that the use of the Scientific Alphabet will tend to confuse the habits of spelling in the traditional fashion. The best spellers can usually give no better reason for their correct spelling of a word than that the right form comes to mind with insistence and is unquestioned. But if the wrong form is often seen, it will also come. Then must come hesitation and an increased percentage of errors. Even the present agitation in the newspapers and journals concerning the proposed simplification of a few hundred words is making many of us unsettled as to which is the traditional spelling of these words.

But such confusion is really to be welcomed by any one who is interested in our real progress in the use of English. When in doubt, the safer way will always be to use the simpler form, and the more doubts arise, the faster will be our approach to a pure phonetic spelling. It is time that American teachers were certain of the plain fact that phonetic spelling is a goal toward which English-speaking people are steadily traveling, although by various roads, and is a goal that will certainly be approximately reached. It is only a question whether we wish to have the immense advantages of such spelling at an earlier day by planning for it, and by enduring, during a perhaps necessary stage of confused spellings, the almost painful feelings that come to many of us when we see a word misspelled.

Those who refuse to use the Scientific Alphabet should adopt or devise some system of dictionary marking which will plainly indicate the silent letters and which will place with each sounded letter that is to be marked some one mark which will constantly represent that sound, no matter what the letter may be. Such a system requires fewer marks, and these marks, having constant sound values, are far less confusing than are those of the systems in current use. The Shearer system, already illustrated, is the best that I know of the kind, and is in my opinion worthy of more attention than it has received from the makers of dictionaries, although it needs certain modifications on the side of legibility. Such a system has the advantage of not suggesting misspellings, visually at least, and of yet familiarizing the child with the use of a strictly phonetic system. It merely hacks the word-trees that are dead, leaving them standing; it gives an unvarying character for each sound, and never represents several sounds by the same character as in the Webster and other systems. Care is to be taken, however, that the child shall not read from a page so marked, although such reading may be of the greatest value to adult foreigners who wish to learn English quickly.

However, all the systems of phonetic writing and marking, often most carefully worked out from the philological and logical points of view, have been conspicuously lacking in revision from the psychological and pedagogical sides. Psychology and pedagogy have now advanced far enough to make such revision quite possible and practicable, and this is now one of the many important problems awaiting solution at the hands of our newly established psycho-educational departments.

CHAPTER XVIII

READING AS A DISCIPLINE, AND AS TRAINING IN THE EFFECTIVE USE OF BOOKS

READING as a school exercise has almost always been thought of as reading aloud, in spite of the obvious fact that reading in actual life is to be mainly silent reading. The consequent attention to reading as an exercise in speaking, and it has usually been a rather bad exercise in speaking at that, has been heavily at the expense of reading as the art of thought-getting and thought manipulating. With the newer and more correct ideal, much that is of the greatest value can be done for the reader in the time that was formerly given to laboriously wading through the pronunciation of the lessons. By silently reading meanings from the first day of reading, and by practice in getting meanings from the page at the naturally rapid rate at which meanings come from situations in actual life, the rate of reading and of thinking will grow with the pupil's growth and with his power to assimilate what is read. We have seen that the rapid readers have the firmest grasp of meanings and retain best what they read. Continued practice in the prompt extraction of what the page has for the reader, irrespective of how it would *sound* if read to others, must result in increasing considerably the average effective rate of reading. And such practice will also develop discriminative reading, and will develop the power to discriminate and to grasp the essential. Pages that are full of meaning, or that carry meanings for which the reader's apperception is not well prepared, will be given the time that they require. But many a page has almost nothing that the reader wants, or only suggests what he is already familiar with. There is simply no sense in reading such matter carefully at the regulation pace. The reader cannot afford it. Such reading costs the reader his time, and one who has been practiced in feeling values in reading will *fly* over such pages, delaying only at the occasional oases that appear in the desert of words. In such cases almost everything is in favor of the rapid reader. Not only does he save valuable time, but having the eye far ahead of the voice, and having, too, a larger amount of what is being read ringing simultaneously and unitarily in the inner speech, he holds in his grasp at every moment a larger total of meaning, and sees each part in a better perspective. The disjointedness of print tends of itself to give an unnatural hobble to reading, and the one who grasps in larger units feels best the meaning-totalities which are given quickly in actual speech, but which may need a long paragraph in print. The contracted speech range of the slow reader simply loses at each moment both ends of the total that is needed for an easy and correct grasp of meanings. It is sometimes necessary to read a difficult passage slowly at first, feeling the full values of each word or of important words. But even in such a case the correct meaning is better appreciated when such dissection is followed by a continuous reading at a rather rapid rate. Of course there are careless rapid readers as there are plodding slow ones. But if the practice has been in *getting meanings* rapidly, and not in covering a maximum number of pages, the rapid rate will not be found to stand in the way of thoroughness. It must be remembered, too, that each reader should be developed only to *his own* maximum rate of effective reading, and that these maximum rates will have as great individual differences as have the rates of thinking generally for these individuals.

With the breaking up of the habits of reading at a dead level of speed and intensity, or rather with readers who have never been led to form such habits, reading may become one of our most effective means of mental discipline. But its value as discipline depends mainly upon how it is done, as in any study, and not upon the mere fact of its being done. There is always the danger that the one who reads much will lose the natural tendency to link action to thought and to feeling. The reader tends to go on reading and to put off to a more convenient season the doing of the suggested deed. The plant that we read about is not there to handle and to care for. The poor people that we are moved to help will be forgotten before the reader finds himself where he can help them. Reading starts multitudes of these impulses, most of which must perforce die because we are not in a position to act them out, and the reading habit doubtless weakens, for many readers, the power to promptly decide and perform.

Doubtless in the early stages of any study it is much safer to learn by direct observation and performance with the objects themselves, and Rousseau's insistence upon the study of things as against words needs constant reiteration and reapplication.

There is the danger, too, that minds will be disintegrated by much reading. The mind which continually passes in review quantities of ideas, impulses, and feelings, without acting upon them and without organizing them, tends to take on itself the shapelessness and disorganization of what it finds in reading. At the best, reading will always have these dangers, and over-reading, or reading pursued mainly for its own sake, will always have some of these results. The natural remedies are, first, to begin each study, as I have suggested, with action and direct observation rather than with reading, and for a long time to read only as actual need arises for the guidance or inspiration of action; second, to nucleate the reading about one's life activities so that it always serves a purpose, so that the reader is always feeling values and choosing such as he can use, while rejecting or ignoring most. If the mind really keeps positively exercising itself and feeding on what may be found worth using, it may deal safely with almost any quantity of any material. But the reader who lets the machinery of reading automatically run through with any and all grists will be found growing to a likeness that is without character.

However, despite the dangers from wrong habits of reading, I repeat that the reading of the mother-tongue may be made one of the most effective means of mental discipline. In the first place, while in the early stages of any study direct observation and experience are better than reading, and the concrete must precede the abstract, there comes a time when overdependence on the object itself cripples the power to think, when the further development of thought-power demands the manipulation of meanings by means of language. The meanings and ideas used in thinking are mainly conceptual, abstract ideas and meanings, and inhere mainly in words. President Hall rightly urges, therefore, that in our present-day insistence on the concrete we are in some danger of arresting the power of thinking, in a stage which is but a preparatory though a necessary one. Certain it is that reading, when carried on as the manipulation of abstract

meanings for the attainment of the reader's purposes, becomes excellent practice in the higher processes of thought. The practice in
silent, *selective* reading, the constant feeling for values and choosing
of what is essential, is of the essence of mental discipline, is golden
practice in the training of the judgment. There has been deplorably
little of such practice, even in the high school years, and the majority
of students who enter college, or even graduate from college, are consequently quite unable to make effective abstracts or to grasp quickly
the gist of what is read or heard. We are not likely to overestimate the
value of such mental training pursued continuously, as it well may be,
from even the earliest days of reading. On every page of reading that
is done with a motive there is the relevant to be set off from the irrelevant, or there is to be the rejection of all as irrelevant. There comes
to be a semi-automatic "feeling its way" of mind among its material,
adding to itself and rejecting according to an ingrown habit that becomes of the mind's very nature. I am convinced personally that the
discipline of such practice in reading English is considerably superior
to that obtained from the reading of the ancient languages. Not only
is there the development of the power to feel values and to choose
the essential, but with proper attention to rate, and with practice
in the prompt gathering of thought and meaning, there comes the
habit and power of *promptly* deciding, of making the selection and the
judgment while the material is being handled, with no loss of time.
This attainment of a proper "pace" of accurate judging is perhaps as
important as the power of judging itself, and I fear that such a pace is
rather hindered by the prevailing practice with the classics.

After all, we get most of our mental and other habits by imitation; and real reading in which the author's meanings are felt, and
felt in a perspective of values in which we actively and sympatheti-
cally follow the ins and outs of his intentions and selections and
associations, and feel his cautions, his fidelity to truth, his accuracy
and method,—such reading cannot but train the mind to modes of
functioning that are similar to his. With this feeling I have, for my
own part, usually been partial to the use of books from the master's
own hand, rather than to use adaptations which, of course, often
have a better pedagogical arrangement. To be sure, this cannot be
made a general rule; but to really read a great book until, as President

Hall puts it, we "get the flavor," gives a higher tone to the whole personality; and it is certain that really exercising one's self in the mental functionings of a great mind at least *acquaints* one with the more effective ways of thinking, and develops them in the reader, unless it happens that the copy has such peculiar individual traits as to make it impossible of adaptation.

In order to obtain the rich disciplinary value of reading, much of the instruction in the subject must consist in teaching the effective use of the library. The library is the reading laboratory, and reading is a laboratory subject. The pupil must be taught to use the catalog and to find the proper books and articles promptly, getting what is needed from them without dissipating energy on irrelevant matter. He must learn to use books of reference and indexes, and to take notes in usable form, to make abstracts, digests, reviews; must learn to do things with what is read and to read so as to get things done. Dr. Winthrop somewhere argues that physicians are apt to be effective readers because they have so little time for reading; and, reading for application in their individual cases, they quickly grasp and retain the gist of what is read in flying moments. Perhaps librarians will sometime be trained to be our most effective teachers of reading, and many of them are so already. The growing practice of having specially trained children's librarians suggests rich possibilities of having the teaching of reading made more effective. Perhaps if all reading classes had to be conducted in the library, the "silence" rule itself would compel a better use of the recitation time; and I am glad to find, too, that in the best libraries the early years are provided for with readings aloud and the telling of stories to the children, giving the literature to the children as the race learned it in its childhood, through the ear, and with the help of an abundance of pictures.

The fact is that school children get little from reading not only because they usually never really learn how to read effectively, but also because, and especially in the grades, they are not given opportunity to read at all. President Eliot, in his address on "An Average Massachusetts Grammar School,"[1] states that "The amount of time given to reading and the study of the English language through the

---

[1] *Educational Reform*, p. 185.

spelling-book and the little grammar which are used in that school, and through a variety of other aids to the learning of English, is thirty-seven per cent of all school-time during six years." Yet he found by actual test that a high school graduate could read aloud at a moderate rate "everything that the children in most of the rooms of that school have been supposed to read during their entire course of six years," *in forty-six hours.* "These children had, therefore, been more than two solid years of school-time in going through what an ordinary high school graduate can read aloud in forty-six hours." No wonder if, as some say, our use of English has been deteriorating for forty years, in spite of our giving more and more time to it. We have had quite too much dissection of small sections of knowledge and of language and much too little of actual constructive use of the mother-tongue. Grammar, linguistics, form, the old age of language, have displaced content and spirit, the professor of English often having only analytical ideals. Thoroughness has often become a fetich, and has too often meant going at the same intensity over every inch of some restricted and perhaps unworthy area, forgetting that just as much thoroughness might be shown in the same time by working selectively through ten times the material, to accomplish some inspiring constructive task.

The deadening effect of too much analysis is especially noticeable at the period of early adolescence, the period when, as Bullock, Lancaster, Kirkpatrick, Vostrovsky, and others have shown, there comes a veritable craze for extensive reading. This interest should be judiciously fed, instead of confining these young people to the usual contracted diet of analytical English and still more analytical Latin or Greek. This time, too, when the language habits are setting, is the very time when the pernicious translation English is allowed to coöperate with the dissection of the mother-tongue in unsettling all that should be smoothly constructing itself.

And yet this is the time when, if ever, the pupil wants life, not death, in literature; when he wants to forage among life's ideals and ring the changes on all the feelings; wants freedom to roam and to look at himself in that best mirror of the soul, the world's best literature. English will not be disliked if the pupil is permitted and encouraged to feed these interests, and especially if his individual interests and even whims are, not crossed in the gratuitous effort to standardize the reading requirements for entrance to college. The best of "required books" are often abhorred by good students who will, nevertheless, take delight in others that are quite as good. At any rate, it is high time that high schools should live for their own pupils and come out of the shadow cast backwards upon all pupils by college entrance requirements and examinations that will be taken by comparatively few. If most of the Latin and analytical English were exchanged for extensive foraging in the world's great classics, all read in the mother-tongue by pupils who have been taught to really read from their earliest contact with the printed page, the conditions would at least be much improved.

Not that better and wider reading will solve all the troubles with English. On the expression side, the excessive amount of perfunctory written work, and technical rhetoric with its excess of formula at the expense of spirit, must give place to far more of oral work, to exercises in using English effectively for the pupil's own purposes. Habits of using the mother-tongue correctly and effectively are formed mainly by practice at a *natural rate*, the rate of speech or thought, and not at the necessarily self-analytical pace of writing. When people wrote as they talked, there was brilliance in literature, and rhetoric to be effective must again become largely what it meant in the days of Greece, oratory, the art of persuading men with the living voice and manner.

Young people are interested in this kind of English expression, if they are encouraged to express their real selves on topics that touch their actual life. And again, on the side of impression, they should hear much as well as read widely, and they are almost always eager to hear good literature well interpreted, however indifferent they may be about reading the same authors. The impression made is stronger and more lasting, and the understanding is better. If reading by ear is more interesting and effective, there is no reason why students of literature should not be given all the benefit that the schools can afford by using this method whenever it is possible. There was a time when telegraph operators read their messages from a paper tape, but the ear has proved itself a far better receiver. We would not think of being satisfied with reading a charming opera from the printed score. The music of speech, too, well repays its proper rendition to the listening ear; and the regular rather than the holiday dramatization of literature may, as Sir Henry Irving urged, yet be made an effective part of our school work in English.

CHAPTER XIX

WHAT TO READ; THE READING OF ADOLESCENTS

THERE remains for brief consideration the question of what should be read in school, and it is clear in the first place that the reading-matter will be of two somewhat distinct classes. First, the pupil will properly read all that will help him live the life of the school, and that will inform him about the activities and studies with which his school life concerns itself. Such reading-matter will review and organize his experiences, as in the Chicago children's printed accounts of their trip to the country, their work in the garden, etc. Letters and other communications and directions concerning the life of the school will be read as the occasion arises. Reading and writing will be, in the little school community, just what they are in adult business,—they will be means of doing effectively whatever is to be done. Colonel Parker urged that reading, as such, should disappear in the study of the "central subjects." Certainly whatever needs to be read in living the natural life of the school is proper subject-matter for "reading lessons"; that is, such reading-matter gives opportunity for practice and for wise direction in reading effectively.

Second, reading from the beginning will be done to feed the child's soul, — to nourish his imagination, his moral impulses, his higher aspirations, for a child has *his* higher aspirations as well as has the adult. In other words, the child should from the first read real humanizing literature. A beginning will have been made in the teacher's story-telling and readings aloud, and the best kind of reader for this period is Old Mother Goose, the rhymes and jingles and stories that are so dear to the child's soul and that have been voted classic by millions of children, not classic because they are old but old because they are classic, the worthless having been allowed to die.

And then there are the myths and folk tales and legends and ballads, through which successive stages literature grew into history and developed poetry. It is the child's natural inheritance that he shall read over this old race trail, and the excellent adaptations of these classic stories and of the Hebrew Scriptures, by men like Lang and Church, give right food for the early period. While it is doubtless unwise to make the child's early reading deal exclusively or even mainly with the unreal, it must be remembered that his fancy is busily playing most of the time, even when he is dealing with sticks and stones and toy horses and harness; and fairy tales and the wildest myths do not exceed the extravagance of his everyday thought, but simply exercise him in more beautiful and ideally truthful ways of doing this his everyday thinking. To insist constantly upon the real in his reading as in his talking and thinking is to make him other than a child and to unfit him as well for adult thinking.

On the other hand, however, the child *knows*, and appreciates *reality* as distinguished from fancy, and he should be helped in making this distinction and in valuing truth and truthfulness by reading much of what is faithful to reality. We have come to have a wealth of true stories well told, in history, natural science, biography, travel, etc. These are of the greatest interest to young readers, and are full of the highest idealism as well. The child's reading should include much of both these classes of matter, and in the main should be done independently of formal "Readers." Many of the old readers had a high culture value through their wise selection of masterpieces from literature, but far too little was read, and the scrappy compilations gave little real introduction to the great body of valuable literature from which the selections were taken. Wider reading is needed, and the reading of literary wholes. Miss Mary E. Burt, in the *Dial* for March 16, 1893, tells of her experiment in teaching reading without "Readers," using "real books" from the library instead. She decided that the reading-book was "of no earthly use," that it "made children timid toward real books," that "the child should never be compelled to buy a reading-book. He should buy only what is desirable to keep through life in a library." She gives the children the Odyssey, Irving's works, Shakespeare, Hawthorne, and later even Plato's Phasdo, Dante, Æschylus, Sophocles, Plutarch, Tennyson, etc. She would have "thirty copies, or enough to go round" of each of these and similar books, for a class, and likes the original books rather than even the best of adaptations. The plan was indorsed by John Burroughs and wife, who followed the experiments; and certainly much is to be said in favor of introducing the children directly to the library.

The absurdity of confining the child's reading to the very limited texts of the grammar school course is most evident in the seventh and eighth grades and in the lower high school classes. The studies upon this early adolescent period not only show that it is usually marked by a mania for reading, but they indicate the unfitness of this age, in interest and capacity, for the usual intensive analytic study of a few standard selections. As President Hall says in his "Adolescence"[1]: "It is the age of skipping and sampling, of pressing the keys lightly. What is acquired is not examinable, but only suggestive. Perhaps nothing real now fails to leave its mark; it cannot be orally reproduced at all, but in emergency it is at hand for use. As Augustine said of God, so the child might say of most of his mental content in these psychic areas, 'If you ask me, I do not know; but if you do not ask me, I know very well,' — a case analogous to the typical girl who exclaimed to her teacher, 'I can do and understand this perfectly if you only won't explain it.'" "School pressure should not suppress this instinct of omnivorous reading, which at this age sometimes prompts the resolve to read encyclopædias, and even libraries, or to sample everything to be found in books at home. Along with but never suppressing it there should be some stated reading, but this should lay down only kinds of reading ... or offer a goodly number of large alternative groups of books and authors like the five of the Leland Stanford University and permit wide liberty of choice to both teacher and pupil. Few triumphs of the uniformitarians, who sacrifice individual need to mechanical convenience in dealing with youth in masses, have been so sad as marking off and standardizing a definite quantum of requirements here. Instead of irrigating a wide field, the well-springs of literary interest are forced to cut a deep cañon and leave wide desert plains of ignorance on either side." Besides, too often, as President Hall says, "the prime moral

---

[1] Vol. II, pp. 474-480. These and the other selections from Hall's "Adolescence" are quoted by permission of D. Appleton & Co., copyright, 1904.

purpose of youthful reading is ignored in choices based on form and style, and a growing profusion of notes that distract from content to language, the study of which belongs in the college if not in the university, develops the tendencies of criticism before the higher powers of sympathetic appreciation have done their work." President Hall quotes with approval the opinion of Quintilian that the simple reading of great works, such as national epics, "will contribute more to the unfoldment of students than all the treatises of all the rhetoricians that ever wrote"; and on the question which remains, as to what the young adolescent should read, I cannot help my readers better than by quoting at length the advice of this our profoundest student of youth, from his Adolescence[1]: —

"At the dawn of adolescence I am convinced that there is nothing more wholesome for the material of English study than that of the early mythic period in Western Europe. I refer to the literature of the Arthuriad and the Sangrail, the stories of Parsifal, Tristram, Isolde, Galahad, Gawain, Geraint, Siegfried, Brunhilde, Roland, the Cid, Orlando, Lancelot, Tannhaüser, Beowulf, Lohengrin, Robin Hood, and Rolando. This material is more or less closely connected in itself, although falling into large groups. Much of it bottoms on the Nibelungen and is connected with the old Teutonic mythology running back to the gods of Asgard. We have here a vast body of ethical material, characters that are almost colossal in their proportions, incidents thrilling and dramatic to a degree that stirs the blood and thrills the nerves. It is a quarry where Chaucer, Shakespeare, Spenser, Scott, Tennyson, Wagner, Ibsen, and scores of artists in various lines have found subject-matter. The value of this material makes it almost Biblical for the early and middle teens, and is increased, from whatever point of view we scrutinize it, for this purpose. In a sense it is a kind of secular New Testament of classical myths. Lancelot's quarrel with Arthur parallels in more modern form that between Achilles and Agamemnon. The skalds, bards, troubadours, meistersingers, and old chroniclers and romancers compare with the Homeridæ; the quest of the Grail with the argonautic expedition for the Golden Fleece; Vivian with Circe; Merlin with Nestor; Asgard with Olympus. The northern myths are more sublime and less beautiful; content predominates more over form; there is more of the best spirit of modern romance, and woman's position is higher. This rich field represents perhaps the brightest spot of the dark ages and the best expression of feudalism. It teaches the highest reverence for womanhood, piety,

---

[1] Vol. II, pp. 442-444.

valor, loyalty, courtesy, munificence, justice, and obedience. The very life blood of chivalry is heroism. Here we find the origin of most of the modern ideas of a gentleman, who is tender, generous, and helpful, as well as brave; the spirit which has given us Bayard and Sidney, as well as the pure, spotless, ideal knight, Sir Galahad. These stories are not mechanically manufactured, but they grew slowly and naturally in the soul of the race. They, too, shape and direct fear, love, pity, anger, essentially aright. The Anglo-Saxon writer never legislates more wisely for the feelings or for the imagination than when he is inspired by and uses this material well. It stirs those subtle perceptions, where deep truths sleep in the youthful soul before they come to full consciousness. Although they have no very definite geography or date, so that such events and persons existed nowhere, they might be realized anywhere. To the mind at this stage of growth nothing seems quite complete or quite actual. The air whispers secrets of something about to happen, because to nascent faculties the whole world seems a little mystic, though very friendly. It is this kind of *muthos* that is the mother of poetry, religion, art, and, to some extent, of morals, philosophy, and science. It is not very examinable material, for it works too deeply and unconsciously, and the best and largest objects of the soul have not yet come to consciousness at this age, but the great lines of cleavage between right and wrong, beauty and ugliness, truth and falsehood, are being controlled, and the spiritual faculties developed. Morals and aesthetics, which are never so inseparable as at this period, are here found in normal union."…"If we have anywhere the material for an ethnic Bible left at the most interesting and promising stages of incompleteness by the advent of the alien culture material brought to the Teutonic races by Christianity, it is here. I have looked over eight of the best known popular digests of all or principal parts of this matter and many lesser paraphrases, but do not find quite the right treatment, and I believe that a great duty is laid upon high school teachers now; namely, that of reëditing this matter into form that shall be no less than canonical for their pupils. Pedagogic art is often, as Walter Pater says of art in general, the removal of rubbish. Excrescences must be eliminated, the gold recoined, its culture power brought out, till, if the ideal were fully realized, the teacher would almost become a bard of these heroic tales, with a mind saturated with all available literature, pictures, and even music bearing on it, requiring written and oral reproduction from the pupils to see what sinks deepest. Some would measure the progress of culture by the work of reinterpreting on ever higher planes the mythic tradition of a race, and how this is done for youth is a good criterion of pedagogic progress."

Perhaps we shall have, by-and-by, such a collecting and editing of this material as has been done for German young people in "Das Deutsche Lesebuch," a ten-volume work of over thirty-five hundred pages. In the preparation of this great "Reader," "many men for years went over the history of German literature, from the Eddas and Nibelungenlied down, including a few living writers, carefully selecting saga, legends, *Märchen*, fables, proverbs, hymns, a few prayers, Bible tales, conundrums, jests, and humorous tales, with many digests, epitomes, and condensations of great standards, quotations, epic, lyric, and dramatic poetry, adventure, exploration, biography, with sketches of the life of each writer quoted, with a large final volume on the history of German literature."[1]

Until this is done for English literature, and indeed always, more or less, we must make our selections with the help of trained librarians, who more and more are becoming ready and efficient assistants and advisers in directing the reading of youth. Extended discussion of the selection of reading-matter belongs rather in a treatise on the study of literature than in such a volume as this; but the few suggestions that have here been made seem to belong here properly in view of the widespread neglect of the real nature of youth in the choice by the schools of what shall be read.[2]

Finally, we may briefly summarize the practical pedagogical conclusions which have seemed to be warranted in our study.

1. The home is the natural place for learning to read, in connection with the child's introduction to literature through story-telling, picture-reading, etc. The child will make much use of reading and writing in his plays, using both pictures and words. The picture writing and reading of primitive peoples has a wealth of suggestion for such practice.

2. The school should cease to make primary reading the fetich that it long has been, and should construct a primary course in which reading and writing will be learned secondarily, and only

---

[1] "Adolescence," Vol. II, p. 480, note.

[2] "The Children's Hour," a ten-volume series edited by Eva March Tappan and just issued by Houghton, Mifflin & Co., comes to my notice as this goes to press. It seems to fill many of the requirements of a comprehensive and careful selection of the best literature for children.

as they serve a purpose felt as such by the pupil, the reading being always for meanings.

3. The technique of reading should not appear in the early years, and the very little early work that should be tolerated in phonics should be entirely distinct from reading.

4. The child should never be permitted to read for the sake of reading, as a formal process or end in itself. The reading should always be for the intrinsic interest or value of what is read, reading never being done or thought of as "an exercise." Word-pronouncing will therefore always be secondary to getting whole sentence-meanings, and this from the very first.

5. There should therefore be much more practice in silent reading than in reading aloud, the latter being practiced not as an exercise in reading, but in the effective use of oral language.

6. Until the speech habits are well formed, the school should have much more of oral work other than reading, than of work involving reading. Grammar and other analytical study of language should play little part in training to the correct use of the mother-tongue, in all the lower grades.

7. The learning of real literature should begin in the home and in the very first days of school, and should continue uninterruptedly, the literature being presented by the living voice and with the help of pictures and dramatization, for a good while, the children reading for themselves as fast as their interest demands. School readers, especially primers, should largely disappear, except as they may be competent editings of the real literature of the mother-tongue, presented in literary wholes, or as they may be records of the children's own experiences and thoughts, or as they may be books needed for information in the everyday life of the school. The children should learn to read books, papers, records, letters, etc., as need arises in their life, just as adults do, and they should be trained to do such reading effectively.

8. The children should from the first read as fast as the nature of the matter read and their purpose with it will permit, but without *hurry*. Speed drills in the effective gathering of meaning from what is read will be very beneficial.

9. The reading of the mother-tongue may be done so as to discipline the mind at least as effectively as in the reading of ancient languages. To this end the pupil should be practiced in grasping the essential meanings, in selecting and gathering from books and papers what they have for his purposes, in ignoring the irrelevant, and in feeling values always.

10. Most of the time usually given to "exercises" in reading aloud, etc., will be far more productive if spent in learning the effective use of the library, of indexes, books of reference, periodicals, in learning to make notes, abstracts, reviews, and to make effective use of these for the reader's purposes.

11. Far more extensive reading should be done in the upper grades and in the high school, as compared with the usual intensive analytical study of a few texts and authors. Analysis generally should give place to synthesis until the college period at least; and especially at adolescence the individual tastes, even though capricious, should be given as wide a range of choice as is possible.

12. The reading and hearing of literature is to be depended upon to impregnate the soul with the race's highest ideals and tastes. To this end reading, as the study of literature, should be of what our race has voted best, or classic, in its successive stages of culture, the child and youth roughly recapitulating these stages in reading interests and needs. The literature of Teutonic feudalism and chivalry and of mediaeval romanticism seems especially suited to the nature and interests of adolescents.

13. Reading of the mother-tongue, learned and always used as a means and not as an end, done effectively and as rapidly as is natural and possible, done so as to serve as an effective discipline, *real* reading, is to increase rather than to diminish in comparative importance among the studies of the school. It will absorb many of the values hitherto set mainly or exclusively upon classical study, and largely displacing the classics will become our most effective means of growth in culture and ideals; just as we pursue the sciences, on the other hand, for information, for control of nature, and for the peculiar discipline which they afford.

PART IV

THE HYGIENE OF READING

CHAPTER XX

READING FATIGUE

READING makes certain severe demands upon the psycho-physical organism, demands which were not foreseen in the evolution of that organism. These demands fall most heavily upon the eye, upon the mechanism of inner speech, upon mind and brain in the rapid functioning of attention, apperception, association, imagery, feeling, etc., and upon the general nervous mechanism. The causes of the peculiar fatigue experienced after continued reading have not all been satisfactorily made out as yet, and the writer hopes to make this the subject of later treatment. Provisionally, we may here point out certain functionings more or less peculiar to reading which condition part of the fatigue and degeneration that is thus induced.

In the case of the retina, in the first place, as Javal long ago pointed out,[1] the stimulations in reading constantly fall on approximately the same regions of the retina, tending to give, as he believes, the same fatiguing effect that is so noticeable in after-image observations. In the ordinary work for which the eye was evolved the stimulations of the different retinal regions are varied and redistributed from moment to moment.

Javal finds, too, that the eyes have much trouble in the effort to make the asymmetrical accommodations needed in near work, especially in reading long lines, when the fixation point is often much nearer to one eye than to the other and the comparative distance is constantly changing. He considers this an important condition of the fatigue and strain of reading, and a strong argument for the use of shorter lines.

Among the more unusual and probably fatiguing functionings of the eye in reading is, of course, the excessive number of eye-movements necessitated. A page that we read in a minute or two has required perhaps one hundred and fifty of these quick movements

---

[1] Revue Scientifique, 1879.

and stops, while the eye in ordinary looking at objects at a little distance would make but a fraction of this number. And not only is the number of these rapid movements greatly in excess of the normal, but during each reading pause the muscles must maintain, with rifle-aim precision and steadiness, a "set" of the eye which will prevent blurring of the letters. That there is in spite of this a certain wavering has been repeatedly shown. But it is perfectly certain that the reading pause requires a much greater accuracy of fixation than would be necessary in ordinary seeing, and there is much reason to believe that these fixations are trying both to the eye-muscles and to the attention.

It is true that whenever we go about, whether walking or moving rapidly in a car, our eyes constantly move whenever we look at objects that are stationary or that have a different motion than our own, the movement being in the endeavor to keep points in the objects fixated. But this movement, at least in walking or driving, is much slower than the reaction movements of reading, does not ordinarily require the same accuracy of fixation, and is of a more free and varied character. When the movements must be rapid and frequent, as in watching objects from a railroad train, they are, as we know, very fatiguing, more so than the movements of reading. Indeed, as Professor Dodge urges in his article on "The Act of Vision,"[1] it is doubtless less fatiguing to read than to look out of the windows, in a swiftly running train. The fatigue peculiar to reading on the cars seems, as he suggests, to be mainly due to the constant blur causing muscular strain in the "vain and persistent attempts to correct the blur by changes in the convexity of the eye lens," and, we may add, by adjusting the convergence. The amount of this eye-strain, of course, depends upon the amount of jolting and vibration. It varies in amount, also, with different ways of holding the reading-matter. To really rest the eyes while riding it will be better, as Professor Dodge suggests, to look at objects within the car, or at any objects having the same motion; and, if the scenery must be observed, look forward or back rather than to the side, and attend

---

[1] Harper's Magazine, May, 1902.

to the more distant objects. Reading on the cars is always at least a little more trying than reading at home, and is a neurally expensive process at best. Readers must not be misled by Professor Dodge's statement that "the eye muscles are at rest more than nine-tenths of the time as we read"[1] into minimizing the fatiguing effects of reading in general. The muscles are "at rest" only in the sense that they are trying to maintain the eye in stable equilibrium, which in reading may possibly mean even more trying work than when they are in rapid movement.

But doubtless the most dangerous artificial condition produced by reading is the great amount of *near* work that is thus forced upon an organ that was planned for dealing mainly with objects at some little distance. The tremendous development of myopia among the peoples who read and are educated and its comparative absence among the others, its usual appearance at about the time at which the reading and other near work of the school begins, its progressive increase up the school grades, and its greater prevalence and degree when the lighting and other conditions are particularly bad, all point to reading and the other near work of the schools as a prime factor in producing this dangerous form of degeneration. The prime cause of myopia is eye-strain, either in the children that are affected or in their ancestors. The strain may occur either in the oculo-motor muscles or in the ciliary muscle, or in both. Javal opposes the common theory that myopia comes from strain of the oculo-motor muscles in convergence, arguing that this violates principles of physics, and holding that some blind persons become progressively myopic. He finds the key to a truer theory in the fact that some myopics have power to change the length of the eyeball as a means of accommodating for distance, instead of by changing the curvature of the lens, and this change in the length of the eyeball becomes permanent. In any case we know that myopia always means a lengthened eyeball, and that muscular strain of some kind has produced it. We are certain, too, that near work is a main cause of this strain. Cohn, in his "Hygiene of the Eye,"

---

[1] "Act of Vision," note.

pp. 46-53, says: "All oculists agree that protracted near work with a bad light is one of the circumstances most favorable to the origin and development of short sight." "In looking at near objects the accommodation is strongly excited, the choroid strained, the convergence forced, and the head bent forward." The straining of the ciliary muscle in accommodating for the near object stretches and pulls the choroid and so induces, near the optic nerve, choroidal attenuation and atrophy. The stooping of the head in near work "produces a congestion in the veins which carry off the blood from the eye. Hence arise irritating conditions and over distentions with blood in the back part of the eyeball, and these may bring on a yielding of the choroid and the sclera." "Short sight is almost always accompanied by atrophy of the choroid, which increases, as has been proved by experience, with the increase of short sight." This atrophy of the choroid at the posterior pole "gradually approaches the yellow spot," and "when once that is attacked by the disease, the central sight is extinguished." "Not less dangerous is the detachment of the retina from which so many highly myopic people suffer," this last being "the last step to incurable blindness."

Donders finds that "in youth almost every kind of myopia is progressive." "This age is the critical period for the short-sighted eye; if during youth the defect does not greatly increase, it may become stationary; but if it once develops into a higher degree, it is difficult to put limits to its further advance. It is, then, in youth that injurious exciting influences must be most anxiously guarded against."[1] As myopia is not only very prevalent in the schools but is absolutely incurable, the importance of avoiding the conditions which originate and develop the disease is obvious enough. It may be remarked that one of these conditions is the fact that many of the children have astigmatism, due to a difference in curvature in the two meridians. Myopia often arises from the strain in trying to accommodate, in reading, to prevent the blur due to this condition. Of course proper fitting with cylindrical lenses will largely remove this blurring and the consequent strain.

---

[1] "Anomalien der Refraction und Accommodation," p. 289.

Near work causes strain of the ciliary muscle not only by the excessive degree of contraction necessary for proper focusing, but by the constancy of that contraction, by what Javal calls the "permanent tension of accommodation," which he finds to be an important factor in producing reading fatigue and myopia. The near work other than reading is not usually so fatiguing or so productive of myopia because the tension is not kept so constant. Of course in the ordinary seeing for which the eye was evolved the tension varies constantly.

Javal finds that this near work of reading is one of the most common causes not only of myopia but of strabismus. The near work is especially harmful when it is continued for long periods at a time. The congestion then becomes very considerable and the muscles are strained to their limit, both conditions increasing the intra-ocular pressure and tending, as Cohn shows (p. 109), to break the tunics at the weakest part, the posterior. Shorter periods of work should be the rule, with complete rest from near work in the intervals. Cohn calls attention to the fact that dispensing with afternoon school sessions often means five consecutive hours in the morning, perhaps with intervals of only five minutes between classes. He urges instead an interval of fifteen minutes after every hour and one of half an hour after three hours. "For the bodily health and eyesight it would generally be better to return to the old arrangement of three hours school in the morning and two hours school in the afternoon."[1]

Next to prolonged near work, especially with small objects, Cohn finds that bad lighting is most conducive to eye-strain, and next to this is bad seats, causing improper postures in reading. The arrangement in which there is a plus distance between the desk and seat, leading the pupil to stoop over, with the resulting congestion of the eye, is especially to be avoided. The desk-top must be at a proper angle and the whole arrangement suited to the height of the pupil. If artificial illumination must be used, the light should be shaded and not too near, the heat from a gas or oil lamp, especially, tending to heat the eye, drying the cornea and causing general congestion with

---

[1] "Hygiene of the Eye," p. 216.

its tendency to myopia. Cohn prefers a well-shaded electric light, as being much cooler than oil or gas. It is very important that the light should be steady, and it should come from over the shoulder or from the side. It is important in writing that the ink should be black and that the paper be placed at sufficient distance. The school assignment of home tasks should be sparing, especially in the earlier years. The home conditions as to light, seats, paper, etc., are often very bad, and much harm may result from doing school work there. It is important that if the children are already myopic, they be sent to a good oculist instead of being left, as often happens, to the mercy of ignorant opticians or spectacle peddlers. Investigations have shown that a very large percentage of myopic school children are wearing improper glasses.

In view of the facts advanced concerning myopia and the other defects of vision, and the evident part that the near work of the school plays in producing and aggravating these, we have additional reason for agreeing with Cohn that the reading and other near work of the lower grades, especially, should be strictly limited, and that the language work here should be largely oral. Indeed we have in the needs of the eye itself quite sufficient reasons for demanding a radical change in the traditional primary course. It must be remembered, too, that eye-strain is in the closest relations with nerve-strain, and that we seldom or never have the former without the latter. The weakening of eyes by the near work of the early grades means the weakening of the entire psycho-physical organism, and the fact that these conditions commonly become hereditary warns us of the danger of race degeneration coming from this abuse of the school.

It is not to be supposed that the eye is incapable of adapting itself, in time, to the artificial conditions incident to reading. Violent environmental changes have been frequent in the course of human evolution, and the organs have met these changes with suitable adaptations of function and structure. It will be so with the new activities that are really required by our complex civilization. There is no need for pessimism on this score if we regard the final outcome. But such adaptations require time, and disaster awaits many in the transition period. When we find, therefore, that the danger is chiefly in the early period of growth, a period that is in any case better suited to active employments, and when we find too, that the danger at all points can be greatly lessened by proper attention to plain hygienic requirements, it is simply the part of wisdom to act upon the warning so sharply given by the myopia and asthenopia which are so prevalent among our young people.

A second class of disturbances which the organism suffers from early reading are those of speech, and these arise chiefly from reading aloud. As a result of two censuses of stutterers, taken by Dr. Hartwell, director of Physical Training in the schools of Boston, he reported that "out of every thousand children in the public schools of Boston at least seven stutter or stammer." This, of course, does not take account of the very many others who are backward, hesitative, bungling, or otherwise deficient in their speech, but who cannot be said to stutter. The causes are often the same for all. Hartwell finds that the period of the second dentition, at about seven years, is a period of disturbance in the nervous system and is a period that is most liable to language disturbance. He thinks that stuttering "is largely due to faulty or misguided methods of instruction in speaking and reading." Clouston, in his "Neuroses of Development," makes "stuttering and backwardness of speech" one of the prominent neuroses liable to occur in this early period, and remarks that "it is during this very period that most children enter school, and are launched upon intellectual pursuits by being taught the rudiments of the art of reading aloud." This takes attention and mental effort, and "it is a comparatively easy matter to induce stammering among Abecedarians." A. Melville Bell, the well-known "inventor of vis-ible speech," called schools the "nurseries of stuttering," and wrote in 1866 that "with a proper initiatory training and school surveil-lance, stammering and its train of silent errors would be altogether unknown." Hartwell calls the elementary schools "the breeding ground" of the stuttering habit. He found a "marked increase of stut-tering among pupils of the primary schools as compared with pupils in the kindergartens," and thinks it "highly significant that the amount of stuttering, both in boys and girls, is greatly augmented at the very time when instruction in reading aloud is begun." It may be remarked, by the way, that from three to four times as many boys as girls are found to stutter habitually.

Hartwell finds that "any one or all of the organs concerned in producing speech may be affected in one who stutters," but that "the respiratory muscles are almost certain to be at fault." Unless these are set right the work on the throat and mouth muscles seems to be "largely wasted." He finds that those most successful in curing stuttering have "instinctively" begun with gymnastic exercises of the breathing muscles, and later have developed phonation, then articulation, — from fundamental to accessory. The means of cure suggest the means of prevention, and Hartwell is doubtless right when he urges that free play and gymnastics will prevent much of it. He dwells on the importance of building up the fundamental system of muscles before working hard with the peripheral muscles, with the eyes, the articulatory apparatus, the fingers, etc. "The highest level centers, in the cortex of the brain, represent the most special, precise, elaborate, and varied of our peripheral muscles," and these, as Flechsig shows, cannot function so early as the centers for the more fundamental movements. We are thus reminded again of the necessity of making the early work of the school largely motor, with little fine work of the fingers or eyes or speech organs.

Of course in the case of the speech organs the danger is not from the exercise of the muscles themselves, but from the attempts to control them through the higher centers. Prevalent methods in phonics and in teaching to pronounce and to read aloud call the child's attention to the particular movements and processes concerned in speaking, and this consciousness of the "how" of speaking arises whenever, in reading or talking, the thought is directed to anything else than meanings. Any analytic work of this sort, done before the speech habits have well set, brings in its train the abnormal functionings that always attend the attempts of consciousness to tamper with processes which are meant to function automatically.

Doubtless the most unusual functionings upon which the psycho-physical organism has fallen in reading are those of mind and brain. Reading fatigue is mainly fatigue of mind and not of eye, though the eye-movements and tensions and over-stimulations are conditioning factors in this fatigue, just as movements of one sort or another probably condition all mental activity. We know how frequently and how closely mental and neural exhaustion is correlated with painful vision and especially with difficulty in reading. Over-use of the eyes in reading and in other near work brings with it a reduction of the general stock of nerve energy such as results from over-use of the mind. Doubtless the nervous mechanism which functions in vision, and especially in the vision of reading, is involved as well in many of the more general functionings of mind, and especially in many of the mental processes that go on in reading. The fatigue, therefore, of mind and eye mutually condition each other, some, at least of the fatigue that seems to be purely of the mind being due to the abnormal or excessive functionings of the eye, — functionings which, however, may never come to consciousness as such, even when abnormally performed.

However, much of the mental fatigue that comes from reading is conditioned otherwise than by the work of the eye. One of the most important characteristics of the mind's work in reading is the unusual amount of attention that is required. There is a certain constant "set" of the mind upon the book or upon the general procedure in reading, having, as its bodily basis (and Ribot and the other analysts of the attention have shown that attention always has certain muscular adjustments and tensions as its basis), certain tensions of the muscles of the neck and head and eye, doubtless with others that are basal to maintaining the mental attitude characteristic of reading. We notice the presence and volume of this attention set when we involuntarily relax and perhaps sigh, yawn, and feel general relief after a period of continuous reading.

Besides this general set of the attention, there is a continued succession of particular sets and quick changes of the attention as the mind fastens upon one after another of the "total ideas" expressed in the sentences read. The attention is mainly upon these total idea-meanings, but these are different with every sentence, and often have sharply varying phases with the sentence's subdivisions as well. Now to be conscious of things focally, to attend, is a normal functioning of mind, practiced in ordinary activities without special fatigue. But in reading, these successive sets of the attention are so very numerous, are forced upon the mind at such a pace, that they must sooner or later become fatiguing. Besides the fatigue due to the rapid succession of apperceptive-attention acts concerned in apprehending the meanings, a certain variable amount of consciousness attends the rapidly succeeding acts of looking at the line itself. The extent to which consciousness concerns itself with the actual "looking," and consequently the extent to which reading fatigue is due to these visual attention-acts, varies with readers and with subject-matter. Normally this visual "looking" should be largely automatic, except when we are dealing with some special kinds of subject-matter, and of course supposing that the matter is properly printed. But it is a fact that very many readers are much concerned with the mere visual looking at the line, and the rapid succession of attention-acts thus necessitated is an important condition of their fatigue in reading. There is no doubt that for all readers the rapid succession of eye-movements and pauses, though unconscious in themselves, condition somewhat a general state of mental tension or attention, fluctuating perhaps somewhat with the movements and pauses, and tending to fatigue when long continued. Besides, reading involves certain general forms of mental as well as physical activity and attitude, in addition to the general set of the attention which we have mentioned, which repeat themselves constantly and are doubtless wearing by their very monotony.

The pace at which mental content moves in reading, and the large amount of mental content which is aroused from moment to moment, furnish additional conditions of reading fatigue. There is a continual shifting and resetting of the kaleidoscope of imagery, feeling, and motor attitude, with a rapidity of the flow of associations, verbal in the main, that is unparalleled in the ordinary life of observation and action for which mind was developed. Not only must a really vast amount of mental machinery function in the mental construction of the words upon any page, in their visual, motor, and auditory elements and in their meaning implications, but a still larger number of words must be sub-aroused, almost to the point of actual construction, as associative expectancy points in their direction before the particular form appears. Large portions of the mind's total vocabulary may thus have to keep "fired up," in reading certain classes of matter, and the total quantity of psycho-neural functioning

is thus much in excess in reading. The fact that the content is mainly verbal doubtless contributes all the more to the fatigue. Words,
as Stout so well shows in his Analytical Psychology, are the most
admirable instruments for thinking because they are susceptible of
such nice and rapid control; but this very *nicety* of control makes it
"near work" for the mind, and as fatiguing as all finely discriminative work tends to be. Words, too, are conceptual, abstract, and their
use in reading involves more or less of the fatigue that comes with
continued use of highly generalized experience.

The rapidity with which such thinking may be done is a source of
illusion as to the amount of energy that is being expended, and thus
becomes a source of danger from fatigue. In reading, thought may
run with "seven league boots," and we are apt not to have the natural
reminders when the mind has done enough. Of course such thinking is far less fatiguing for its being a game of "follow your leader,"
and much more of it can be done with safety than when the mind
must blaze its own trail. But many sympathetic readers read almost
as actively and constructively as though doing the thinking on their
own initiative, and for them reading is quickly though often insidi-
ously reductive of nervous energy. In cases of nerve exhaustion, with
this type of reader, the feelings of head strain and of being wrought
up with nervous tension come quickly on attempting to read, and are
especially aggravated by doing hurried reading. The trouble is often
referred mainly to the eyes, and much time and money are wasted in
attempting to correct these. Eye fatigue and mind fatigue here have
their common denominator in nerve exhaustion. We must remember that, even for all classes of readers, reading even at its best and
pleasantest requires the expenditure of much energy and is reductive
of nerve reserve. Though often a helpfully recreative employment,
it lacks the freedom and the rejuvenating effect of free play. Our
organism is always working at a considerable expense while taking
such recreation.

I have elsewhere urged the great advantages of rapid and selective reading. On the side of hygiene we must remember that such
reading will be more fatiguing, when continued for long periods,
and especially in the first attempts to hurry the pace and vary the
method. It is to be remembered, however, that the fast rate becomes

habitual as well as does the slow rate, and the hurry feeling then disappears. In the selective reading, too, while certain parts are thought more intensely, far more is quietly ignored, and the feeling of values and using them as they appear becomes a habit of mind which functions almost as automatically as other aspects of the reading process. The slow reader who with painstaking "thoroughness" works as hard at one line as at the next expends so much energy in lifting dead weight and in handling useless débris that his work is doubtless more fatiguing, to obtain equivalent results, than that of the rapid and selective reader. Of course, all selective mental activity, in which the mind really acts, judges, and constructs for itself, whether in reading or otherwise, naturally causes far more fatigue per hour than when the performance is mainly passive. We cannot get something for nothing even in psychic economics. Here, as everywhere, a hard pace means a short course and frequent change. It should be remembered, however, that a rapid pace is not always the hardest of paces, for organisms that are trained to it. And it is a safe and needed rule for all kinds of reading that it should never be continued uninterruptedly for long periods of time, seldom indeed for longer periods than two hours at the most.

CHAPTER XXI

HYGIENIC REQUIREMENTS
IN THE PRINTING OF BOOKS AND PAPERS

PROBABLY the most important and most feasible means of lessening the fatigue and strain of reading is by bringing it about, so far as possible, that all books and papers shall be printed in such type and arrangement as shall fall within certain recognized limits of hygienic requirement. As to some of the requirements which should be made of the printer we are still uncertain, and further experimental investigation rather than the present excess of opinion is in order and is cryingly needed. Of other requirements we can now be certain, and these should be enforced rigorously, in the printing of schoolbooks and government publications at least. If enforced here, they will tend to extend to all printing.

The size of the type is perhaps the most important single factor. The experiments of Griffing and Franz showed that fatigue increases rapidly as the size of the type decreases, even for sizes above eleven point, or above a height of 1.5 millimeters for the short letters like v, s, etc. The various investigators are generally agreed that this should be made a minimum for the height of the short letters. Matter printed in this size of type is read faster and individual words are recognized more quickly than where the type is smaller. Besides, Griffing and Franz found that the effect of insufficient illumination is less marked with the larger type. Preferably the height of the small letter should be somewhat above the minimum stated, though when the height is much above 2 millimeters Weber's experiments indicated that the speed of reading is decreased.

The thickness of the vertical strokes of the letters should not be less than .25 millimeter, according to Cohn; preferably .3 millimeter, according to Sack. This thickness of the letters has been found by Javal and others to be a very important factor in increasing legibility, and thus in decreasing fatigue. Griffing and Franz found, however, that hair lines might form parts of the letter without decreasing the legibility provided the other parts were thick. They find it possible, however, that such hair lines may increase fatigue. The minimum of thickness stated above should be insisted on for the main lines.

The space within the letters between the vertical strokes should not be less than .3 millimeter, according to most investigators. Sack finds .5 millimeter to be preferable. There is probably little to be gained by increasing the distance between the letters beyond that which is usual in the better printed books of the present time. Burgerstein and Netolitzky would require that this distance should be greater than the distance between two "neighboring ground strokes" of a letter, and Sack would make the minimum distance .5 to .75 millimeter. Burgerstein and Netolitzky would not allow more than six or seven letters per running centimeter and would require as much as 2 millimeters between words. With these requirements Sack is in agreement. It should be remembered that any very unusual sep-aration of the letters of a word is distracting and should be avoided. These minimal norms, as stated by Burgerstein and Netolitzky, should be made requirements, except that possibly the distance between letters is not so important as they urge. The minimum of six or seven letters per running centimeter is a convenient approxi-mate gauge which can be quickly applied and is not too stringent.

Griffing and Franz found that legibility increased somewhat, though not greatly, with increase in the distance between the lines, with the leading, as it is called. Cohn thinks it important that there should be a minimum leading of 2.5 millimeters, and Sack requires the same. Javal does not find that leading increases legibility appreciably, and thinks that the space used for this purpose would far better be given to an increased size of letter without leading. The leading is doubtless a mistake when the size of type is below the requirements made above. The size of type should by all means be increased instead, as this is by far the most important of the factors conditioning fatigue. However, a certain amount of leading should be required in schoolbooks, at least, but hardly more than Cohn's minimum of 2.5 millimeters.

As to length of lines there is a general consensus in favor of the shorter as against the longer lines, with a tendency to favor 90 milli-meters as a maximum, some placing the maximum at 100 millimeters.

The latter is doubtless too high. Javal, who has studied the matter very carefully, insists that the maximum should be considerably below even 90 millimeters. As already noted, he names as one of the principal causes of fatigue in reading, and a cause tending to produce and aggravate myopia, the considerable amount of asymmetrical accommodation required as the eye moves along a long line, the amount increasing always with the length of the line. Even with the page squarely before the reader, unless he makes constant and fatiguing movements of the head while reading, the reading-matter is always farther from one eye than from the other, except at the middle point of the line, and the reader strains to accommodate for both distances, especially for objects held so near as is the page in reading.

Against the long lines is also to be urged the difficulty and distraction incident to finding the place at each turn to the next line, increasing always as the lines are longer. Besides, the longer lines require a greater extent of eye-movement for a given amount of reading. This comes from the fact, verified by various experimenters, that the eye does not traverse the whole line in reading, but begins within the line and usually makes its last pause still farther within, the reader reading the first and last parts of the line in indirect vision. The amount of this indentation tends to be a constant amount somewhat irrespective of the line's length, and is consequently a larger proportion of the line's length in the shorter lines. There is thus an important lessening of eye-work in using the shorter lines. Indeed I found that readers could read matter printed in lines of 25 millimeters in one downward sweep without any lateral movement of the eyes. With lines 30 millimeters long the lateral movement was sometimes almost nil, and seemed to be due mainly to habit. In reading such lines in this way the eye's extent of movement is hardly more than one-fourth or one-fifth the amount needed for the same matter when printed in long lines.

With the shorter lines, generally, more words were read per fixation than with the longer ones. A magazine column having lines 60.5 millimeters long was in one case read at the rate of 3.63 words per fixation, while columns having lines 98 to 121 millimetres long required a fixation for every two words. Lines of a length approximating 60 millimeters are usual in newspapers, and in my experiments were read with a minimum of eye-movement. The makers of the modern newspaper have felt the reaction of readers more, perhaps, than have the makers of books. Out of this experience has evolved the present practice of printing newspapers in narrow columns, the line-lengths of which are perhaps as near the optimum as can be determined at present, when we consider that much shorter lines give great inconvenience to the printer.

For books, also, the newspaper line-length is near an optimum so far as ease and speed of reading are the conditions to be considered. In the case of large books, where the question becomes one of printing in one or in two columns per page, the latter alternative should undoubtedly be chosen. For books of ordinary sizes a somewhat longer line may be used where this will contribute to convenience or beauty; but a book should not be used whose lines are more than 90 millimetres in length, and somewhat shorter lines are generally to be preferred.

One of the great advantages of the shorter lines is that they constantly permit the reader to see in indirect vision what his eye has just passed as well as what is just coming. Though the words of this related matter may not be clearly perceived, they furnish visual clews which keep the reading range further extended at each moment, a most desirable condition for all reading and especially for fast reading or for skimming. With such lines a hurried reader may glance straight down a page with only an occasional short stop and may yet be sure that he has gathered the gist of everything.

Dr. Dearborn, in experiments made recently at Columbia University, found that the eye makes its longest pause near the beginning of the line, thus permitting a preliminary general survey. A secondary pause of more than average duration is made near the end of the line, perhaps partially in review. He finds that lines of only moderate length facilitate these general surveys better than the longer lines, and finds also that they facilitate a rhythmical regularity of eye-movement, both being conditions which contribute to speed and ease of reading. His tests showed that such lines (a little longer than newspaper lines) were read at greater speed and with shorter pauses than lines of twice the length.

Dearborn argues, and correctly I think, in favor of uniformity in the length of lines, particularly in books for children. The reader drops quickly into a habit of making a constant number of movements and pauses per line, for a given passage, and broken lines confuse and prevent the formation of such temporary habits. However, a *slight* indentation every other line may, he thinks, be of distinct advantage. Dearborn thinks that a line of 75 to 85 millimeters combines a good many advantages, and we are certainly safe in putting 90 millimeters as a maximum, with a preference for lines of 60 to 80 millimeters.

The smaller books, which can be easily held in the hand during the reading, are to be preferred, and on the whole have grown in popular favor. The larger books usually have to lie on a support which exposes the letters at an angle, greatly lessening their legibility and producing the equivalent of a material decrease in the size of type.

As to the forms of particular letters, many changes are cryingly needed. However, further investigation is needed before we are warranted in requiring changes of the printer. We know that such letters as t, z, o, s, e, c, i, are comparatively illegible. C, e, and o are often confused with each other, and i with l, h with k, etc. This confusion can be avoided by making certain changes in these letters, and their legibility can be increased. Certain excellent recommendations of changes in particular letters have been made by Javal, Cohn, Sanford, and others.

However, there are many things to be considered in making such changes, and further thorough and mature investigation is needed before any letter is permanently changed. The whole matter should be placed in the hands of a competent specialist or committee of specialists, to be worked over experimentally and advised upon in the light of the psychology of reading, the history of typography, aesthetic considerations, the convenience of printing, and the lessons of experience generally. Changes should not be made on the single basis of experiments upon the comparative legibility of isolated letter-forms. A letter whose legibility in isolation is bad may sometimes contribute most to the legibility of the total word-form. Studies now being made of the comparative legibility of letters as seen in context will doubtless throw light on this point. The subject is too complex to permit the adoption of recommendations that are based on study, however careful, of any single aspect, or on anything that does not include a careful study of all the factors. It is high time that there should be a rationalization of these printed letter-forms that have come down to us in such a happy-go-lucky fashion, and it is to be hoped that either the Carnegie Institut on or some department of research in a well-equipped university may take hold of the matter and see that the work is thoroughly done.

Among further printing requirements that are important and that should be insisted on, the letters should have sharp, clear-cut outlines, and should be deep black. The paper should be pure white, but without gloss, the latter being especially trying to the eyes. According to Cohn and Sack the paper should have a minimum thickness of .075 millimeter.

Paper of a slightly yellowish tinge is probably not injurious and is preferred by Javal. But in general the legibility depends on the contrast between the black of the printed forms and the white of their background, and colored or gray papers lessen this difference and thus diminish legibility. Pure white light gives the greatest legibility.

The print of one side must not show through from the other, and the printing must be so done that it will not affect the evenness of surface of the other side.

It is important that wall charts and maps should not contain more names than are absolutely necessary for purposes of instruction, and that these should be in large, clear type; or the most important names for reference at a distance and by classes may be in the large type, with the others in type fulfilling the requirements for schoolbooks, and for use by individuals at the ordinary reading distance from the chart or map. Burgerstein and Netolitzky advise that school maps should not present the physical and political features on the same map, in the interest of greater legibility. Names printed on colored map surfaces need to be in larger rather than in smaller type than that used in books if legibility is to be maintained, as any other background than white means diminished legibility.

The writing upon slates is considerably less legible than that upon good white paper. In the case of blackboards the surface is apt to be gray after erasing, and this, of course, lessens the legibility very considerably. It is important that the blackboard surface be deep black, without gloss from reflection so far as this is possible, and that it be kept clean, avoiding the gray effect. Teachers and pupils should acquire the habit of writing on the blackboard in a large plain hand, as the greater distance at which the writing is read and the usually diminished legibility makes this of importance, and especially in the primary school grades.

In stating the requirements above I have had in mind the needs of adult readers and of the older school children. The younger children must have a type much larger than the minima there stated. The reading of young children has not been sufficiently studied to warrant a final statement of what should be required in the printing of their books. As the most usable approximate statement of what may properly be insisted on, and for the sake of uniformity, I quote here the requirements made by Shaw in his "School Hygiene," with his illustrative examples. These requirements are none too stringent, except that sometimes some of the leading may well be sacrificed in favor of a type that is a little larger, for the third and fourth grades especially: —

"For the first year the size of the type should be at least 2.6 millimeters and the width of leading 4.5 millimeters, as shown in this example:—

Then there is a turn in the road. The long train runs over the bridge and swings round behind a hill. The children cannot see it now.

For the second and the third year, the letters should not be smaller than 2 mm., with a leading of 4 mm. Some of the more carefully made books for the second and the third years are printed in letters of this size, as shown in the following example:—

She must climb the tree.   She held on, first to one branch and then to another, and tried to reach the golden plums.   Her hands, her face, and her feet were scratched and torn by the thorns.   Try as hard as she could, she

For the fourth year, the letters should be at least 1.8 mm., with leading 3.6 mm., as follows: —

On the way down, an Indian who was in a canoe stole something from the ship.   One of the crew saw the Indian commit the theft, and, picking up a gun, shot and killed him.   This made the other Indians very angry and Hudson had several fights with them."

For some grades succeeding this the type should be kept well above the minimal requirements for adult readers.

Examinations of the schoolbooks in use in Germany, Russia, and other European countries, made at various times and places, have shown that usually from fifty to eighty-five per cent of the books came short of hygienic requirements American books are somewhat better, but include very many that are very bad. Even when the principal part of the book is in good type, there will often be large sections printed in a type so small as to be very injurious. The dictionaries and other books of reference have notoriously small print, and those with the smaller and poorer types should be mercilessly discriminated against. As Shaw rightly says, "Principals, teachers, and school superintendents should possess a millimeter measure find a magnifying glass and should subject every book presented for their examination to a test to determine whether the size of the letters and the width of the leading are of such dimensions as will not prove injurious to the eyes of children. If every book, no matter what its merits, were rejected if its type were too small, the makers of such books would very quickly bring out new editions with a proper size of type."

CONCLUSION

READING AND PRINTING
OF THE FUTURE

CHAPTER XXII

THE FUTURE OF READING AND PRINTING. THE ELIMINATION OF WASTE

READING is the means by which the world does a large part of its work. The printed page is a contrivance used for hours daily by tens of millions of people. The slightest improvement either in the page or in the method of reading means the rendering of a great service to the human race. Human thought has been busy rationalizing. It has rationalized the traditional methods of transportation and locomotion until we have the steam and electric locomotive and the economy and comfort of modern travel. Means of communication at a distance have had the keenest and most persistent efforts of inventive genius, and the modern marvels in telegraphy and telephony are the results. Even printing and the making of books has had attentive study and continuous improvement until wonders of the printer's art are within easy reach of all. Yet with it all the essential characteristics of the printed page itself, and of the reading process by which we gather its meaning for so many hours of the working day, have never been rationalized in the interest of the reader's time or energy or comfort.

To take a trite example, note the spelling of our printed page. Like the ancient Egyptians, who spelled out their words in letters and then laboriously added the useless picture hieroglyph, we compel "practical" moderns, pressed for time as they are, to traverse one-fifth or one-sixth more of printed matter than is needful, on every page, in order that a few scholastics may enjoy a luxurious thrill from the sight of the silent-letter relics. Again, we have never seriously worked out to a conclusion what form of any letter would give the greatest legibility, and we have never used the results of the meager though very valuable investigations already made in this field. Indeed, who knows but that Broca and Sulzer may be right in their contention[1]

---

[1] *La Nature*, Paris, February 13, 1904.

that the extreme of simplicity, in letter-forms, means the maximum ease of recognition, recommending therefore such forms

as **O** ⟶ **>>** ⅃ ⅂ ⌐ ϕ **<** **⌐** ∕ for the capitals, and

⎮⎮⎮ ∨ ⌐ ⫪ √ ⫪⎸ for the small letters. Certainly the letter-

forms that have come down to us through the ages have never been pruned to meet the *reader's* needs, though the writer and printer have made conservative changes for their own convenience. There is not the slightest doubt that forms can be devised which will be much more legible than these ancient traditional symbols. From the point of view of Messmer's analysis of letter-forms, it may well be that the legibility of words will be increased by adding to the number of characteristically formed, or dominant, letters. We certainly have many words whose letters are optically very similar, and these words would be much improved by such additions.

And then we have never canvassed the possibilities of improving the total word-form, for particular words. We know how the German use of initial capitals, for instance, and the imitation of this practice by such writers as Carlyle, gives greater prominence to the capitalized words. If by using capitals or by changing the shape, size, or even color of constituent letters we bring into prominence the total word-form and characterize it better, total form will thus come to play a still larger part than at present in mediating the recognition of what is read. Such recognition in larger units favors speed in reading and lessens the strain on eye and mind. The special temporary characterization of the important words or phrases in any given article, by changes in type, etc., may also aid much in speed and ease of reading whenever the reader's aim is selective, purposing to get quickly the kernels or gist of the matter read. Even the present somewhat crude use of such characterization, by our daily newspapers, shows that such a method meets a need of busy readers. Any arrangement which makes comprehensive skimming an easy matter will be of great benefit for large parts of our reading.

We are likely, indeed, soon to consider the possibilities of a total rearrangement of our printed symbols, in the interest of economy of time, energy, and effectiveness in getting thought from the page.

The history of writing has a wealth of suggestion here which may well be pondered. Consider, for instance, the Egyptian representation of the name "King Sent," as compared with the narrow row of little black strokes by which modern printers present the words. In the figure, [~~~ ∩] the S (vertical hook within the oblong, at the right), N (upper left wave line), and T (D or T, the hand) represent "Sent," while the surrounding oblong represents "King." Such bunching of the letters of words into a characteristic total form, with even such substitutions of simple forms, like oblongs, squares, etc., for oft repeated words, would agreeably distribute the stimulations on the retina, would permit the eye to cover several times as much reading-matter with the present extent of movement, would encourage the more facile and more speedy reading in total forms, — would have, on the whole, advantages so vital that the possibilities of such rearrangement are at least well worth careful consideration.

Consider, for instance, the traditional arrangement of our words into straight horizontal lines, already referred to in our introductory chapter. We read so because, a good many thousand years ago, the scribes found it convenient to write their characters that way. The Egyptian, on the other hand, found the arrangement in vertical lines to be very readable, and the Chinese and Japanese still prefer it. The writer made an extended series of experiments, a few years ago,[1] to determine the relative speed of reading-matter printed by our present method as against reading equivalent matter arranged in columns of words, the individual words in the latter case standing horizontally, one below the other, down the page. The results showed that for reading aloud at maximal speed nonsense matter could be read as quickly in vertical arrangement as in horizontal. With sense matter the vertical reading was only from seven to ten per cent slower. In silent reading the vertical method reduced the speed considerably, the distraction from the novel arrangement seeming to have more effect in the silent reading, But in view of the tremendous amount of practice which each reader had had with

---

[1] American Journal of Psychology, IX, pp. 375-386.

the horizontal lines and the consequent distraction produced by the unusual vertical arrangement, it seemed entirely likely that the vertical arrangement might ultimately give even greater speed than the horizontal. The further great advantages would be that in reading down vertical columns in the Japanese fashion the eye may cross-section its words, reading the lateral parts in indirect vision and thus getting the visual data needed for reading four or five words with the movement now needed to traverse one lengthwise. Not only might we thus save at least three-fourths of the fatiguing eye-movements and three-fourths of the pauses as well, but we would constantly be able to use the upper and lower retinal periphery in getting far more data than at present for the perception of the immediate context just past and just coming. The reading range of each moment would thus be materially increased, with the accruing advantages. It is probable, too, that with such an arrangement of printed symbols there would be much less distraction in "keeping the place," less distraction from the remotely related matter in the neighboring lines, and greater freedom in the choice of fixation places. Of course, on the other hand, such an arrangement would have certain disadvantages both to the printer and reader. But enough has been said to show that this is an important direction for experimentation in the rationalization of the printed page.

The economy that may come from a more general and effective use of illustrations is already being recognized, and the psychology and pedagogy of picture-printing of itself is worth a volume. What a development here already since the days, in the memory of men now living, when illustrated books were a rarity, and when boys were flogged for bringing them to school! Johnson gives an interesting account of this in his "Old-Time Schools and School Books." How very much of the reader's time may be saved by judicious use of graphic methods of presentation, by charts, maps, globes, the stereopticon, etc. What possibilities for beautifying and increasing the effectiveness of our printed page, and for easing the work of the eye, may come from using the wealth of suggestion in ancient and modern pictography, and indeed in modern cartooning and advertising.

The history of Egypt, of China, and of other ancient peoples shows that they endured untold wastes for hundreds and even thousands of years because they failed to rationalize their systems of reading and writing, regarding the traditional ways as "good enough." It behooves the modern world to appropriate the benefits that are sure to come from eliminating our own very evident wastes in these same arts. Our printed page, as we have seen, may be made a far more economical one. And with this improved page, with a simpler alphabet and a natural phonetic system of spelling, much of the present waste in learning to read will disappear. A thorough rationalization of the methods of learning to read, on the basis of the psychology and history of reading, will give additional economy. When our schools take up their proper work of teaching all readers to utilize the library and all printed matter effectively and rapidly, and to substitute real selective reading for mechanical plodding at the customary uniform, "aloud" pace, another great waste will disappear from the school and from life. In this training the opportunities for mental discipline in reading, largely neglected hitherto, will be utilized, and certain subjects long studied mainly for the sake of discipline may consequently be advantageously omitted. Further, it may be said that the learning of foreign languages, ancient or modern, will in many quarters undergo considerable revision in the direction of economy, when the facts are clearly grasped as to what constitutes the essence of natural reading. It will then be even more clearly and demonstrably evident than hitherto that much of our academic "reading" of languages has been but a gloss and hollow parody upon reading, lacking the free rhythm and melody play of inner speech, lacking the dominance of all parts by total unifying idea-meanings, without the habits of associative expectancy that are absolutely essential for the control of a language either in speaking or in reading, and wanting still other earmarks of real reading.

A certain waste of the reader's time has already been lessened by the improvement in the style of writing English, since the Elizabethan times at least. Professor L. A. Sherman, in his "Analytics of Literature" (p. 256 ff.), calls attention to the fact that the early English prose had either crabbed or heavy sentences, which demanded "re-reading" or even "pondering" before the meaning would reveal itself. He finds that "ordinary modern prose, on the other hand, is clear, and almost as effective to the understanding as oral

speech." Still he admits that few of us to-day really "write as idiomat-
ically and naturally as we speak," and most men's written language is
very different from their spoken language. This difference is partly
due to the slowness of handwriting, which makes an author fini-
cal, self-conscious, and unnatural. On the whole, however, Professor
Sherman finds that "from the lyrical bards to the present the language of books and the language of men have been growing rapidly
alike." If this development continues, and the modern habit of dic-
tating at a natural rate to stenographers and even to graphophones
may hasten it, reading, as the translation of what is written into
natural inner speech, may have further facilitation by this change,
and perhaps from still further changes in composing to be suggested
from studies, already overdue, in the psychology of style.

Indeed there are those who go further than any of these legit-
imately warranted prophecies of future economy in the time and
effort of the reader, and predict the displacement of much of reading,
in toto, by some more direct means of recording and communicating.
Just as the telegrapher's message was at first universally read from
the tape, by the eye, but has come to be read far more expeditiously
by the ear; so, it is argued, writing and reading may be short-circuit-
ed, and an author may talk his thought directly into some sort of
graphophone-film book which will render it again to listeners, at
will; reproducing all the essential characteristics of the author's
speech, which, as we have seen, are not recorded by written language
and which the reader must construct for himself at a considerable
expense of energy. This latter proposition is, of course, as yet, the
wildest of speculations. But the plainly possible changes in the direction of eliminating present wastes in reading are so important
that they demand the early institution of organized research upon
the various problems, to determine, at least, the ideals toward which
we should strive in the making of our page and in the practices of
reading and learning to read. All these problems are complex and
demand maturity of judgment, as well as mastery of technique, in
their solution. And they are problems in which the points of view
of the psychologist, the philologist, and the educator must receive
a practical synthesis. Too often, as in the working out of systems
of phonetic spelling by philologists, a system excellent from the

philological or logical standpoint has lacked fitness to the psychic or hygienic conditions involved in reading, or it has lacked the pedagogical adaptations needed to permit its making a successful appeal to the masses. The need is, first, for more of particular researches such as we have had, on specific problems, to furnish much more of fact and of suggestion. Second, the problems of determining optima, along the more important lines already suggested, should be placed in the hands of committees of competent specialists, to be worked out as a part of the duties of our institutions for higher research, if necessary with government supervision and provision. It is important that we should have before us, as early as possible, correct and authoritatively promulgated ideals in all these matters. Conformity to these will come but gradually, but will come the earlier for their being definitely stated. The increasingly effective means for the dissemination of information is making possible the hastening of reforms; and the possibilities of controlling conditions as to reading and even printing, through the government supervision of the practice of the schools, gives promise of early improvement in conditions when once the specialists have reached final conclusions. When the world comes to put aside the false sentiment and traditions that have clouded the subject of reading, and sees it as the everyday means of doing a large part of our work; and when the proposed reforms are shown to mean definite savings of time, money, and health, and definite improvement in mental habits as well, practical sense will sooner or later see to it that they are duly installed.

BIBLIOGRAPHY

Bibliography of the works referred to in this book, and of a few others which may be of service. For most of the topics the bibliography is, of course, not even approximately complete. It introduces, however, to the literature that has been found most helpful in my study of the subject.

Abell, Adelaide M. Rapid Reading. *Educational Review*, 8, 283.

Ahrens. Die Bewegung der Augen beim Schreiben. Rostock, 1891.

Bagley, W. C. Apperception of the Spoken Sentence. *American Journal of Psychology*, Vol. XII, pp. 80-130.

Ballet. Le Langage Interieur.

Barnum, Edith C. *Reading*, in the series of articles on the curriculum of the Horace Mann School. *Teachers College Record*, January and September, 1906. The work of the higher grades is to be presented in later numbers.

Bawden, H. Heath. A Study of Lapses. *Psych. Review Monograph Supplements*, Vol. III, No. 4, April, 1900.

Baxt, N. Ueber die Zeit welche nothig ist, damit ein Gesichtseindruck zum Bewusstsein kommt. *Pflüger's Archiv für Physiologie*, Vol. IV, 1871, pp. 325-336.

Becker. Experimentelle und kritische Beiträge zur Psychologie des Lesens bei kurzen Expositionzeiten. *Zeitschrift für Psych. und Phys. der Sinnesorgane*. Bd. 36, H. 1 u. 2, pp. 19-73.

Brown, Alex. C. The Relation between the Movements of the Eyes and the Movements of the Head. Oxford, 1895. pp. 28. See also *Nature*, Vol. LII, 1895, p. 184.

Calkins, Mary W. Association. *Psych. Review Monograph Supplements*, No. 2, February, 1896.

Cattell, J. McK. *Brain*, Vol. VIII, p. 305 ff.

——*Philosoph. Studien*, II u. III.

——*Mind*, 1886, p. 65 and p. 531 ff.

——*Mind*, 1889.

Cattell, J. McK. Time and Space in Vision. *Psych. Review*, Vol. VII, 1900, pp. 325-343.

Dearborn, Walter F. The Psychology of Reading. *Columbia Univ. Contribs. to Philosophy and Psychology*, Vol. XIV, No. 1. New York, The Science Press.

Delabarre, E. B. A Method of Recording Eye Movements. *American Journal of Psychology*, July, 1898.

Dodge, Raymond. Die Motorischen Wortvorstellungen. Halle, 1896. pp. 65.

——Visual Perception during Eye Movement. *Psych. Review*, Vol. VII, 1900.

——Eye Movements and the Perception of Motion. *Psych. Review*, January, 1904.

——Five Types of Eye Movement. *American Journal of Physiology*, Vol. VIII, pp. 307-329.

——Act of Vision. *Harpers*, May, 1902.

——The Illusion of Clear Vision during Eye Movement. *Psychological Bulletin*, June 15, 1905.

——An Experimental Study of Visual Fixation. *Psychological Review Monograph Supplements*, Vol. VIII, No. 4, November, 1907. This article was received after Part One had been electrotyped.

——*See* Erdmann und Dodge.

Egger, V. La Parole Interieure. Paris, 1904.

Erdmann, B. Die Psychologischen Grondlagen der Beziehungen zwischen Sprechen und Denken. *Archiv f. Systemat. Philos.*, III, 1897.

Erdmann, B., und Dodge, R. Psychologische Untersuchungen über das Lesen, auf Experimenteller Grundlage. Halle, 1898.

Exner. Entwurf zu einer Physiol. Erklärung der Psychischen Erscheinungen. Erster Theil. Leipsic und Wien, 1894.

——Versuche über die zu einer Gesichtswahmehmung nothige Zeit. *Sitzungsbericht der Acad. d. Wissenchaft in Wien*, Bd. LVIII, Abth. II, 1868.

Flournoy. Temps de Lecture et Omission. *L'Année Psychologique*, II, 1896, pp. 45-53.

Gale, Harlow. Psychology of Advertising. *Psychological Studies*, No. 1, July, 1900. Published by the author, Minneapolis, Minn.

Galton, Francis. Inquiries into Human Faculty. New York, 1883. Macmillan Co.

Gildersleeve, B. L. Pindar (Preface). *Olympian and Pythian Odes*, 1885. Am. Book Co.

Goldscheider, A., und Müller, R. F. Zur Phys. und Path. des Lesens. *Zeitschrift f. Klin. Med.*, Bd. XXIII, p. 131.

Gutzmann. Das Stottern, p. 178 ff. Frankfurt-a.-M., 1898.

——Die Praktische Anwendung der Sprachphysiologie beim ersten Leseunterricht. Berlin, 1897.

Helmholtz. Optique Physiologique.

——Physiologische Optik. Voss, Hamburg, 1896.

Holt, E. B. Eye Movement and Central Anaesthesia. *Psych. Review Monograph Supplements*, Vol. IV, January, 1903.

Huey, E. B. Preliminary Experiments in the Physiology and Psychology of Reading. *American Journal of Psychology*, July, 1898.

——Psychology and Physiology of Reading. *American Journal of Psychology*, Vol. XI, pp. 1-20, and Vol. XII.

James, William. Psychology (Advanced Course), Vols. I-II. Henry Holt & Co.

Javal, Emile. Notice sur les Travaux Scientifiques de Emile Javal. The author, Paris. (The *Notice* reviews the twenty-five articles which constitute the bibliography of Professor Javal's personal researches. See also the various numbers of *Les Comptes rendus de l'Ecole des Hautes Études*, Paris.)

——Conditions de la Lecture facile. *Comptes rendus de la. Société de Biologie*, 1879, p. 8.

——Sur la Physiologie de la Lecture. *Annales d'Oculistique*, 1878 et 1879. (Several articles.)

——Physiology of Writing. Eng. trans. Harison, No. 59 Fifth Ave., New York.

Lamansky, S. *Pflüger's Archiv*, 1869, p. 418 ff.

Lamare. Des Mouvements des Yeux pendant la Lecture. *Comptes rendus de la Société française d'Ophtalmologie*, 1893, p. 354 ff.

Landolt. Nouvelles recherches sur la physiologie des mouvements des yeux. *Archives d'Ophtalmologie*, II, 1891, pp. 385-395.

Meringer und **Mayer**. Versprechen und Verlesen. Stuttgart, 1895.

Messmer, Oskar. Zur Psychologie des Lesens bei Kinder und Erwachsenen. *Archiv für die gesamte Psychologie*, December, 1903, Bd. II, H. 2 u. 3, pp. 190-298.

Meumann, E. Die Entstehung der ersten Wortbedeutungen beim Kinder. *Wundt's Philosoph. Studien*, XX. Festschrift 2.

Münsterberg, Hugo. *Beiträge zu Exper. Psych.*, H. 4, p. 17 ff.

Pillsbury, W. B. A Study in Apperception. *American Journal of Psychology*, Vol. VIII, No. 3, April, 1897.

Preyer, W. Development of the Intellect. Appleton & Co. 1898.

Quantz, J. O. Problems in the Psychology of Reading. *Psych. Review Monograph Supplements*, Vol. II, No. 1, December, 1897.

Ribot. Enquête sur les Idées Générales. *Revue Philosophique*, October, 1891.

——— The Evolution of General Ideas. Open Court Co., Chicago, 1899.

Romanes, G. J. Mental Evolution in Animals. Appleton & Co., New York.

Schumann, F. Psychologie des Lesens. *Bericht über den Il Kongress für Exper. Psych. in Würzburg*, 1906. pp. 31.

Scripture, E. W. Elements of Experimental Phonetics. Chas. Scribner's Sons, New York. 1902.

Secor. Visual Reading. *American Journal of Psychology*, Vol. XI, pp. 225-236.

Stout, G. F. Analytical Psychology, Vols. I-II. London, 1896. The Macmillan Co.

——— Manual of Psychology. Hinds & Noble, New York.

Stratton, G. M. Eye Movements and the Æsthetics of Visual Form. *Wundt's Philosoph. Studien*, XX. Festschrift 2.

Stricker. Studien über die Sprachvorstellungen.

Sweet, Henry. Primer of Phonetics. Oxford Univ. Press, London. Henry Frowde, Agent, New York.

——— A Practical Study of Languages. Holt & Co., 1900.

Talbot. *American Journal oj Psychology*, Vol. VIII, p. 414. (Describes an attempt at training in visualization.)

Taylor, Clifton O. Ueber das Verstehen von Worten und Sätzen. *Zeitschrift f. Physiol. u. Psych. der Sinnes-Organe*, Nov. 30, 1905.

Wallin, J. E. Wallace. Researches on the Rhythm of Speech. *Studies from Yale Psych. Lab.*, Vol. IX, 1901. pp. 143.

Whitney, W. D. Life and Growth of Language. New York, 1880. Appleton & Co.

Wirth, W. Zur Theorie des Bewusstseins Umfanges und seiner Messung. *Wundt's Philosoph. Studien*, XX. Festschrift, 2.

Woodworth, R. S. Vision and Localization during Eye Movements. *Psychological Bulletin*, Vol. III, No. 2, Feb. 15, 1906.

——— in *Proceedings Am. Psych. Assoc.*, 1905-1906.

Wundt, Wilhelm. Völker-Psychologie, Die Sprache. W. Engelmann, Leipsic.

Zeitler, Julius. Tachistoskopische Versuche über das Lesen. *Wundt's Philosoph. Studien*, Bd. XVI, H. 3, pp. 380-463.

THE HISTORY OF READING AND WRITING

Bouchot. The Printed Book; its history, illustration, and adornment, from the days of Gutenberg to the present time. Translated and enlarged by Bigemore. London, 1887. 312 pages.

Budge. Egyptian Language. Kegan Paul, Trench, Trübner & Co., Ltd. London, 1899.

Chambers. Encyclopædia, article on Babylonia, p. 632.

Clodd, Edward. Story of the Alphabet. Appleton & Co., New York. Copyright, 1900.

Deniker. The Races of Man. Walter Scott Pub. Co., Felling-on-Tyne, England. 1900.

Evans, Sir Arthur. Primitive Pictographs. *Journal of Hellenis Studies,* XIV, ii. 1894.

——Cretan Pictographs and Pre-Phœnician Script. 1896.

——Further Discoveries of Cretan and Ægean Script. 1898.

Forsyth, W. History of Ancient Manuscripts. John Murray. London, 1872.

Hirn, Yrjö. Origins of Art. London, 1900. The Macmillan Co.

Hoffman. Beginnings of Writing. Appleton & Co., New York. Copyright, 1896.

Hogarth. Authority and Archaeology. John Murray. London, 1899.

Homer. Iliad, vi, 169.

Judd. Genetic Psychology for Teachers. Appleton & Co. Copyright, 1903.

Plomer, H. R. Short History of English Printing. London, 1900.

Rawlings, Gertrude B. The Story of Books. Appleton & Co., New York.

Taylor, Isaac. The Alphabet, Vols. I-II. Copyright by Edward Arnold, publisher. London.

Thompson. Greek and Latin Palæography. Appleton & Co., New York. 1894.

Tylor, E. B. Early History of Mankind. Holt & Co., New York. 1878.

Vogt, C. L'Ecriture, etc. *Rev. Scientifique,* June 26, 1880, p. 1221 ff.

Wundt, W. Völker-Psychologie, Die Sprache. W. Engelmann. Leipsic.

THE HISTORY OF READING METHODS

Comenius. The Great Didactic. Translated by Keatinge. London, 1896, pp. 468.

——Orbis Pictus. Edited by C. W. Bardeen. pp. 197. Bardeen, Syracuse, 1891.

Fechner, H. Die Methoden des ersten Leseunterrichts. Wiegandt und Grieben, Berlin, 1882.

Fechner, H. Grundriss der Geschichte der Wichtigsten Leselehrarten. Wiegandt und Grieben, Berlin, 1884. pp. 72.

Johnson. Old-Time Schools and School Books. TheMacmillan Co.

Leigh. Pronouncing Orthography. N. E. A. Report, 1873, pp. 207-219.

Mann, Horace. Seventh Report of the Secretary of the Massachusetts Board of Education. Published by the state.

New England Primer. Boston, 1777. Reprinted by Ginn & Co.

Prior, Matthew. Alma, Canto II.

Reeder, R. R. Historical Development of School Readers and of Method in Teaching Reading. *Columbia Univ. Contribs. to Philos., Psych., and Ed.,* Vol. VIII, No. 2. The Macmillan Co., 1900, pp. 92.

Scudder. Life of Noah Webster. Houghton, Mifflin & Co., Boston.

Thornton. Cadmus, or a Treatise on Written Language. *Common School Journal*, Vol. II, 1840.

METHODS AND GENERAL PEDAGOGY OF READING

Adler, Felix. Moral Instruction of Children. Appleton &Co., 1895.

Arnold, Sarah L. Waymarks for Teachers. Silver, Burdett Co., 1894, pp. 152-186.

——Reading, How to Teach it. Silver, Burdett Co.

Atlantic, July, 1890, Vol. CXLIII, Pace in Reading.

Broca and Sulzer. Reading and the Alphabet. *La Nature*, Feb. 13, 1904. Reviewed in *Lit. Digest*, March 12, 1904, p. 367.

Bryan, E. B. Nascent Stages. *Ped. Sem.*, Vol. VII, p. 357.

Bullock, R. W. Some Observations on Children's Reading. N. E. A. Report, 1897, p. 1015 ff.

Burt, Mary E. On Teaching Children to Read. *New Eng. Mag.*, Dec., 1889, pp. 426-429.

——Experiments in the Teaching of Reading. *The Dial*, March 16, 1893.

Chadwick, in *New York Teachers' Monographs*, June, 1902.

Chambers, Will Grant. How Words get Meaning. *Ped. Sem.*, March, 1904.

Clark, S. H. How to Read Aloud. The author, University of Chicago.

Conradi. Children's Interests in Words, Slang, Stories, etc. *Ped. Sem.*, Vol X, pp. 359-404.

Cooke, Flora J. Articles in the *El. School Teacher*, October, 1900, p. 111 ff. and April, 1904, p. 544 ff.

Dale, F. H. The Teaching of the Mother Tongue in Germany. Special Reports Ed. Dept. Great Britain. London, 1896-1897, pp. 536-578.

Dewey, John. The Primary Education Fetich. *Forum*, Vol. XXV, pp. 315-328.

——in *New York Teachers' Monographs*, November, 1898.

Eliot, Chas. W. *Educational Review*, July, 1891.

——*Educational Reform*. The Century Co., New York.

Everett, Cora E., in *New York Teachers' Monographs*, June, 1902.

Farnham. The Sentence Method of Teaching Reading. C. W. Bardeen, Syracuse, N.Y. 1887.

Funk & Wagnalls. Standard Dictionary, pp. 2104-2107, and elsewhere. Funk & Wagnalls Co., New York.

Gordon, Emma K. The Comprehensive Method of Teaching Reading. Heath & Co. Copyright, 1902.

Hancock. Children's Tendencies in the Use of Written Language Forms. *N. W. Monthly*, Vol. VIII, pp. 646-649.

Iredell, Harriet. Eleanor learns to Read. *Education*, Vol. XIX, 1898, pp. 233-238.

Judd, Chas. H. Genetic Psychology for Teachers, Chaps. VII-VIII. Copyright, 1903, by D. Appleton & Co.

Kehr, K. Geschichte der Methodik des deutschen Volks-schulunterrichts, Vol. I, on Lese-unterricht.

——Geschichte der Methodik.

Lukens, H. T. Children's Drawings in Early Years. *Ped. Sem.*, Vol. III, pp. 79-110.

Lukens, H. T. The Joseph Story. *New York Teachers Mag.*, April, 1899.

March, Francis A. The Spelling Reform, U. S. Bureau of Ed. Report, 1893.

McMurry, C. A. Special Method in Primary Reading and Oral Work with Stories, 1903. Special Method in the Reading of Complete English Classics, 1903. The Macmillan Company, New York.

Merry, Robert. Book of Puzzles.

New York Teachers' Monographs, June, 1902, and November, 1898. (Devoted to reading and language work.)

Parker, Francis W. Talks on Pedagogics. A. S. Barnes & Co., New York. 1894.

Patrick, G. T. W. Should Children under Ten learn to Read and Write. *Pop. Sci. Monthly*, January, 1899, pp. 382-391.

Peck, H. T. Psychology of the Printed Page. *Cosmopolitan*, Vol. XXXI, p. 161.

Pollard, Rebecca. Synthetic Method of Reading and Spelling. Copyright by Am. Book Co., New York.

Rein, W. Encyklopädisches Handbuch der Pädagogik, Vol. IV. Das Lesen.

Scott, W. D. The Theory of Advertising. Boston, 1903.

Scripture, Mrs. E. W. In the Japanese Way. *Outlook*, 1897, Vol. LV, pp. 556-557.

Scudder. Childhood in Literature and Art. Houghton, Mifflin & Co.

Search. The Ideal School. Appleton & Co.

Sherman, L. A. Analytics of Literature. Ginn & Co. Boston, 1893.

Trettien, A. W. Psychology of the Language Interest of Children. *Ped. Sem.*, June, 1904.

University Quarterly, Vol. XX, p. 120. Science of Reading.

Vaile, E.O. Reading as an Intellectual Process. *Pop. Sci. Monthly*, Vol. VIII, pp. 212-225.

Ward, E. G. Rational Method in Reading. Silver, Burdett & Co., New York.

—— in *New York Teachers' Monographs*, November, 1898.

Wheaton, Margaret, in *New York Teachers' Monographs*, November, 1898.

PRIMERS AND READERS

Alger, Edith G. Primer of Work and Play. Boston, 1901.

Arnold-Forster, H. O. The Citizen Reader. London, 1885.

Beard and **Van Marter**. Bible Symbols, or The Bible in Pictures. Hertel, Jenkins & Co., Chicago.

Burt, Mary E. Poems that Every Child Should Know. Doubleday, Page, & Co., New York.

Deutsches Lesebuch für Höhere Anstalten, Vols. I-V.

Fuller, Sarah. An Illustrated Primer. Copyright, 1898, by D. C. Heath & Co., Boston.

Funk & Wagnalls. Standard First and Second Reader. Funk & Wagnalls Co., New York.

Judson and **Bender**. Graded Literature Readers, First and Second Books. Maynard, Merrill & Co., 1899.

McMurry and **Cook**. Songs of the Treetop and Meadow. Bloomington, Ill., 1899.

McMurry, Lida B. Classic Stories for the Little Ones. Bloomington, Ill., 1904.

Norton, Chas. Eliot. Heart of Oak Books. Heath & Co., Boston. 1894.

Shearer, J. W. The Combination Speller. Published by F. B. Johnson, Richmond, Va.

Smith, Jessie R. Four True Stories of Life and Adventure.

——The Story of Washington. Copyright by E. H. Harison, publisher, New York.

Smythe, E. Louise. Old Time Stories Retold for Children. Am. Book Co., New York.

Spears and **Augsburg**. Preparing to Read. New England Pub. Co., Boston. 1892.

Summers, Maud. The Thought Reader, Bk. I. Ginn & Co., Boston.

Taylor, Frances Lilian. First Reader. Am. Book Co., 1900.

——The Werner Primer. Am. Book Co.

Turpin. Classic Fables. Maynard, Merrill & Co.

Williams, Sherman. Choice Literature, Bk. I. Am. Book Co., 1898.

WHAT TO READ

Burton, Richard. Literature for Children. *N. Am. Review*, September, 1898, pp. 278-286.

Chase, Susan F. Adolescence, Choice of Reading Matter. *Journal of Adolescence*, January, February, and March, 1901, and *Ch. Study Monthly*, Vol. VI, pp. 322-328.

Dana, J. C. A Librarian's Experience on what the American People are Reading. *Outlook*, Dec. 5, 1903.

Elmendorf, H. E. Some Things a Boy of Seventeen should have had an Opportunity to Read. *Rev. of Reviews*, December, 1903, pp. 713-717.

Griffith, George. *Ch. Study Monthly*, February, 1899.

Hall, G. S. How to Teach Reading and What to Read in Schools. Heath & Co., 1874, pp. 40.

——Adolescence, Vol. II. D. Appleton & Co. Copyright, 1904.

Haultain, Arnold. How to Read. *Blackwood's Mag.*, Feb. 1, 1896.

Irving. Home Reading of School Children. *Ped. Sem.*, Vol. VII, No. 1.

Tappan, Eva March. The Children's Hour; a comprehensive and careful selection of the best literature for children. Ten vols. Houghton, Mifflin, & Co., 1907.

Vostrovsky. Reading Tastes. *Ped. Sem.*, Vol. VI, No. 4.

Williams, Sherman. Supplementary Reading. *New York Teachers' Monographs*, November, 1898.

Wissler, Clark. Children's Interests in Reading. *Ped. Sem.*, Vol. V, No. 4.

HYGIENE OF READING, AND REQUIREMENTS OF THE PRINTER

Allport, Frank. Tests for Defective Vision in School Children. *Educational Review*, New York, 1897.

Blasius und **Lüdieke**. Deutsche Vierteljahrschrift f. off. Gesundheitspflege, Bd. XIII, p. 432.

Bravais, V. Du Mouvement des Yeux dans la Lecture. *Lyon Medical*, Nov. 29, 1891.

Burgerstein und Hetolitzky. Handbuch der Schulhygiene, zweite umgearbeitete auflage. Jena, 1902.

Clouston. Neuroses of Development.

Cohn, H. Hygiene of the Eye. Midland Educational Co., Ltd., Birmingham, England, 1886.

——Lehrbuch der Hygiene des Auges. Wien und Leipzig, 1892.

——L'Ecriture, La Typographie, et le Progres de la Myopie. *Rev. Scientifique*, 1881, p. 297 ff.

Dodge, Raymond. Act of Vision. *Harpers*, May, 1902.

Donders. Anomalien der Refraction und Accommodation.

Griffing and Franz. Conditions of Fatigue in Reading. *Psych. Review*, Vol. III, 1896.

Hartwell, E. M. Report of the Director of Physical Training, Boston, 1894. *School Document*, No. 8, 1894, pp. 69-85.

Javal, Emile. Myopia. *Rev. Sci.*, 1879, p. 494 ff.

——L'Evolution de la Typographie. *Rev. Sci.*, June 25, 1881.

——Bulletins et Memoires de la Société française d'Ophtalmologie, Vols. I-VI. Paris, 1883-1888.

Mosso, A. Fatigue. Translated by Drummond. *Putnam's*, 1904, pp. 334.

Sack, Dr. N. Die Ausseren Eigenschaften unserer Schulbücher vom Standpunkte der Hygiene des Auges. Reviewed by Erisman in *Zeitschrift für Schulgesundheitspflege*, Nos. 4 and 5, 1898.

Sanford, Edmund C. Relative Legibility of the Small Letters. *American Journal of Psychology*, Vol. I, May, 1888.

Shaw, Edward R. School Hygiene. The Macmillan Co. 1902.

Weber, A. Ueber die Augenuntersuchungen in den höheren Schulen zu Darmstadt. Referat und Memorial, erstattet der grossherzoge Ministerial-Abtheilung für Gesundheitspflege. 1881.

INDEX